To hester,

With very best wishes

[signature]

March 4 '95.

Do voters in large-scale democracies reliably vote for the electoral outcomes they want? Is voting essentially like choosing a job or selecting an asset portfolio? Or is it more like cheering at a football game? And if the latter, what are the implications for the functioning of democracy when policies are determined by who cheers the loudest? This book is concerned with answering these questions. In the most narrow construction, the book offers a critique of the interest-based theory of voting behavior characteristic of modern "public choice" theory – and does so using the decision-theoretic apparatus of standard economics. The central claim is that fully rational voters will not reliably vote for the political outcomes they prefer. The broader objective of the book is to present an "expressive" theory of electoral politics as an alternative to the "interest-based" account. The authors argue that this expressive theory is both more coherent and more consistent with what is observed than is the interest-based orthodoxy. In particular, they believe that this theory can explain, for example, the propensity of democratic regimes to make war, the predominance of moral questions (the sexual conduct of candidates or the abortion issue) on the political agenda, and the distributive activities of democratic governments – facts that represent something of a challenge to the interest-based account.

The significance of this account should be clear. If, as economists frequently assert, proper diagnosis of the disease is a crucial prerequisite to treatment, then the design of appropriate democratic institutions depends critically on a coherent analysis of the way the electoral process works and the perversities to which it is prone. The claim is that the interest-based account incorrectly diagnoses the disease. Accordingly, this book ends with an account of the institutional protections that go with expressive voting.

Democracy and decision

Democracy and decision

The pure theory of electoral preference

GEOFFREY BRENNAN
Australian National University

LOREN LOMASKY
Bowling Green State University

CAMBRIDGE
UNIVERSITY PRESS

Published by the Press Syndicate of the University of Cambridge
The Pitt Building, Trumpington Street, Cambridge CB2 1RP
40 West 20th Street, New York, NY 10011-4211, USA
10 Stamford Road, Oakleigh, Victoria 3166, Australia

First published 1993

Printed in the United States of America

Library of Congress Cataloging-in-Publication Data
Brennan, Geoffrey, 1944–
Democracy and decision : the pure theory of electoral preference /
Geoffrey Brennan and Loren Lomasky.
p.   cm.
Includes bibliographical references and index.
ISBN 0-521-35043-3
1. Voting.   2. Social choice.   3. Pressure groups.   4. Democracy.
I. Lomasky, Loren E.   II. Title.
JF1001.B74   1993
324.9 – dc20   92-14265
                                                        CIP

A catalog record for this book is available from the British Library.

ISBN 0-521-35043-3 hardback

To James Buchanan,
colleague and friend

Contents

vii

Preface

The writing of this book has spanned a decade, and several continents. It was begun during the fall of 1982 at the Center for Study of Public Choice in Blacksburg, Virginia, where Lomasky was spending the year as a visiting fellow. It was finally completed during a fortnight's visit at the Australian National University in August 1991. The world may not have "eagerly awaited" the emergence of the book, but the authors certainly did.

The period of its gestation is partly a testament to the difficulties of trans-Pacific collaboration – particularly when one of the authors is a devotee of nineteenth-century technology. Collaboration for us, at least on this project, has required face-to-face contact: the opportunity to talk things through and the discipline of having one's door battered down by an irate colleague when drafts are overdue. We have become converts to the view that live theater has no satisfactory substitutes.

The delay is also partly attributable to difficulties in collaboration across disciplines. There has been no great difficulty in coming to a mind on the central argument of the book or on the more detailed aspects developed in the various chapters. Our problems have not been ones of communication with each other, but rather of communication with our various imagined audiences. Each of us has wanted in the writing, naturally enough, to address our respective disciplinary peer groups. And here, such matters as style, technical complexity, the nuance of argument, even the meanings of terms, have become serious problems. A line of reasoning that is utterly familiar to philosophers will be novel, even controversial, to economists, and vice versa. To be inclusive, as we have aimed to be, runs the risk of being tedious to everyone (though, we hope, tedious at different points). But at least no reader should be able to lodge a complaint over the technical complexity of the argument. Those points at which a little technique appears (some of Chapter 4 and a few parts of Chapters 5 and 8) can be skipped without loss of the central thread. This book should, we reckon, be accessible to economists, political scientists, political philosophers, and even that much-mentioned but uncommon breed, "intelligent laypersons." And with luck it should be intriguing to them as well.

We do concede, however, that this book is written with a particular audience primarily in mind – namely, those who believe that voters vote their interests. This group is wider than the set of "public choice" scholars, although public choice scholars *do* make the notion of self-interested voting an axiom for their analysis. Also included are those who adopt more casually the presumption that politics is essentially a battle of rival interests and those who take it for granted that elections reliably aggregate expressions of private interest into some version of the "public interest." In our experience, the total group is broad indeed, and we have tried to make our argument available to the whole of it. Even so, mainstream public choice scholarship is a central target. We aim to persuade scholars in that tradition – as we ourselves have become persuaded – that one central component of their models is seriously defective. That central component is the claim that electoral choice and market choice are essentially alike. Our claim, by contrast, is that electoral choice and market choice are radically different. This difference, we argue, has profound implications for our understanding of electoral politics – of its problems and possibilities. But arguing all this represents the substance of the book. The intellectual context of that argument we attempt to set out in Chapter 1. The argument itself occupies Chapters 2 through 11.

Because the argument is critical of public choice orthodoxy, it may seem a trifle strange to be dedicating this book to James Buchanan, a man who more than any other is identified with the public choice movement. After all, the "integration of the theories of economic and political decision-making" for which Buchanan won his Nobel Prize is, on our argument, more problematic and decidedly more complicated than public choice theorists allow. Nevertheless, the approach we follow is very much in the public choice tradition, and although we believe the argument is entirely general and will be of interest to the whole range of political theorists and political philosophers, the particular influence of Buchanan's work will be evident. We have both at different times collaborated with Buchanan – and for Brennan in particular the collaboration has been an academically and intellectually crucial one. We both count Jim as a friend and regard him with great affection and deep respect. Besides, the ideas here were foreshadowed by early Buchanan pieces; and in Buchanan's most recent work, he has been inclined to distance himself from the use of the homo economicus model, except in restricted analytic settings. Indeed, earlier versions of the central argument here were originally developed in collaboration with Buchanan and most notably in Brennan and Buchanan (1984).

Although our debt to Buchanan is the most notable, it is not the only one. Parts of the book have been aired in various settings over the decade of its writing, and we have had useful comments from a wide array of persons. We want to make particular mention of John Head, Dennis Mueller, Philip Pettit, Jonathan Pincus, John Quiggin, Perry Shapiro, and Viktor Vanberg. Ken Shepsle at the eleventh hour read the entire manuscript and provided many useful suggestions.

It is apt that this book has had its origins and completion in two institutions that have been, in different ways, quite critical to its creation. We wish to place on record our debt to the Public Choice Center (now at George Mason University) and to the Research School of Social Sciences, Australian National University, for stimulation and support – and to Betty Tillman and Eileen Berry, who at different times had the tedious job of typing the bits and pieces of the manuscript. We should also express our gratitude to the University of Minnesota, the National Endowment for the Humanities, and the Social Philosophy and Policy Center at Bowling Green State University for financial support. And finally, we wish to express our thanks to Liberty Fund Inc., Indianapolis, which first brought us together and has nurtured us on occasion since.

1 Ethics, politics, and public choice

The burden of proof should rest with those who suggest wholly different models of man apply in the political and economic realms of behaviour.
                                    James M. Buchanan, *"Politics Without Romance"*

Introduction

This book offers a theory of electoral preference. That is, it aims to give an account of what it is – or more particularly, what it is not – that voters do when they go to the ballot box in the large-scale collective decision-making processes that are characteristic of Western democracies. The basic analytical arguments generalize to a whole range of "collective" activities, but our focus throughout the book will be on electoral behavior, and our discussion proceeds almost exclusively in terms of that particular (and highly significant) example.

The topic is an almost totally neglected one; and this is, in itself, extraordinary. For one thing, the role of electoral considerations in shaping actual political decision making in most Western democracies seems entirely beyond dispute. For another, electoral constraints, and the connection these are presumed to imply between electoral outcomes and citizens' preferences over those outcomes, are commonly taken to be crucial features of genuinely democratic institutions and basic ingredients in establishing the normative case for democratic rule. Other bits of democratic apparatus may be important, but without periodic elections in which parties and/or candidates compete for office and/or alternative policies are offered for popular electoral scrutiny, we would simply not have democratic order as it has come to be understood.

Accordingly, one would have thought that the systematic analysis of the choice behavior of individual voters would occupy a central place in our formal theories of democratic process. Not so. Political theory is otherwise preoccupied with the question of whether electoral constraints are sufficiently binding, with the quality of political decision makers, or with the properties of majority rule in transforming individual votes into social "decisions," but not, it seems, with the nature of the votes themselves. Apparently, it is simply taken for granted that votes are what they seem to be: straightforward statements of voters' preferences over electoral options whether those options are parties, candidates, or the politics those parties or candidates stand for.

We shall argue that such complacency is utterly misplaced. We shall try to show that voting in large-scale elections is disconnected in a fundamental way from citizen preference over electoral outcomes. And we shall try to spell out the implications of this disconnection for the positive predictive science of politics and for the normative theory of democratic rule.

1

The account we give of electoral behavior is basically a decision-theoretic one. It involves an application of the kind of rational actor theory most fully developed in mainstream microeconomics. In that sense, this book is properly to be construed as an exercise in what has come to be known as "public choice theory." By public choice theory here, we mean simply the application of the techniques and methods of mainstream economics to the study of political processes. And we want at the outset to identify ourselves clearly with the public choice tradition so defined. That is, we are faithful to the individualist method; we take it that actors are rational (in a sense we shall have to specify with some care); we believe in the role of relative prices, and of changes in them, in explaining human affairs; we hold, within limits, to the virtues of abstraction; and our tools of analysis are drawn almost entirely from the mainstream economist's kit bag.

Yet if our argument is properly construed as an application of public choice theory, it is also a *critique* of it. More particularly, it is a critique of one important element in the public choice approach – namely, the wholesale importation of homo economicus into electoral politics. We shall argue, against public choice orthodoxy, that consumer choice and voter choice are fundamentally different in decision-theoretic terms and, hence, that market behavior and political behavior are likely to be distinctly different. We shall argue that while interests may predominate in market behavior, they are strongly muted in the ballot box. At the same time, ethical considerations, which are muted in the marketplace, are likely to play an increased role in democratic electoral politics. In other words, we shall offer a decision-theoretic foundation for a kind of "two-hats" thesis – for the thesis that actors have two personas: one for markets and a different one for the ballot box (and analogous collective activities).

This critique of public choice theory may seem to cut very deep. After all, the homo economicus behavioral assumption – the assumption that all political actors are predominantly egoistic, and that their egoism is expressed mainly as a desire for income or wealth broadly conceived – is often seen by both critics and proponents alike as the characteristic feature of the public choice approach. For example, Dennis Mueller in his book-length survey of the field states that "the basic behavioral postulate of public choice, as for economics, is that man is an egoistic, rational, utility-maximizer."[1] And Alistair Cooke, in the particular "Letter from America"[2] in which he discussed the award of the Nobel Prize to James Buchanan, described public choice as embodying the homely but important truth that politicians are, after all, no less selfish than the rest of us. What then, one may ask, is left of public choice if homo economicus is removed? This is one question we want to address in this opening chapter, partly for its own sake and partly because it helps to establish something of the intellectual context within which the argument of this book is set.

---

[1] Mueller (1979), p. 1. Mueller does go on to state that a "second salient characteristic . . . of modern public choice literature [is that it] employs the analytic tools of economics" (p. 2), a definition we prefer to follow. It is worth noting that Mueller is effectively distinguishing the homo economicus assumption from the "analytic tools" of economics.

[2] Broadcast sometime late in October 1986.

There is, however, more at stake here than homo economicus, or indeed any other particular behavioral model. Many public choice scholars may be prepared to retreat from the strict homo economicus model – to allow for considerations of benevolence and virtue, and a richer psychology generally, in plotting human behavior. What they are likely to find more objectionable is the "two-hats" aspect of our argument – the idea that human behavior is institution dependent in the manner we shall argue for. That is, the idea that human behavior is uniform across alternative institutional forms could be argued to be a much more central part of the public choice enterprise than the use of the homo economicus model, as such. Why this is so is a matter that we shall also explore in what follows.

We shall develop this chapter in the following way. First, we describe the public choice enterprise in terms that we think substantially reflect those in which public choice theory sees itself. In the process we shall distinguish between two strands of public choice theory (or "rational actor" political theory more broadly) – one essentially positive strand that aims to develop a predictive political *science* with the same claims to intellectual rigor, analytic clarity, and predictive power that economics makes in the analysis of market behavior; and a strand that is normatively driven and has as its aim the *evaluation* of political institutions on the same basis and using the same criteria as are used in the evaluation of market institutions. We shall then focus on the role that motivational assumptions play, both in these two strands of the public choice program, and in traditional economics. On this basis, we shall try to isolate what drives the egoistic behavior assumptions within the public choice approach, and to specify at what point in the whole intellectual scheme we depart from orthodoxy and what of orthodoxy we retain.

What is public choice?

An analogy: just price theory

To give an account of public choice theory from *within* (i.e., in the terms that public choice scholars themselves might see it) it is useful to pursue an analogy with an earlier development in intellectual history. The medieval doctrine of "just price" no longer plays any role in the economist's theory of markets. Economists, naturally enough, believe that this is a good thing. They have a theory that explains why prices (and quantities) are as observed. The explanation in question runs in terms of "demand" and "supply" – categories that are essentially descriptive. In the face of such explanation, the question of whether the price in question is "just" or not is seen to be somewhat beside the point. Prices are what they are; they reflect the forces of demand and supply, and the *justice* of any particular price is simply irrelevant to the exercise of explaining how the market works.

The triumph of demand–supply analysis over just price theory is then to be seen not merely as the replacement of worse theory by a better one (like, perhaps, the demise of phlogiston theory in chemistry): It is to be seen rather as the triumph of science over superstition. Just price theory involves a kind of category error: It treats as an object of ethical concern something that, like the weather, should properly be recognized as arising from "natural" causes. The relation between modern price theory and the just price doctrine is rather like that between meteorology and rain dancing. Or at least, this is how most economists see it.

The just price enthusiast might make several responses. He might seek to reintroduce considerations of justice into the account of how markets work by asserting that demanders and suppliers are, in fact, strongly influenced by their perceptions of justice and will not pay (or charge) prices that depart too far from those they see justice to require. On this line, just price theory is not so much categorically inappropriate as poorly expressed. Once filtered through the proper demand–supply language, it becomes a hypothesis to be empirically explored. The modern microeconomist's reaction to this reformulation may be of two kinds. As far as the pure logic of demand–supply analysis is concerned, there would be some adjustment to be made: Agents' utility functions would need to include as arguments prices as well as quantities, and the basic consumer and producer equilibrium conditions would have to be modified accordingly. But such adjustments could be made easily enough, and not a great deal would be at stake at this level. As far as the practical economist-qua-scientist-dentist is concerned, however, the just price theorist's response is to be rejected: The basic hypothesis can, of course, be explored, but only to be exploded. As an account of agent behavior rivaling the standard egoistic model of consumer choice, just price theory fails: When the relevant empirical work is actually done, considerations of justice are found not to bear on the behavior of economic agents in any significant way. Or at least this is what economists generally believe the empirical evidence would show. It is interesting that direct tests of such matters are uncommon[3] and that many of the indirect "tests" do not actually prove that conceptions of justice are irrelevant.

It is worth emphasizing here that even if considerations of just price did bear on actual market behavior, it would be the participants' own conceptions of justice that would be relevant and not some putatively "correct" notion derived from independent ethical axioms or from a careful reading of Aristotle via Thomas Aquinas. In arguing the empirical relevance of just price conceptions, one would need to appeal to a purely positive account of the prevailing morality: There would be no prescriptive element as such.

The just price enthusiast might, at this point, try another tack. He might argue that just price doctrine is not to be seen as a rival predictive theory of market behavior, but rather as a set of instructions as to how market participants ought to behave. The fact that such instructions are much more honored in the breach than in the observance (so much so that they seem to have negligible predictive power) does not necessarily imply that the instructions are ethically defective. On its face, this may seem to be a reasonable response. But the modern economist, adopting his standard normative posture, would reject it entirely – and this for two reasons. First, because proper ethical theorizing must, in the economist's view, take account of what is *feasible* – otherwise, the central core of practical ethics is simply swept

---

[3] Amartya Sen (1987) makes a similar point in commenting on relevant remarks of George Stigler's.

away – and second, and relatedly, because just price analysis applies normative evaluation at the *wrong level*. Both points merit brief elaboration.

Economists have always insisted that social ethics should be informed by a proper sense of scarcity. Extrapolating from their account of individual choice behavior, they see ethics as a matter of choosing among alternative *feasible* states of the world. Indeed, some (most notably Milton Friedman) have been inclined to argue that most disagreements in social ethics, including ideological ones, are actually disagreements about which states of the world are feasible or about which states of the world follow from various policies rather than how those states should be valued. By implication a lot of ethical theorizing is a waste of time: Ethicists would more profitably expend their energies in trying to understand how the social order works. Furthermore, in deriving claims about what states of the world are feasible, one must take account of the scarcity not merely of the standard resources – time, ingenuity, and so on – but also of human benevolence and individual ethical sensibility. As Dennis Robertson remarks, one of the chief roles of the economist is to offer a warning bark whenever someone proposes a policy arrangement that demands much in the way of the scarce human resource "love." On this view, an ethical theory of social phenomena that fails to take adequate account of how people *actually* behave is at best irrelevant to real-world decision making and at worst deeply misleading. Just as an individual chooser in the standard economic calculus will choose wrongly if she fails to perceive the set of feasible options accurately, so the social ethicist will make mistakes if the specification of feasible worlds is inaccurate. Just price theory fails on these grounds, so the argument goes, because that theory takes benevolence and a sense of justice to play a larger role in human conduct than they actually do.

If the just price theory fails on these grounds, this does not mean the death of ethics entirely. Rather, armed with a theory of how markets actually work, the relevant normative question changes. The focus of normative attention switches away from the behavior of particular market agents and the ethical properties of particular prices, to the properties of the market system as a whole. And the analytical apparatus relevant to this more abstract, systemic evaluation is rather different from that which just price theory (or for that matter much conventional morality) offers. A different task requires different tools. In the case at hand, attention focuses on the coordinating capacity and incentive structure of the market system, on the "invisible hand" properties of market organization and the circumstances under which those properties fail to apply. Considerations of justice may obtrude, but in a way unlikely to be enlightened by the niceties of just price analysis. For this reason just price categories are not merely irrelevant to the explanatory exercise of how markets actually work: They are also substantially irrelevant to proper ethical evaluation. The case against the just price theory is complete.

This small excursion into the history of economic thought may seem to be somewhat beside the point. It is, in fact, highly germane, for public choice theorists see themselves engaged in an exercise in the analysis of political processes almost exactly analogous to that in which economist-crusaders against just price theory were engaged two centuries or so ago. That is, public choice theorists have insisted that the direct application of normative categories is inappropriate to the explanation of how politics actually works. They have identified, rightly or wrongly, most conventional political theory as representing an inappropriate amalgam of normative and positive analysis, pretty much at the level of the just price doctrine. As they see it, accepted "political theory" is characterized by prescriptive definition and heroic assumption, stronger on "hope" than on analytic reasoning. The requisite, hard-nosed insistence on feasibility is almost entirely absent – and this because there has been inadequate attention to political *science* properly understood and too much attention to political *ideals*. Public choice scholars have insisted that a proper *positive* account of political process is a critical exercise in its own right, and that any subsequent ethical evaluation must be undertaken at the more abstract level of political institutions – the rules of the political game – rather than at the level of particular policies or policy platforms. And of course it is exactly in such terms that public choice scholars have seen their own enterprise: to provide a properly positive scientific account of political processes, using the techniques of economic theory; and to bring to bear in evaluating political institutions the same abstract normative apparatus, the same concern for incentive structures, coordination of information, invisible hand structures, and so on that economists have used in the evaluation of markets.

The positive strand of public choice

Within this enterprise, the two strands – the purely positive "political science" strand and the normatively driven "comparative institutional evaluation" strand – are conceptually separable and have developed to some extent along independent lines. As in traditional economics, some theorists have been entirely content with the purely explanatory dimension. To such theorists the application of the methods and analytic techniques of economics to the study of political process promises to provide for political science the same sort of theoretical undergirding and framework for empirical investigation as economic theory provides for economics. Their object has been positive analysis: the working-out of the logical implications of basic axioms, and the testing of resultant hypotheses. They have secured the cultivatedly sharp separation of the positive and normative by the simple expedient of leaving the normative dimensions of the enterprise to others.

Indeed, for scholars with this strictly scientific ambition, the introduction of any normative element at all is likely to represent a distraction, and in some ways a highly unwelcome one. After all, an explicit object of the whole exercise is precisely to stake a claim for positive analysis *against* a tradition in which normative considerations have played too immediate and undisciplined a role (as they see it). To answer just price doctrine with an alternative conception of justice, even one that emphasizes the indispensability of a proper positive undergirding, is arguably less likely to cure just price exponents of their superstition than is a purging diet of pure hard science. Accordingly, this scientific strand of public choice scholarship has been inclined on occasion to try to distance itself from its more normatively driven counterpart (which we shall discuss later in greater detail).[4]

One feature of this scientific strand is worth special emphasis – namely, its aspiration to provide a fully unified social theory, a theory of human behavior in the entire range of social institutions (of which markets and political processes are to be seen as particular cases). Of course, a unified social theory might conceivably be developed on other than rational actor foundations; but it is perhaps not too surprising that those with a taste for the elegance and austerity of a single unified social theory should be attracted to the abstract analytics and deductive methods of modern economics. In any event, and for whatever reason, positive public choice theory can be seen as the major contemporary articulation of an Enlightenment aspiration – to build a *single* theory of social phenomena. For at least some scholars that aspiration is fundamental to the whole enterprise of public choice or rational actor political theory.

The normative strand of public choice

We must all recognize, I think, that the ultimate purpose of positive analysis, conceptual or empirical, must be that of modifying the environment for choices, which must in some basic sense be normatively informed. (Buchanan, 1979b, p. 176)

In politics, even more than in traditional economics perhaps, positive analysis tends to be driven by normative concerns. And indeed, as a matter of intellectual history, public choice inquiry did emerge largely as an explicit counter to a perceived anti-market bias embedded in the welfare economics treatment of so-called market failure. The object of that welfare economics literature had been precisely to provide an ethical justification for government intervention in the economy. As Samuelson puts it in motivating his seminal work on public goods: "We can formulate the grand Walrasian model of competitive general equilibrium so stringently as to leave no economic role for government at all. What strong polar case shall the student of public expenditure set alongside this pure private economy?" (1955, p. 350). The strong polar case developed was precisely an extreme case of "market failure." Public choice theorists have not, of course, objected per se to the demonstration of market failure, or to more general ethical scrutiny of market arrangements. Indeed, many of them have contributed, one way or another, to that enterprise. What they have objected to, quite strenuously, are the terms on which that ethical scrutiny had been conducted; for it had simply been taken to be self-evident that the demonstration of market failure is *sufficient* to establish a case for government intervention. That this is so is reflected in the predominant method in public economics – a method that seeks to evaluate alternative policies directly in

---

[4] To the extent, e.g., that it sometimes describes itself in terms other than "public choice" – say as "positive political economy," as in Alt and Shepsle (1990). Interestingly, this "political *science*" strand of public choice is more to be found in political science departments than in economics departments, where the welfare economics strand is more predominant. Scholars who would identify themselves with this "positive political economy" camp include, e.g., Bill Riker, Gerald Kramer, Ken Shepsle, James Alt, John Ferejohn, Morris Fiorina, and Barry Weingast, to mention a few names that spring to mind.

terms of their effects on "efficiency" and "equity" in a way more or less analogous to that in which just price theorists evaluated prices. Implicitly, government is viewed as a benevolent despot – as one who has the power to decide on policy unilaterally, and whose sole inclination in doing so is to promote the conception of the good society promulgated by economic advisors. It is precisely this implicit benevolent despot model of government behavior that public choice theory set out to criticize: "Public choice theory offers a 'theory of governmental failure' that is fully comparable to 'the theory of market failure' that emerged from the theoretical welfare economics of the 1930's and 1940's" (Buchanan and Tollison, 1984, p. 13). As public choice theorists conceive it, the central issue in normative public choice is the scrutiny of political process on terms exactly analogous to, and on all fours with, the normative scrutiny of markets: What is required is a piece of "comparative institutional analysis." To simply *assume* that government will somehow correct any imperfections we may observe arising out of market interactions is "to imply, by neglect, preference for the collective alternative." It is to act "like the judge who awarded the prize to the second singer after he had heard only the first" (Buchanan, 1979a, p. 272). And in particular, the ascription of heroic motivations to political agents, without a corresponding ascription of heroic motivations to those agents in their market roles, seems bound to bias the whole comparative institutional exercise.

To the extent that an enterprise can be understood as much by what it is *opposed* to as by what it is in favor of, public choice theory, particularly in its normative guise, can then be understood in terms of its implacable opposition to the benevolent despot model of government. That benevolent despot model treats government as a kind of deus ex machina. The public choice scholar opposes both the deus and the ex machina elements – the former because it assumes what is to be tested (namely, whether political forces are or are not on balance benign); the latter because it sweeps off the explanatory agenda all questions about how exactly government operates.

To summarize briefly, public choice insists on a radical separation of positive and normative elements in the analysis of political process (just as of market process). Public choice identifies the relatively abstract level of "the system as a whole" as the appropriate level for normative evaluation and focuses largely on the issue of comparing the properties of political and market processes – or more generally the properties of centralized versus decentralized decision-making mechanisms. For public choice theorists, as for welfare economists more generally, the central normative questions have been: What should government do? What activities should government pursue? And equally, and no less crucially, what should government not do? What restrictions on government action should be imposed? This orientation remains central in the normative agenda. However, to deal with such issues adequately, public choice theorists insist, requires a substantial, purely "positive," analytical component entirely comparable with what economics provides for markets. The workings of market process are, on the whole, well understood – or at least so economists believe. The workings of political process are, by contrast, poorly understood. In traditional "theories" of politics, so the argument might go, we are still pretty much at the level of the just price doctrine – at a level where prescriptive definition, heroic assumption, and "romantic" conceptions abound. Public choice analysis sees itself as attempting to set all this to rights.

The role of homo economicus

What is the role of homo economicus in this whole enterprise? Before attempting to answer this question, we ought to make it clear what exactly the homo economicus assumption amounts to. How, for example, does homo economicus relate to Mueller's specification that "man is an egoistic, rational utility-maximizer"?

In fact, there is some confusion on this matter at both popular and professional levels. We do not aspire here to settle the issues once and for all, but we do want to make it clear what we shall understand by the various terms "egoistic," "rational," "utility maximizing" and how we shall define homo economicus in this book in terms of that vocabulary.

Defining homo economicus

Consider, first, utility maximization. What we shall mean by "utility maximization" is that each agent has purposes that her action is designed to promote, and that such purposes are commensurable, so that the agent's ends can be represented by a function[5] connecting achievement of the various purposes to a single measure. This measure we shall call "utility," for want of a better term, and the related function, a "utility function." Only if the agent acts to maximize this utility function can she be considered "rational."

"Rationality" requires rather more than this, however. Specifically, it imposes a *structure* on the utility function so described. In particular, we require that the utility function be continuous and continuously differentiable (so that small increases in the achievement of one's purposes involve small increases in utility) and "convex." Roughly stated, "convexity" means that generalized demand curves slope downward. It is this assumption that allows us to predict agent behavior in response to changes in relative prices: The more costly some object is in terms of other valued objects forgone, the less of that object the agent will choose to take. On this reading, rationality implies utility maximization, but not vice versa.

None of this requires any assumption about the particular purposes the agent has. *Egoism* is an assumption of this latter kind. It postulates that the agent's purposes are selfish in the natural everyday sense. When we speak of self-interest here, we refer to the *object* of the interest not the *subject*. It is uninformative to be told that, when an agent acts, the reasons underlying the action are his; for that is just what it is for a bodily movement to be an action. Each of us necessarily is moved by reasons that are, in the last instance, our own rather than someone else's. To be interested is to be the subject of one's actions; to be self-interested is, in addition, to be the object of one's actions – that is, to be concerned with the flourishing of oneself. So, for example, we will normally take it that to feed someone else is

---

[5] This is unnecessarily strong, but specifying the weakest axiom set sufficient to generate the results is a distraction here.

to act in an other-interested way, while to feed oneself is to act self-interestedly. Even such simple examples, however, invite psychological speculation. Though it is plausible that feeding another is grounded either in a concern for the other's well-being or perhaps in a commitment to a moral principle requiring succor of the hungry, it may of course be that I am acting to assuage pangs of guilt or to garner the approval of spectators. Equally, feeding myself may (in bizarre cases) be an other-interested act. Jones, for example, in pursuit of his own well-being, is dieting and judges that it is better for him to go hungry than to eat. Jones's mother is, however, distressed at the knowledge of her son's hunger, and Jones decides to eat after all to relieve his mother's distress: Eating then is interested, but not self-interested.

Economists have never been much interested in this kind of motive unraveling. Their concern in specifying the content of individuals' utility functions has been to assist in the development of empirically testable hypotheses – to develop a "science of choice" beyond the pure "logic of choice" that derives from the rational actor axioms themselves. For this purpose, even egoism may be slightly too complex, as the simple eating example indicates. In at least some instances it will simply not be clear what egoism implies.[6] For purposes of empirical application – and for deriving hypotheses that show some prospect of being conceptually testable – something rather more specific will be required.

Economists have typically taken the logical contender here to be wealth (or income) maximization. Wealth can be more broadly or narrowly defined for these purposes. In the limit it can be taken as the capitalized money value of all the goods the actor values (including leisure, and nonmarketed activities for which some "shadow price" can be adduced). But the broader the definition, the less empirically manageable; and hence economists have tended to settle for income/wealth definitions that accord more or less with common usage and statistical convention. Such a usage is sufficient to generate a rich array of testable predictions about agent behavior, and it is on this basis that homo economicus makes his appearance on the analytical stage.

In our usage, then, homo economicus is to be understood as the embodiment of three independent assumptions:

1. that agents are rational (which includes the notion of utility maximizing as we shall understand it);
2. that agents are egoistic; and
3. that egoism takes the form of economic self-interest, narrowly understood. Homo economicus is a personal-wealth maximizer.

Homo economicus in politics

With this as background, let us return to the grounds on which public choice theory has imported homo economicus into the study of political processes. What role does homo economicus play in public choice? Is he really necessary?

---

[6] David Gauthier's (1986) *Morals by Agreement*, e.g., argues that an entire apparatus of morality can be derived from agreement among rational egoistic actors.

The answer depends in part on which strand of public choice scholarship one is concerned with. For the political scientist qua scientist, the answer seems clear enough. The assumption of wealth-maximizing behavior is used extensively in economics; it has been found to be a useful abstraction in developing theory and hypotheses about market behavior; and empirical tests have provided what, in general, the profession has taken to be adequate corroboration. Given a general predilection for the "simplicity" and "generality" of hypotheses,[7] it is natural to postulate that a motivational assumption that has proven useful in one area of human activity will prove useful in another.

It is, however, worth noting that for many purposes in conventional economics, the assumption of wealth maximization – that agents have wealth as a single argument in their utility functions – is unnecessarily strong. Pretty well all of the relevant comparative static propositions of the kind that predict the direction of response to changes in relative prices can be derived with a more general utility function in which wealth is not the sole argument, but merely one among possibly many. For example, one does not need to postulate wealth maximization as the only consideration in portfolio choice to predict that individuals will tend to shift away from assets whose rate of return (net of tax) suddenly declines relative to the rate of return on assets of a different type. One does not need to postulate wealth maximization as the sole objective of academics to predict that if salaries decline in location A relative to location B, the number and quality of academics remaining in A will tend to decline. All that needs to be assumed is that wealth is one argument in utility functions. Of course, if one wants to explain the world – or an aspect of it such as portfolio selection or academic location – nothing less than a complete specification of the utility function will suffice. But if one merely wants to predict changes in the state of the world, specification of part of the utility function may be enough.

The explanation of political outcomes in public choice terms involves the more stringent formulation. In that sense, the use of homo economicus in public choice theory is more ambitious than is its use in much of economics. Although homo economicus is sufficient to generate most of the standard results in conventional economics, it is not necessary, whereas it is necessary for much of the public choice orthodoxy. Accordingly, empirical support for those standard results in economics cannot properly be adduced as evidence for the stronger formulation of the homo economicus construction.

At the same time, it is quite clear that wealth maximization is an extremely potent assumption in the public choice context. Among other things, it enables the theorist to predict the pattern of electoral support for various policies directly from a knowledge of the incidence of those policies (who benefits and who loses). We can also predict that politicians and bureaucrats will exploit available opportunities for their own ends, unless the institutional framework is such as to constrain them to do otherwise. And we can further predict the *direction* of such exploitation – namely, toward the ultimate wealth maximization of the political agents.

---

[7] Two of Quine and Ullian's five "virtues" for hypotheses. See Quine and Ullian (1978), chap. 6.

But for the positive analyst, homo economicus is ultimately dispensable. If an alternative hypothesis of similar austerity and simplicity can be found that is capable of explaining human behavior better than the homo economicus rival, then so much the better. Some debate may proceed as to just how much austerity and simplicity in motivational structure one really wants, and why such austerity is to be valued – but there should be no loyalty beyond that which is empirically warranted to the homo economicus construct as such.

Loyalty will, however, be engaged at the level of uniformity across institutional forms. As we noted in the previous section rational actor political theory draws much of its appeal from its promise of providing a single, unified social theory – one that will be capable of treating behavior in markets and in politics as special applications of the one general analysis. Motivational uniformity seems, on its face, to be a crucial ingredient in any such general analysis. Accordingly, rational actor theorists may retreat from homo economicus tout court, but they are likely to show great reluctance in retreating differentially across different institutional forms. Yet as we shall argue, it is just such *differential* retreat that is called for.

So much for homo economicus within the positive strand of public choice theory. Within the normative strand, there is rather more at stake. As mentioned in the previous section, if a properly unbiased account of the relative merits of market and political arrangements is to be offered, the assumption of motivational neutrality is required on purely methodological grounds. It is, of course, precisely this assumption that public choice's arch enemy, the benevolent despot of government, violates. That model, and any analogous model that assumes political agents to be more benevolently motivated than market agents, seems bound to smuggle a collectivist bias into the relevant institutional comparisons.

Moreover, the crucial normative test that economists have sought to apply to markets and to extend to political processes amounts to isolating the presence of Smithian "invisible hands." What is under scrutiny is the capacity of institutions to transform egoistic motivations into publicly beneficial actions. For this purpose, the assumption of egoistic motivations seems entirely natural. As Adam Smith remarks in the well-worn quotation, "It is not from the benevolence of the butcher, the brewer and the baker that we expect our dinner, but from regard to their own interest" (1930, p. ii). Smith does not here deny the existence of benevolence: He merely notes that "man has almost constant occasion for the help of his brethren, and it is in vain for him to expect it from their benevolence *only*" (p. ii, our emphasis).[8] Benevolence may or may not be present, but it cannot be relied on as a basis for all social interactions. Given that this is so, the natural question for the public choice theorist to pose is whether the transformation of self-interested motives into other-interested conduct, which Smith identifies in idealized markets, works

---

[8] On the more specific issue of Smith's views as to the *extent* of benevolence, there is an instructive remark in the *Lectures on Jurisprudence* to the effect that a beggar would "die in a week" if he were dependent on others' benevolence alone – though there is some suggestion that this is because dependence on benevolence is being contrasted with exchange, and that the beggar would die not because his total remuneration were inadequate but because he could not exchange the old coat someone had given him for food or lodging or another coat that fitted him better.

within *political process* – and specifically in *democratic* political process where market-like constraints, such as electoral competition under majority rule, apply.

If this is the question at issue, it hardly makes analytic sense to assume benevolence at the outset. To test whether institution J transforms A into B, we cannot begin by assuming that B exists in adequate amounts irrespective of whether J is operative or not. Indeed, once the scarcity of benevolence is so much as acknowledged, the issue of how to recognize and mobilize invisible-hand processes becomes significant. Once the significance of that issue is accepted, the assumption of egoism follows quite naturally in its wake.[9]

However, it is clear that a significant retreat from pure egoism would be perfectly acceptable *in principle* within normative public choice provided that the principle of motivational neutrality were applied. Comparative institutional analysis requires a ceteris paribus exercise in which the institutional form *and that form only* alters. If persons are assumed to be benevolent in their political roles, they must equally be taken to be benevolent in their market roles – and there are no prima facie grounds for believing that the assumption of such benevolence will radically affect institutional rankings. Within markets, monopolists can be presumed to be constrained in setting prices by benevolent concern for their customers, polluters will take account of the interests of pollutees in their technology and production decisions, would-be free riders will not free-ride to the same extent out of concern for others, and so on. In short, although political processes will work "better," the market failure that might otherwise be taken to justify political intervention will be substantially moderated. No direct institutional implications follow.

The general conclusion to be drawn from all this is that although the homo economicus assumption may have its uses in rational actor political theory, it is a less significant piece of the enterprise than the assumption of motivational neutrality. In both the positive political economy and comparative institutional analysis strands that can be identified within the public choice project, the assumption of motivational neutrality is critical – though for different reasons in two cases.

The implication of this fact is that if any attack on the use of homo economicus in public choice analysis is to be successful, it will either have to include in its ambit the use of homo economicus in *economics* or it will have to undermine the principle of motivational neutrality – at least as that principle has been understood in public choice circles.

Once motivational neutrality is accepted, any critique of homo economicus in politics is necessarily a critique of homo economicus tout court; and equally, any evidence for homo economicus adduced from behavior in markets is evidence for homo economicus across the board. It is, we think, for this reason that relatively little work has been done by public choice theorists in testing out the use of homo economicus in the political setting specifically: Given the market evidence,[10] no additional such testing has been seen to be a particularly high priority.

---

[9] See Brennan and Buchanan (1981, 1985) for a fuller discussion of this line.

[10] In what has been interpreted as market evidence, the interpretations are, as we have already noted, sometimes excessively generous to homo economicus.

But *criticism* of the public choice enterprise has certainly focused on the empirical dimension: Critics have determinedly asserted that "politics just isn't like that" and sought to defend their criticisms by appeal to the "real world." We shall ourselves examine the empirical literature as it relates to voting in Chapters 6 and 7. Like much empirical work, the results are subject to alternative interpretation, though it would be hard to assert that homo economicus gets the best of the argument. Probably, the weight of evidence is not sufficient to make many people change their minds. It is perhaps only in methodology textbooks that hypotheses are decisively rejected!

For the most part, therefore, we shall in this book attend to purely logical matters – partly because the "facts" do not speak with a single voice and partly because it is the logic of the argument that generates the firmly held prior beliefs. Critics of public choice theory have not, on the whole, attended to the logic by which public choice has extrapolated from market behavior. That, so they might say, is the public choice theorist's problem. But whoever owns the problem, it surely is one. Either critics are asserting that homo economicus is inappropriate in *economic* applications or they are attacking the principle of behavioral-motivational neutrality. They cannot simply avoid the issue.

One critic who has not avoided this issue is Mark Kelman. In a wonderfully extravagant, "boots-and-all" assault on public choice theory he has this to say:

> To insist that the picture of political man be fully integrated with the ordinary picture of "private man" is, in a very weak sense, an unexceptionable claim; it is not especially plausible that people would exhibit in one sphere character traits that were wholly invisible in other areas. The fundamental problem with the way public choice theorists use this insight is that the picture of human character that economists posit governs other realms of social life is so shallow and incomplete that extending the caricature to another sphere simply serves to extend the domain of distorted understanding. (1988, p. 206)

In other words, Kelman basically accepts the principle of motivational neutrality and simply doubts the usefulness of the homo economicus construction more generally. Here, if nowhere else, there seems to be some agreement with Buchanan. As Buchanan puts it: "I do not want to enter into either a defense of or an attack on the usefulness of homo economicus, either in economics or in any theory of politics. I would say only as I have said many times before, that the burden of proof should rest with those who suggest that wholly different models of man apply in the political and economic realms of behavior" (Buchanan and Tollison, 1984, p. 13). For Buchanan as well, the principle of motivational neutrality seems central, the use of homo economicus decidedly more provisional.

Behavioral neutrality under fire

It is time to indicate where our own argument bites in the public choice intellectual scheme. The object of our critique is the principle of motivational neutrality or, rather, what that principle is taken to imply. We agree with Buchanan's dictum, quoted at the outset of this chapter, that the burden of proof should rest with those who suggest wholly different behavioral models in political and market settings. It is a burden of proof we accept: We aim to provide grounds for the claim that market and political behavior will be predictably different.

We do not, however, dispute the principle of motivational neutrality, appropriately abstractly interpreted. In fact, our argument ultimately depends upon it. We believe that the agent carries the same basic motivational structure, the same utility function, into market and political arenas. However, the way in which that uniform motivational structure fleshes itself out in behavior is, we argue, likely to be radically different in the two institutional settings. Each institutional structure engages, as it were, with different aspects of human motivation: Each magnifies one dimension of that total motivation vis-à-vis others, so that the behavior that emerges will be different. In brief, we accept *motivational* neutrality, at least at an appropriately abstract level; but we reject *behavioral* neutrality in favor of what we earlier referred to as a two-hats thesis.

The particular motivational structure we shall assume is not, however, the extreme form of homo economicus often adopted in public choice circles. We take it that the utility function *includes* wealth as an argument – but that it includes other things as well, which we shall be at pains to specify as we proceed. We shall not be profligate in this respect: We shall not treat the utility function as a kind of carryall in which motivations can be thrown in at will as problems of explanation arise. We too have a taste for austerity. But we equally do not want to make of austerity a fetish, and we hold no particular belief for homo economicus. We shall throughout, nevertheless, maintain the apparatus of rational actor theory and the assumption of predominant egoism.

The central analytic proposition in establishing behavioral nonneutrality (the two-hats proposition) is developed in the next two chapters at considerable length. At this point all we need to do is to suggest how the argument will go. In our account the crucial difference between the market and the ballot box that gives rise to the behavioral nonneutrality is this: In the market the agent is *decisive*. Faced with a choice between market options *a* and *b*, the agent genuinely *chooses* one or the other. It is a genuine choice because the opportunity cost of opting for *a* is *b* forgone. The chooser actually gets what he chooses. This feature of market choice is distinctive. At the ballot box, in particular contrast, the agent is nondecisive. The opportunity cost of "choosing" electoral option *A* is not the other option *B* forgone (or, at least, not in any except very remote cases): Whether option *A* or option *B* actually emerges as the electoral outcome is a matter not of how I vote, but of how everyone else does. Electoral outcome is *detached* from electoral "choice" for each voter in a crucial way. This fact radically alters the account we must give of electoral behavior. It implies that unlike the case in analogous market settings, there is no one-to-one connection between voter preference over outcome and voter choice. Consequently, the considerations that predominate in market choice cannot be presumed to predominate in electoral choice. Specifically, market behavior reflects agent "interests" in a way that electoral behavior does not.

If electoral behavior is not "interested," at least in any normal sense, what is it? What kind of account within the rational actor tradition can we offer for it? The account we shall give is in terms of "expressive" behavior, in a sense yet to be defined. What we conjecture is that, often enough, though by no means invariably, expressive behavior will reflect various kinds of ethical and ideological principles that are suppressed in the market setting. Politics therefore gives much freer range to ethical considerations than do markets. For example, to the extent that popular ethics include a concern for "just" prices, just price considerations may be relevant in explaining political intervention in markets, even though in the absence of such political intervention just price considerations would play no role in the market process as such. Just price ethics might, in this way, provide an explanation of policies like rent control, minimum wage legislation, and the pricing strategies of state enterprises – and this not because those policies were imposed by some benevolent despot, but because ethical considerations dormant in market behavior become significant in the polling booth. For this reason, the political process may often enough look rather like the sort of quest for "truth" and "justice" (and "the American way of life" perhaps) that public choice scholars identify with the benevolent despot conception. Political process may look like this because these terms (truth, justice, etc.) are pregnant with symbolism and likely to mobilize support in the electoral arena. The benevolent *despot* model of politics may be grossly defective, but the benevolent *voter* model of politics may be much closer to reality than public choice orthodoxy recognizes.

Having said this, we should emphasize that our claim is not that interests play no role in democratic politics at all. Our critique of public choice orthodoxy is restricted to the behavior of *voters*. The argument has no direct implications for the behavior of politicians and bureaucrats. The argument might well have some indirect implications: Electoral constraints are a sufficiently central piece of democratic machinery that it would be surprising if voters' behavior did not have its echoes throughout the whole political process. But initially, at least, and except where otherwise specified, we shall maintain the public choice hypothesis that politicians and bureaucrats are predominantly self-interested and that they operate to serve their individual interests except where constrained to do otherwise by institutional arrangements (and by electoral competition specifically). Note also that our arguments do not bear on questions of lobbying, or paying of bribes, or making campaign contributions, except possibly indirectly. In some public choice models, lobbying is conceived as the primary mechanism by which particular interests are fed into public policy making. The connection between lobbying group and politician (or bureaucrat) is an ordinary transaction of a market type in our typology: There is a direct quid pro quo. There may be other puzzles associated with lobbying, but they will not be our concern here. The only possible aspect of the lobbying question on which our argument bears arises when the lobbyists themselves are elected or are the agents of persons elected, under reasonably large-number electoral procedures.

More generally, it is worth offering the reminder that the elections are by no means unique to politics. The boards of corporations are elected by shareholder ballot, union officials are elected by union members, producer associations elect their "representative bodies," and so on. The account of electoral decision making we give in what follows bears on these arrangements as well. Generalized applications of our reasoning are clearly called for. However, we shall not pursue these generalizations in this book. The political setting is quite rich and complex enough.

A road map

In this initial chapter, we have offered a brief description of public choice theory and of how our application and critique of it fits into a broader scheme. In particular, we have tried to expose the concerns by which public choice analysis is impelled and to show how the homo economicus behavioral postulate is relevant to those concerns.

Briefly put, public choice theory (or rational actor political theory as it may more aptly be called), in both its positive and normative variants, is much more committed to the principle of motivational neutrality than to homo economicus or any other particular motivational model. Or at least, public choice theory ought to be so committed, given its ambitions. Those ambitions as we see it are twofold: to develop a single, unified social theory on rational actor foundations, in which behavior in markets and political arenas are encompassed as special cases of the more general theory; and to evaluate the normative properties of alternative institutional arrangements via an analytical procedure that avoids implicit bias. Motivational neutrality is a critical piece of both enterprises.

The principle of motivational neutrality is, in any event, one that we accept and are prepared to defend. We assert, however, that when the logic of rational action is faithfully applied, motivational neutrality implies behavioral nonneutrality. We claim that although homo economicus may be a useful abstraction in explaining market behavior, he is unlikely to be as useful in a theory of electoral politics. Voters cannot properly be modeled as choosing the electoral option that would, if it prevailed, best satisfy their interests, and in this critical respect the standard public choice account of democratic political process is flawed.

The implications of this fact for the particular ambitions of public choice theory are discomfiting. The possibility of a unified social theory is not totally undermined, but there must be some retreat from its more simple and direct articulations. The sciences of economics and politics remain related, but there are significant differences of method – differences significant enough to require that the two sciences be pursued as distinct enterprises. Equally, comparative institutional evaluation will remain a central part of any proper normative exercise; but it will have to reckon with the effects of institutional choice on the "preferences" that agents reveal, and in doing so will have to appeal to a richer and less abstract normative theory than standard welfare economics provides.

The relevant underlying reasoning is set out in the substance of the book. In Chapter 2 we develop the decision-theoretic logic that underlies our argument, and in Chapter 3 we attempt to put some psychological flesh on those decision-theoretic bones. Chapter 4 considers some analytic details concerned with the probability of being decisive. Chapter 5 traces out the implications for public choice theory more generally. Chapters 6 and 7 consider the empirical warrant for our general claims. Chapter 8 extends the treatment from majority rule to unanimity. In Chapter 9 we consider the analysis of "merit goods" and the broader issues of individual sovereignty that the merit goods concept engages. Chapter 10 examines the implications of our reasoning for the evaluation of democratic rule as distinct from other forms of political organization. And Chapter 11 deals with the constitutional-institutional implications of the whole argument.

A final remark is in order. As the range of epigraphs to the various chapters suggests, the argument in this book is not entirely new. Pieces of it can be found in a wide variety of places, particularly where rational actor political theory is under scrutiny. Specifically, complementary statements of the same or similar ideas can be found in Colm (1965), Barry (1970), Goodin and Roberts (1975), Margolis (1982), and Meehl (1977). We address the Meehl arguments explicitly in Chapter 10, but we have not attempted to connect our discussion directly to the other statements mentioned. We reckon our own account to be more detailed and analytically explicit than these earlier versions; and we have tried to offer a more extensive working-out of the argument's implications than is available anywhere else in the literature.

2 The logic of electoral choice

It may of course be that people just enjoy voting. This could explain why people vote in large elections. But once this type of consideration is brought in, even the ordinal correspondence between votes and preferences is damaged . . . There will not be a one-to-one correspondence between voting for x . . . and preferring x.

Amartya Sen, Collective Choice and Social Welfare

Introduction

The analysis of the choice behavior of individual voters must be recognized as occupying a central place in any theory of democratic politics. This is so whether the ultimate purpose of the theory is normative or purely explanatory, and whether the theorizing is of the formal kind characteristic of modern public choice scholarship or rather more informal. Specifically, the theory of voter behavior has the same logical status in political analysis as the theory of consumer behavior in the analysis of markets. Voters are the *demanders* in the process of political exchange: To ignore voter calculus is therefore like trying to construct standard microeconomics without a theory of demand.

As we have already noted, within the public choice approach to political analysis no distinctive theory of demand is either offered or, in fact, deemed necessary. It has simply been taken for granted that the logic of choice applied in market contexts can be transferred without amendment to the electoral setting. Agents act *rationally,* whatever the institutional environment. Accordingly, the axioms of rational actor theory are all that one needs. Utility functions can be presumed to include as arguments the candidates or policy platforms, or more particularly the political outcomes those candidates/platforms represent; and it can simply be taken as given that each voter will vote for the candidate/platform that maximizes expected utility. Anything else would be to act irrationally, or so the argument would seem to have it.

In fact, there have been one or two quibbles about this among public choice scholars themselves. In the first place, it has long been recognized that public choice orthodoxy has some difficulty explaining why individuals bother to vote at all, at least in the numbers they do. Given the turnout levels that are characteristic in democratic elections, no single voter can reasonably expect to have any influence on the outcome of an election. She will in fact influence the outcome of the election only in the remote case in which there is an exact tie among all other voters: In all other instances, the electoral outcome is entirely independent of her action. If she pulled the wrong lever by mistake, or misread her ballot paper and voted for the wrong candidate, the world of politics would be no different: Unless there is a dead heat as a result of the votes of all other voters, nothing would change. And the possibility of such a tie must be counted as extraordinarily remote. Just what the prior probability of a tie among all others is, is a matter we take up in greater detail in Chapter 4. But using the conventional procedure, the relevant probability in a typical U.S. presidential election is, at most, of the order of one in twelve and a half thousand, and is almost certainly very much smaller. Consequently, unless the returns to the voter from securing the victory of her favored candidate are enormous, or the cost of voting is negligible, or voters expect turnout to be very much smaller than anything historically recorded, it simply does not pay the individual to bother to go to the polls. Those vast numbers of American voters who do not vote on election day – and who are the despair of the U.S. Democratic Party – are the only people who behave consistently with the standard public choice account. Whether they ought to do so, in the face of much moral urging to the contrary, is a matter we shall take up in Chapter 10. At this point, we simply note that electoral outcomes are determined by the behavior of individuals who, in the standard account, must be counted as acting irrationally – or at least whose rationality must be a matter of considerable doubt.

In the second place, and along somewhat similar lines, it has been generally accepted following Downs's influential early contribution (1957) that voters will rationally be underinformed about political options. (Downs's phrase is "rationally ignorant.") Because political decisions are collectively made, information about public policies and their consequences becomes a pure public good in the strict Samuelsonian sense and, hence, will tend to be underproduced by rational agents. This is a contrast here with information about private goods, which is itself technically "private" and which individuals have incentives to acquire as a direct result of their utility maximization calculus. Voters will not, then, have as much incentive to acquire information about electoral options as those same individuals would have in connection with ordinary market choices.

For our purposes, these arguments are highly suggestive. But they have not been allowed to bite very deep into the standard account of voter behavior. They have been treated pretty much as footnote complications in the broad sweep of the public choice saga. The theory may have some difficulty in explaining *why* people go to the polls in the numbers they do, but such difficulties have never obtruded much into the account of what those people do when they get there. Whatever impels them to go, natural self-interest can be relied on to explain *how* they vote. And equally, though the voter may, because of Downsian "rational ignorance," only dimly perceive how policies/candidates translate into her interests, it is nevertheless those dimly perceived interests that drive the direction of her vote. In this way, public choice orthodoxy has been largely insulated from the real thrust of the rational ignorance–irrational participation arguments.

And it is, perhaps, easy enough to see why. Consider the following:

"Definition" 1. i votes for $s^* \in S \Leftrightarrow U_i(s^*) \geqq U_i(S)$ for all $s \in S$, where S is the set of electoral options, and U_i is i's utility function over those options.

For the economist at least, merely to contemplate that definition is to be drawn to its self-evident validity. "Definition" 1 describes, so it appears, exactly what rational action requires, and to give up on it would seem to sacrifice the whole apparatus of rational actor analysis.

But appearance here is misleading. Treated not as a definition, but as a proposition derived from a more general decision-theoretic framework, "Definition" 1 is false. Put another way, the strict one-to-one logical connection between preference and choice behavior, characteristic of market choice, is severed at the ballot box. We may legitimately talk of agent choice as "revealing preference" in appropriately idealized market settings, but this revealed preference logic simply does not go through in the electoral context. Demonstrating that this is so is the central object of this chapter.

It is because we believe that "Definition" 1 is not properly to be taken definitionally but rather treated as a proposition, and moreover as a proposition that is false, that we have placed quotation marks around the word "Definition." It is, however, useful at this point to introduce a piece of terminology. We will describe behavior in accordance with "Definition" 1 as being "pseudorational." "Definition" 1 thereby *defines* pseudorationality. And the central proposition in this chapter is as follows:

Proposition 1. Rational action $\not\Rightarrow$ pseudorational voting.

Before we proceed to prove this central proposition, one final preliminary remark is in order. Note that the claim is a negative not a positive one. We are aiming to show that a "natural" extrapolation from market to political behavior is inappropriate. We are not offering here a fully fledged theory of electoral conduct; that is for later. Moreover, our reasoning here is logical not empirical. Specifically, although we shall demonstrate – in our view conclusively – that there is no one-to-one *logical* connection between voter preference over electoral outcomes and choice at the ballot box, we do not deny that there may be an *empirical* connection. We do not claim that we can, by logic, show that there cannot be any such connection. That is, we do not and cannot deny here that some individuals may vote in accordance with their preferences over electoral outcomes some of the time – or even that most do so most of the time. What we do deny is that the axioms of rational behavior *require* that they will do so. Consider the argument – all swans are white; this creature is white; therefore is a swan. To recognize that this argument is logically flawed is not to deny that the creature may, after all, be a swan: It is rather to recognize that the argument itself provides no reason for thinking so. In the same way, we shall argue that the axioms of rational choice do not in any way support the assumption of voter pseudorationality, and we deny as a consequence that behavior patterns evident from market settings can legitimately be transferred to the electoral context without a great deal in the way of further argument. We can, in short, declare open an issue that public choice theory has declared to be closed – the issue of what voters do when they vote. And having declared that issue open, we can proceed to develop, from the underlying rationality logic *properly interpreted,* our own theory of electoral behavior.

The central result

Our strategy in arguing for Proposition 1 is to attack the principle of behavioral neutrality, as outlined in the previous chapter. We seek to argue that market and electoral behavior are not logically equivalent. To do so, we shall conduct a conceptual experiment of the kind characteristic of so-called comparative institutional analysis and somewhat analogous to comparative static analysis in conventional economic theory. That is, we compare the actor's decision calculus in the two institutional settings – market and ballot – holding everything else constant.

A brief comment about the use of the ceteris paribus device in this context is in order. The shift from market to ballot typically involves changing more than the decision-making mechanism. If the archetype of ballot decision is taken to be elections in national politics, then both the frequency and the domain of choice are very different from that involved in most market choices. Individuals do not choose in the marketplace whether to go to war or to pursue peace; they do not choose among alternative macroeconomic policies or whether to legalize abortion. And even if we restrict electoral decision making to a particularly quite narrow issue, one that is close to standard consumer choice, there is the fact that in the market the individual chooses only for himself, whereas at the polling booth he chooses for everyone, himself included. If individuals care at all what happens to others, that concern would be expected to influence electoral choices differentially. Moreover, political options typically present themselves as candidates for office rather than as specific policies; and the connection between those candidates and the bundles of goods and services for the voter's consumption those candidates imply is often rather obscure. All these differences between market and electoral choice are important, but for our purposes it is best to suppress them and to focus, thereby, on matters of more immediate concern.

On this basis, consider the rational individual presented with a choice between exactly the same options, designated a and b, in the two institutional settings – marketplace and ballot box. By assumption, a and b involve the same bundle of goods and services to be selected for consumption by the chooser.

The market choice has been the object of extensive study by economists and needs little analysis here. It is to be emphasized, however, that in the market setting the chooser is *decisive:* The opportunity cost of choosing a is b forgone. It is this latter fact that enables the observer to conclude that the chooser prefers a or b and, equivalently, that allows the economist to speak of the individual's choice as "revealing" her preference.

The contrast with choice in the electoral setting is notable. In casting his vote, the individual can reckon on three possible contingencies: where a majority of others vote for a, where a majority of others vote for b, and where there is an exact tie among all other voters.[1] Clearly, it is only in the third of these cases that the op-

---

[1] For simplicity, we take the total number of voters to be odd, so that an exact tie among all others is a contingency that each recognizes is feasible. Otherwise, one has to contend with the prospect of making rather than breaking a tie and, specifically, of how the outcome is decided when a tie prevails. For our purpose here this is a minor complication, and we shall assume it away for expositional reasons.

portunity cost of a vote for *a* is *b* forgone. In both the former cases, the voter receives one or other bundle irrespective of the preference he himself exhibits. In that sense, it is misleading to describe electoral "choice" as a choice between *a* and *b:* It is, rather, a choice between expressing a preference for *a* and expressing a preference for *b* – between a *vote* for *a* and a *vote* for *b*. Voting for *a* actually brings about the electoral outcome voted for only in the case where there is an exact tie among the other voters. It is only in this, presumably rather remote, case that the opportunity cost of voting for *a* is *b* forgone: In all other cases, the opportunity cost of voting for *a* is simply not voting for *b*, with no implications for the electoral outcome at all.

The magnitude of the probability of an exact tie among all other voters is obviously an important question in this context and has been a matter of some controversy in public choice theory circles. We shall examine the relevant literature in Chapter 4. For our purposes here, the question of just how big or small that probability is turns out not to be crucial, as we shall show. In any event, we simply take it as given that the probability of a tie will be quite small and conceivably not much different from zero in plausible cases. As we have noted, the probability of being decisive in a U.S. presidential election with an electorate of around 150 million voters is at most 1 in 12,500 and is almost certainly much smaller. In some ways, given the electoral size, this probability may seem surprisingly large: It implies though that the voter would have to live for several thousand years in order to expect to have a fifty–fifty chance of actually *choosing* a president.

Our interest here, however, is not in the exact magnitude of the probability of being decisive as in what one can induce from voters' behavior at the polls about voters' preferences over electoral outcomes. In dealing with this latter issue, it is useful to compartmentalize the individual's choice of the direction of the vote into two elements:

(i) The instrumental or outcome-causal element, denoted Y_i. This is the value of a vote for *a* that derives from the contribution the vote makes to bringing about the desired electoral outcome. That is,

$$Y^i = R_A^i - R_B^i \qquad \text{if voter } i \text{ is decisive,} \qquad (2.1)$$
$$= 0 \qquad \text{otherwise,}$$

where R_J^i is the money value that voter *i* places on outcome *j*. The *expected* instrumental value of a vote for *a* is then

$$Y^i = h(R_A^i - R_B^i), \qquad (2.2)$$

where *h* is the probability that *i* will be decisive (i.e., the probability of a tie among all other voters).

(ii) The "expressive" or input-causal or "intrinsic" element. This is the value that the voter places on expressing a preference for *a*, rather than *b*, in and of itself (i.e., independent of any effect of the voting act on the electoral *outcome*). Denote this by E^i, again expressed as a money value, where

$$E^i = L^i_A - L^i_B, \tag{2.3}$$

L^i_j being the expressive return to i of expressing a preference for j.

In the standard choice calculus of rational decision theory, no such distinction between instrumental and expressive elements is either customary or necessary. In ordinary market choice, where the chooser is decisive, the various considerations that enter into the individual's "revealed preference" for a over b are all gathered up in the one single calculus and weighed equally dollar for dollar. In *market* choice, therefore, the individual will choose a over b if and only if

$$R^i_A + L^i_A \geqq R^i_B + L^i_B. \tag{2.4}$$

Indeed, economists have tended to regard it as a strength of the revealed preference method that it obviates any need to inquire too deeply into the motives of actors: All the relevant psychological impulse is taken to be subsumed under the single act of choice. The economist can proceed to her analysis on the basis of the observation of that choice, without any further attempt to read the chooser's mind. Accordingly, the economist may have some difficulty in imagining what is at stake in the intrinsic/expressive element of preference revelation, and may doubt whether in fact any such element is present in most choices. We shall, in the next chapter, have both to establish that such an element does exist and to specify something of its nature. However, at this point in the argument we simply introduce the expressive dimension to choice for reasons of logical completeness and will postpone any further discussion of its content.

On this basis, we denote the total expected value W^i of i's voting for a as

$$W^i = Y^i + E^i. \tag{2.5}$$

The rational individual i will vote for a if $W^i > 0$, will vote for b if $W^i < 0$, and will be indifferent if $W^i = 0$. That is, i will vote for a over b if and only if

$$hR^i_A + L^i_A \geqq hR^i_B + L^i_B. \tag{2.6}$$

Comparison of conditions (2.4) and (2.6) reveals that market and electoral choice are different. In the former setting, expressive and instrumental elements in preference revelation are weighed equally; in the latter setting, instrumental elements are h times less important than expressive elements are. Accordingly, we can state our central "comparative institutional" claim as follows.

Proposition 2. The relative price of expressive elements in any act of choice, measured in terms of instrumental benefits forgone, is higher in markets than in electoral settings. As we move from the marketplace to the ballot box, all other things equal, the relative significance of expressive elements increases by a factor equal to the inverse of the probability of being decisive.

Proof. The proof follows directly from a comparison of equations (2.4) and (2.6).

Three remarks

Before proceeding with the main argument, there are several aspects of the fore-going line that are worth emphasizing. First, we have deliberately cast our central proposition in terms of a change in relative prices – the price of intrinsic relative to instrumental benefits in the two institutional settings. Although to some readers that formulation may seem contrived, it exploits language that is significant for all economists and, by extension, all public choice theorists. Economists have a professional predisposition to believe that relative prices matter: If prices change, behavior tends to alter in an entirely predictable manner. If Proposition 2 is valid, then the economist ought to expect market and political behavior to be different. In markets, the agent's choices and the supply responses those choices generate will be relatively strongly oriented toward the consequences of his actions – not least the consequences for his own well-being, or his "private interests." "Political behavior" – by which we here mean electoral choices and the supply responses, if any, that such choices generate – will be relatively strongly oriented toward purely expressive or symbolic action, action that is undertaken for its own sake rather than to bring about particular consequences. Both elements will be present in both contexts, but the rule of consequences and, hence, private interests in the electoral context will be heavily muted and the purely expressive or symbolic greatly magnified. This is simply a matter of relative prices. We should, moreover, emphasize that the relative price change at stake is of an order of magnitude that is enormous in comparison with those with which economists normally deal. Comparative static propositions in microeconomics typically depend on relative price differentials of 20% or perhaps 50% – in unusual cases, like the 1970s oil price hike, three- or fourfold. Here, the relative price effect is of the order of several thousands, at least! Given a relative price change of this magnitude, it must seem to the economist somewhat unlikely on the face of things that market and electoral choice behavior would not be different. And since the price effect is so enormous, one might be forgiven for conceptualizing the resultant institutional differences in qualitative rather than quantitative terms. Equally, however, even if the price differential were not quite so large, the expectation of behavioral differences would remain. As a relative price proposition, this particular one involves comfortable overkill.

This brings us to our second point. Consider the role that the probability of being decisive plays in our reasoning. Even if that probability turned out to be quite high, it must still take values considerably less than unity, and our logic would be un-impaired. It is important to make this point for several reasons. In the first place, some attention has been devoted by certain public choice scholars to the value of this probability in an attempt to salvage the "private interest" theory of electoral participation. Clearly, if the probability of being decisive were large enough and if voters could be assumed to have a great deal at stake in the election, then it may be possible to explain voter turnouts of the size we observe without recourse to any purely intrinsic benefit derived from the act of voting per se. Conceivably this is so, although we ourselves do not find the reasoning at stake here particularly persuasive (for reasons outlined in Chapter 4). But whether the expected instrumental benefits of voting are large enough to explain voter turnout or not, the logic of Proposition 2 remains unimpaired. That is, although the presence of intrinsic benefits may not be necessary to explain the fact that people vote in the numbers they do, these intrinsic benefits must nevertheless be differentially potent in influencing the direction of the vote cast. It is one thing to argue that the probability of a tie is above some threshold level necessary to explain attendance at the polls, another entirely to argue that it is negligibly different from unity. Casual reflection on electoral history should be enough to persuade us that dead heats and single-vote victories are, if not entirely unknown, quite rare. What we claim is that the precise value of the probability of a tied vote, although clearly an important parameter quantitatively, is not crucial to the *qualitative* difference between market and electoral institutions. In this sense, much of the literature on the probability of a tie is somewhat beside the point for our purposes. That literature seems to have been motivated primarily by the issue of explaining voter turnout. In some ways, that focus is regrettable. The implications of nondecisiveness for the logic of electoral choice are, as we see it, much more significant.

Third and relatedly, it should be emphasized that Proposition 2 is not restricted in its coverage to large-number general elections characteristic of Western democracies: The qualitative claim – if not the magnitude of the effect – remains valid for the case of small-number elections, and collective decisions of boards, assemblies, and committees. In an academic board of fifty-one members, the probability of an exact tie among all other voters is (using standard methods of calculation) at most of the order of one in twelve. Even here, then, the consequential element in expressing a preference on such a board is significantly muted as compared with the choice in an analogous market setting: The role of expressive elements in individuals' revealed preferences will be relatively important even in this small-number context. In other words, Proposition 2 applies generally to the whole range of collective decision-making procedures in which the outcome is determined by a direct aggregation of votes rather than the decentralized decision procedure characteristic of market organization. For the most part in what follows, we shall have the large-number setting in mind. Our major interest here is in the workings of majoritarian electoral politics and, particularly, in the normative properties of democratic decision making. However, it is worth noting that our central logic is more general than this: Political and market behavior will tend to be different even where politics is a matter for the "central committee" and not for the populace as a whole. If we imagine a spectrum running from the case in which the chooser is decisive through cases in which the chances of his being decisive are increasingly remote, then the role of expressive relative to instrumental elements in preference revelation increases along that spectrum until, in the limit, expressive considerations become the sole determinant of "choice" behavior. Large-number democratic elections lie well toward the latter pole; small-number committees lie toward the former. The idealized case of market choice, to which the conventional decision-theoretic apparatus fully applies, is to be seen as the limiting polar case of complete agent decisiveness.

Table 2.1. *Electoral choice as a game of each against all*

Each	All others		
	Majority for *a*	Majority for *b*	Tie (probability *h*)
Vote for *a*	$L_A + R_A$	$L_A + R_B$	$L_A + R_A$
Vote for *b*	$L_B + R_A$	$L_B + R_B$	$L_B + R_B$

An alternative formulation

It is useful for the discussion that follows to present the voter's decision-making calculus in a slightly different form – as an *n*-person game among all voters. The *n*-person interaction can without significant loss be collapsed into a simple two-"person" game, of "each" against "all others." Since each is the decision maker, it is sufficient to show only the payoff to each in the relevant cells of a conventional matrix: The outcome for all can simply be induced from the behavior of each. The strategies or actions available to each voter are vote for *a* and vote for *b*. As we have noted, the voter can reckon on three possibilities: a majority of all others for *a*, a majority for *b*, and a perfect tie, the probability of which is rather small. The relevant payoffs to each are depicted in the cells of Table 2.1 using the notation already introduced.

Assuming that voters are risk neutral, it can easily be verified that each will vote for *a* if and only if

$$(L_A - L_B) \geqq h(R_A - R_B), \tag{2.7}$$

which is simply an alternative formulation of 2.6. We can use this matrix to isolate the two polar extremes. The choice in the idealized market setting corresponds to that in the final column: In that case the chooser is decisive, and what she chooses will be what she genuinely prefers. The opposite extreme appears as the probability *h* goes to zero. In this event, the final column of Table 2.1 disappears, and the voter is left with an unambiguous dominant strategy: vote for *a* or *b* depending on which renders the higher expressive benefit. Further, in those cases in which the expressive and instrumental benefits yield *different* rankings of *a* and *b*, then the game in Table 2.1 may take on the properties of an *n*-person prisoners' dilemma. A simple example illustrates: Suppose $L_A = 5, L_B = 0, R_B = 100, R_A = 0$ for all voters, and *h* is negligibly small. Then, the particular payoff structure is that illustrated in Table 2.2. Each voter is led (as if by an invisible backhand, one might say) to vote for an electoral outcome that none wants. Each will vote for *a*, though each would prefer that *b* prevail (i.e., even though each would choose *b* if she were decisive).

The numerical example is, of course, generalizable. For a risk-neutral voter, the necessary condition for market choice and electoral choice to go in different directions is that

$$(R_B - R_A) > (L_A - L_B) > h(R_B - R_A) > 0, \tag{2.8}$$

Table 2.2. *Electoral choice as a quasi-prisoners' dilemma*

| | All others | | |
Each	Majority for *a*	Majority for *b*	Tie (probability → 0)
Vote for *a*	5	105	5
Vote for *b*	0	100	100

where *b* is taken without loss of generality to be the genuinely preferred outcome. Attitude to risk will of course modify condition (2.8) but cannot, in general, rule out such prisoners'-dilemma-like outcomes. There is indeed nothing in the standard decision-theoretic logic that can rule out the possibility that market and electoral preferences can diverge. Accordingly, our central logical claim must be sustained. The one-to-one logical connection that obtains between choice and preference in idealized market settings simply does not hold in the analogous electoral setting. Pseudorational electoral behavior, as set out in "Definition" 1, does not follow as a theorem from the axioms of rational choice theory.

The normative implications

The degree of individual decisiveness establishes, we have suggested, a notional spectrum across which instrumental and expressive concerns play differentially significant roles in accounting for rational choice behavior. In that continuum of possible cases, however, the polar extreme of ideal market behavior represents a normatively salient point – a benchmark against which all other cases can be set; for it is only at that extreme that the agent's behavior reveals his *true* preferences. That is, only in the limiting case of individual decisiveness does the revealed preference logic go through. In all other cases, action is "distorted" in the sense that behavior and preference diverge: It cannot be presumed that rational individuals will choose the option they genuinely prefer. Accordingly, we can state the following corollary to Proposition 2:

Proposition 3. Preferences revealed in electoral settings do not possess the same normative authority as those revealed in an idealized market context.

For the standard economist, well acculturated to the normative authority of individuals' preferences in purely private goods, the claim will perhaps seem an entirely natural implication of Proposition 2. The formulation of electoral choice as an *n*-person interaction with properties that will, in plausible cases, be those of the prisoners' dilemma tells its own story: Citizens may, entirely rationally, vote for outcomes they would not choose if decisive – outcomes that, in the standard decision-theoretic formulation, they can be recognized not to want. In short, if the preferences revealed at the ballot box diverge systematically from those revealed in ideal markets, then electoral institutions are normatively inadequate. Even if political institutions were such as to ensure that political outcomes accurately reflect individuals' electoral preferences (e.g., as in the median-voter/spatial-competition model under single peakedness), those political outcomes would not necessarily be normatively desirable. The electoral preferences themselves are potentially distorted through the peculiarities of the ballot box as a revelatory device. Individual sovereignty at the ballot box and in the marketplace mean very different things, and only the latter has the full normative authority of revealed preference.

Now, of course, this observation may serve to direct attention to questions about the revealed preference framework itself. Are agents really rational even in idealized markets? Might expressive preferences exhibit certain virtues that instrumental concerns lack? These are important questions that we shall take up in some detail in later chapters. But it is clear that within conventional welfare economics and much normative democratic theory, the capacity of institutions to deliver the outcomes that individuals want is the acid test of acceptability; and that within the rational actor tradition, the outcomes that individuals want are those that maximize their utility functions. Since the preferences to which *collective* decision mechanisms give rise do not do this, then there must be a strong normative presumption against those decision mechanisms and in favor of institutions in which agents' choices are decisive (such as idealized markets). It might equally be charged that any comparison of electoral choice with *idealized* market choice begs all the relevant questions. It is, after all, nothing new to observe that the case for the use of electoral decision making depends on markets not being idealized. The theory of the state that is developed in conventional welfare economics is based precisely on generalized "market failure": This is what "public goods theory" is all about. Accordingly, so the argument might go, the relevant institutional comparison must be with markets that are afflicted with externalities, monopolies, and other barriers to optimality. And within such real-world markets, the preferences "revealed" by agent choice do not prepresent those agents' true preferences either.

We have no difficulty with this argument. Indeed, in some ways, the argument makes our point. Anyone who embraces the theory of government activity implied by public goods analysis is logically compelled to recognize that the excessive intrusion of the expressive element in collective choice is a problem just as the free-rider option is a problem in public goods provision in the marketplace: Analytically, the problems are of the same type. At another level, however, the anxiety is beside the point. Just as in market failure theory we compare actual market outcomes with some benchmark ideal, so we do here. The object is to isolate "political failure" in the same terms as we do market failure. Ultimately, a comparison of actual market and actual political institutions will be required. But as a first step, we need to focus on the normative properties of collective decision-making processes per se. And for this purpose, the crucial contrast is between cases in which the chooser is *decisive* and those in which she is not. It is the entries presented in the final column of Tables 2.1 and 2.2 that indicate the true value of the options *a* and *b* to the chooser. Whether those entries correspond to the values attached to outcomes in some actual market setting is an important question, but it is a different one. No problems in interpretation should arise providing it is understood that the notion of idealized markets is an analytic artifact rather than a reference to an actual operational institutional form.

However, there is a sense in which the problem with electoral process that we expose here occurs at a different, and more basic, level than market failure problems do. The notion of an ideal market is at least conceptually coherent. By contrast, because electoral choice is intrinsically nondecisive and because, as a result, expressive considerations obtrude excessively *as a logically necessary feature of the institutional form,* electoral choices are, by the standards of ordinary welfare economics, intrinsically flawed in a way that market institutions are not.

Coda

The argument so far has been one concerning the decision-theoretic logic of electoral "choice." That logic has the same status as the logic of rational actor behavior that underlies the orthodox theory of market behavior. But the logic of electoral choice can take us only so far. The public choice economist might well accept that one cannot logically derive pseudorational (or self-interested) voting from the basic axioms of rational behavior, but deny that this failure has any real empirical bite – that it lacks empirical teeth. Specifically, he might simply argue that, as a matter of fact, the assumption that voters are entirely self-interested "works" well enough in explaining electoral outcomes and certainly better than any comparably abstract and tractable behavior assumption.

Such a claim is, of course, perfectly coherent and cannot be rejected on logical grounds. Whether homo economicus "works" in electoral contexts becomes an empirical question and can only be settled by consulting the empirical record. The relevant evidence will be examined in Chapters 6 and 7. Like most empirical evidence, it is not totally conclusive. In this area as in most others, the debate tends to be decided on the basis of where the onus of proof is taken to lie.

And it is in this allocation of the burden of proof that the "logic of electoral choice" carries great weight. If one accepts that there is no reason to believe that rational voters will cast ballots for the candidate/policy whose victory most conduces to their own self-interest – if one accepts that the evidence about human behavior gleaned from market contexts is logically irrelevant for explaining electoral behavior (and the political outcomes that might be driven by it) – then one has no independent reason to defend the homo economicus model in politics. But the vigor with which the use of homo economicus in democratic politics is defended by public choice scholars suggests that the defenders believe there is a great deal at stake in relinquishing that use – that giving up on homo economicus in politics would be to give up on the whole rational actor paradigm. As we have shown, this is not so. Public choice theorists have generally assigned the onus of proof to those who would dispute the hypothesis of self-interested voting. They have extrapolated directly from market behavior in the mistaken belief that pseudorational voting is what the axioms of rational choice require. In other words, it has been the logic of choice, incorrectly applied to be sure, that has served to allocate the burden of proof. Given that the burden of proof plays so significant a role in the argument, it is quite crucial to get the basic choice logic right.

But the argument against self-interested voting (and pseudorational voting more generally) that we want to develop in this book is stronger than this. We believe that the empirical claims, as well as the logic, of orthodox public choice theory are mistaken. To attack homo economicus in electoral politics in the context of our decision-theoretic language requires us to argue two things – first, that these expressive elements in preference revelation do actually exist; and second, that they do not mirror instrumental elements all the time. The need for the former argument is clear. A relative price change in favor of some object that has no value at all does not induce the rational chooser to buy more of it: The object must be an object of desire – it must actually enter the agent's utility function. The reason for the latter argument is that if rankings of all options according to expressive and instrumental valuations are virtually identical, then individuals can be treated *as if* they vote pseudorationally without great violence to reality. In other words, it is the claim that electoral and idealized market choice are likely to *differ* that is interesting, both for predictive and for normative purposes. We want in what follows to argue for this "difference" claim. If we can make a credible argument to that effect, we will have grounds to reject the narrow self-interest theory of voting behavior characteristic of most public choice analysis, and grounds also to accept the relevance of prisoners' dilemma problems at the level of voter "preference."

And if we can make such an argument, we shall also be able to offer pieces of a conceptually testable theory of electoral behavior. Our ambition is then not just to reject the self-interest model: We also want to be able to explain something of what we observe in politics. To do this, we need to explore the content of expressive preferences. That is the object of the ensuing chapter.

3 The nature of expressive returns

The pyro-technics of party management and party advertising slogans and mar-
ching tunes are not accessories. They are the essence of politics.
Joseph Schumpeter, Capitalism, Socialism and Democracy

Introduction

The argument developed in the preceding chapter depends crucially on a distinction
between instrumental and intrinsic elements in preference revelation. To the economist at least, and possibly to others, any such distinction may seem somewhat
bizarre. The notion that preference revelation can be a consumption activity generating benefits in and of itself (and distinct from the benefits derived from the consumption of the object chosen) is hardly an integral part of the standard theory of
consumer behavior. In that standard account, the individual chooses *A* over *B* because he prefers *A* over *B,* not because he prefers to prefer *A* over *B:* The individual
is presumed to derive utility directly from the consumption of goods and services,
rather than from having a particular utility function. It may well seem excessively
contrived, and even rather suspicious, to invoke any such possibilities. Consequently, while intrinsic elements in preference revelation may be included for reasons of logical completeness in a purely theoretical exposition, there comes a point
at which we must indicate why it is reasonable to suppose that such intrinsic elements are present and what they consist of. Such is the object of this chapter.

As we have already mentioned, the line of reasoning in Chapter 2 can be de-
flected by either of two claims: first, that intrinsic elements in preference revelation
do not exist; or second, that intrinsic and consequential elements invariably lead in
the same direction (that the L_i and R_i terms introduced in equations (2.4) and (2.6)
are perfectly positively correlated). It will be our aim to refute these claims. In the
process we shall hope to offer something by way of specific hypotheses concerning
the content of electoral preference from which a "science," as distinct from a
"logic," of voter choice can be developed.[1]

The arguments we present must, by their nature, involve some speculation about
the sorts of considerations that weigh in the chooser's mind in deciding to express
a preference for any object of choice. The speculation necessary for our purposes
does not require any particularly detailed analysis of chooser psychology, but it is
clear that some minimal foray into what we might call "the psychology of choice"
is required. It is worth emphasizing that this is an area that modern economics
makes some effort to avoid. Within the standard account of market choice, there is
no need to inquire why it is that the individual chooses *A* over *B*. Once rationality

---

[1] We appeal here to James Buchanan's (1980, chap. 2) distinction between the science of choice and the
logic of choice in conventional economics.

is assumed, the fact that A is chosen is enough: Further inquiry into exactly what motivated the choice is taken to be entirely unnecessary. For this reason, one point needs to be established at the outset: Any argument that seeks to deny the importance of intrinsic elements in preference revelation is itself a claim about the chooser's mind. And of course, the same goes for any claim to the effect that intrinsic and consequential elements tend to be mutually supporting. In other words, no coherent defense of the assumption of self-interested voting is possible without making substantive psychological claims. It is simply a fact that any theory of voter choice demands a rather richer psychological apparatus than economists typically rely on, or believe to be necessary. So, with a certain girding of the economist's loins, we proceed.

Do intrinsic returns exist?

The claim that intrinsic elements in choice exist and are nonnegligible is, in our view, almost trivially obvious. There are, for a start, a range of quite familiar situations in which individuals reveal preferences or express desires quite independently of any capacity to bring the preferred/desired outcome about. Every Saturday afternoon in the relevant season, for example, vast numbers of sporting fans toddle off to the game of their choice or sit glued to the live television coverage. While at the game they will cheer their favored teams. Indeed, cheering is not entirely unknown in certain domestic living rooms. The fans in question clearly have a preference as to which team they would like to win, and this is a preference that their cheering and booing unequivocally declare. But even the most enthusiastic partisan does not and cannot believe that his cheering brings about the outcome for which his cheering is expressed. The fan does not go to the game and cheer as a means to the end of securing his team's success: He goes to support his team, but does not choose its victory. A fortiori, the television viewer may yell encouragement to the players and even, in extremis, kick the screen in when his team is being beaten, but he cannot believe that by doing so he affects the outcome. The fan's actions are *purely expressive.* They arise from a desire to express feelings and desires simply for the sake of the expression itself and without any necessary implication that the desired outcome will be brought about thereby. Revealing a preference is a direct consumption activity, yielding benefits to the individual in and of itself.

Consider an alternative example. Ms. A's friend, Mr. B, is ill. A sends B a get-well card expressing the desire that B recover speedily. The card (possibly quite an expensive one) expresses a desire, but it is not itself conceived to bring about the end concerning which the desire is expressed. Although receipt of the card may have mild therapeutic value, it is no substitute for medical treatment and is not normally construed by the sender to be so. The expression of desire is detached from instrumental action. There is no object in the card sending except the card sending. It is not a means to an end; it is itself the desired end.

The two examples are capable of generalization. Within the rational actor tradition in social theory, all human action can be conceived as the outcome of an act of choice. Consider then an activity that is often isolated as being the distinguishing activity of the human species – speech. Clearly, some speech is of an instrumental kind – giving instructions, asking a price, requesting directions. But much is also of a purely expressive kind, a consumption activity generating direct benefits: Storytelling, playacting, and most ordinary conversation are examples. The object of this sort of talking is to reveal something about oneself – one's feelings, desires, or attitudes. It can hardly be argued seriously that this is an uncommon activity. People do it all the time. And what is true of talk is true of the whole range of expressive, self-revelatory, or symbolic actions. When I shake my fist at a passing motorist, expressing thereby my irritation at his having run over my foot, this is an action with a purpose: The purpose is to express my irritation.

Such examples are ones in which the only purpose is expressive – where the intrinsic element is the sole one in the relevant decision-theoretic calculus. They are also cases that are somewhat remote from conventional economic analysis. But it seems clear to us that intrinsic elements in preference revelation are also present in many ordinary consumer decisions. Consider for example the nature of much modern advertising. Recall in doing so that competitive pressures in the advertising industry, together with the standard logic of markets, suggest that advertising will tend to reflect fairly accurately what it is that makes potential consumers tick: Advertisers have the greatest incentive to understand buyer psychology, and only advertisers with such understanding will survive. What seems self-evident in this connection is that the consumer is swayed by the symbolic resonance of a product as well as by its functional characteristics. Buy the London *Times* and show yourself to be an intellectually alive and socially successful person! Buy a Volvo and wear the badge of the fashionably humane (a subscription to the Audubon Society, a copy of the UN *Monthly Chronicle,* and an Ethiopian Famine Relief Appeal Envelope come supplied automatically in the glove compartment). Smoke Peter Stuyvesant cigarettes and proclaim yourself a member of the international jet set, and so on. Of course, product characteristics like reliability, taste, fuel economy, or whatever are sometimes mentioned; but interestingly, one is likely to find more of that sort of thing in *Choice* magazine and *Consumer Reports* than on the television screen or the newspaper page. It is difficult, therefore, to resist the conclusion that at least part of what weighs in the typical consumer's choice calculus is the demonstration to herself and others that she is a particular sort of person – the sort who prefers A to B. The articulation of the preference expresses the individual's personality and character, and the individual can be presumed to derive benefits from this articulation as well as from the object over which the preference is expressed.

In the market setting the isolation of specifically expressive benefits from preference revelation may seem contrived because the expression of personality is as much attached to the act of consumption as it is to the act of preference revelation. Ms. Y is as much the person who drives a Volvo as she is the one who prefers a Volvo. However, as we have emphasized in Chapter 2, it is a characteristic feature of choice at the ballot box that the act of preference revelation and the act of consumption are separated. It is only the former that is available for unilateral determination by the individual voter. Accordingly, it is important in the analysis of voting behavior to break down into separate parts what in market analysis may legitimately be treated as a single consumption choice.

And what of expressive returns and/or intrinsic elements to choice at the ballot box specifically? As we noted in Chapter 2, public choice economists have long recognized the need to make appeal to something of the sort in explaining the size of electoral turnouts. It is certainly true that some scholars (most notably Palfrey and Rosenthal, 1983) have disputed that such considerations are necessary to explain turnouts: Their claim is that the probability of being decisive is high enough to make the act of voting quite rational. In our view, however, the arguments offered to support the instrumental view of voting are ultimately unpersuasive. And it is clear that the balance of professional opinion favors our assessment (see, e.g., Riker and Ordeshook, 1978; Grofman, 1983; Mueller, 1987). Various pieces of evidence can be cited to support our position on this matter. For example, given modern vote-counting techniques, it is not inconceivable that if there is a sufficient uniformity in outcomes in the eastern states in the United States, voters on the West Coast will know the outcome of a presidential election before the polls have closed. This was in fact the case in both the Reagan victories in the 1980s. Yet voters continued to go to the polls and to cast votes for one or other presidential candidate long after the result was known. In this case, the voters knew with complete certainty that they could not alter the outcome. Yet they continued to cast presidential votes – in apparently moderated, but still substantial numbers. Presumably they derived benefits from doing so: It is simply that the benefits were not of an instrumental kind.

As we have mentioned, this line of reasoning has been widely accepted in public choice circles in connection with the issue of turnout. But the simple straightforward extrapolation to the issue of voter choice among electoral options has been essentially ignored. Public choice orthodoxy seems to assume that though noninstrumental considerations are relevant in getting voters to go to the polls in the first place, such considerations cease to bear once the voter slips behind the curtain to pull a lever or mark a card. The argument seems to be that while considerations of duty, or a sense of public responsibility, or the desire to participate in a public event may explain attendance at the polls, the voter once there has already "paid the price of attending" as it were and so will rationally proceed to vote his interests. In determining *how* to vote, the cost in deciding *whether* to vote (in terms of other activities forgone) is a sunk cost, and the considerations that were weighed in the decision to bear that cost are therefore irrelevant. Any such argument strikes us as hopelessly implausible. Indeed, it is not an argument at all so much as an appeal to the "why not" question. Although the voter has already recognized that whether and how he votes will exercise negligible influence on the political outcome, he is nevertheless presumed to vote his interest on the grounds that he might as well do so – voting his interest will provide some (very small) benefit as compared, say, with voting randomly. But this line is simply to assume that the voter has no reason to do anything other than vote his interest. It is to assume that random voting is the only sensible alternative, that to vote randomly would be consistent with the considerations that induced the individual to attend the polls in the first place. Is it really the case that civic duty requires only presence at the polls? Does it not entail also some ''responsibility'' in deciding which vote to cast? If the act of voting is a matter of sufficient moral seriousness to induce the individual to go to the polls, it would surely be surprising if moral considerations did not bear on what the voter does when he gets there. After all, the decision to vote entails the decision to vote for someone. It is difficult to see how a coherent case could be made for the view that the former decision is morally or otherwise significant without the latter decision also being so.[2]

Public choice analysis has been insistent on avoiding any assumption of schizophrenia in dealing with actors in their electoral and market roles: This has been a major consideration in advancing the self-interest theory of voting. Here, we detect just that assumption of voter schizophrenia that public choice theorists seem to find so objectionable: Attending the polls is predominantly an activity undertaken for its own sake, while casting a vote once there is to be explained as a means to something else. In our view, antipathy to schizophrenia is well grounded. The burden of proof lies on those who claim violent changes in motivational structure. Whatever motives are construed to carry the individual to the polls should be presumed to carry through to the act that gives attendance at the polls its point.[3]

And, from casual observation, it seems clear that such motives do carry through. Individual voters are to be concerned not only that they attend the polls: They also care how they vote. Voting is a public activity that resonates with social significance: What one does in the voting context is taken to be significant even if the particular individual vote cast has negligible effect on the political outcome. Indeed, individuals can be observed to express preferences in voting forums relating to matters of much less significance than national elections. We recall an episode of the television show ''Saturday Night Live'' in which the burning question put to a nationwide telephone poll of viewers was whether Larry the Lobster was to be consigned to the boiling pot or, instead, saved to clutter around for another day. Thousands of voters contributed their say on this matter, despite the apparent insignificance of the issue.[4]

In summary, then, there seems ample evidence to suggest that expressive elements in preference revelation do exist, are relevant to a wide range of individual choices, and are relevant specifically to those choices undertaken in electoral or electoral-like contexts. Once their existence is granted, of course, the pure logic of choice as developed in Chapter 2 is sufficient to indicate that they will be predom-

---

[2] Issues concerning voter responsibility receive extended discussion in Chapter 10.

[3] Amartya Sen (1970) provides an earlier suggestion along similar lines: ''Indeed, in large elections it is difficult to show that any voter has any real prospect of affecting the outcome by his vote, and if voting involves some cost, the expected net gain from voting may typically be negative. Nevertheless, the proportion of turnout in large elections may still be quite high, and I have tried to argue elsewhere that in such elections people may often be guided not so much by maximization of expected utility, but something much simpler, viz., just a desire to record one's true preference'' (p. 195). Of course, whether the preferences so recorded are indeed ''true'' and what exactly that means must be a matter of contention, which we take up in greater detail in Chapter 8.

[4] A majority of the callers voted to spare Larry. The Lobster's bright red mortal remains were, nonetheless, exhibited by Eddie Murphy to the show's viewers. Might there be some deep lesson to be derived concerning the basic workings of democratic processes?

inant in the electoral setting. Casual observation and introspection of the sort we have engaged in here does, however, seem to strengthen the force of that logic, rather than call it into question.

One final clarification is in order. There are many purely expressive activities that are not connected to preference revelation. When Ms. A remarks that she is content, this is expressive but not of a preference or desire. Any preference or desire by its nature concerns an outcome and possibly alternative outcomes with respect to which the preference is expressed. In that sense, a preference necessarily *relates* to outcome. The intrinsic element in preference revelation – or what we have here called the "expressive" element in order to provide psychological connotation – is therefore not noninstrumental in the sense that it does not *refer* to ends other than the preference revelation itself: It is noninstrumental in the sense that it is not causally connected to the outcome preferred. A spectator may, for example, conceivably simply enjoy cheering. He may even cheer for both teams. His cheering might be said to express a preference for cheering. But such a person is not by his cheering expressing a preference over the outcome of the game. The intrinsic element in preference revelation occurs when the act of revealing a preference *over outcomes* generates benefits. The person who votes just because he likes voting is relevant to electoral outcomes, but hers is not the sort of motivation we are focusing on here.[5] Electoral outcomes are *relevant* to the voter; but they are not relevant in the same way as they would be if the voter were unilaterally to bring the outcome about.

Do expressive and instrumental elements diverge?

On this basis, we shall take it that expressive benefits in preference revelation do exist. Given this, the next question to be answered is whether they are likely to motivate different electoral preferences from those motivated by an instrumental cost–benefit calculation; for as we have already noted, nothing of any normative or explanatory consequence would follow from the argument in Chapter 2 unless there are such differences. All that would be involved would be certain niceties in the way public choice arguments are formulated – matters of interest solely to the logical purists. Needless to say, we believe that there is much more at stake than this. We believe that such differences do exist and that something systematic can be said about them. We must, however, be careful not to overstate our case. We shall in fact argue that there are reasons why expressive and instrumental benefits may be positively correlated in at least some and possibly many cases. But we shall also argue that there are good reasons to believe that such benefits will be negatively related in other cases, and shall endeavor to isolate the circumstances under which these latter cases are likely to arise.

[5] In that sense, the Sen quotation cited as the epigraph to Chapter 2 is apt to be misleading. The one-to-one correspondence between voting for x and preferring x, in the full sense of preference familiar from decision theory, is broken even where people do not "just enjoy voting." Sen's reasoning seems to imply that the reasons one might have for voting are of only two kinds: either outcome oriented or connected with a preference for voting in the same way that the random cheerer has a preference for cheering. We do not know whether or not this is Sen's view, but it is a mistake.

At first sight, the possibility of any divergence between the directions in which expressive and instrumental preferences lead may seem absurd. To appeal to our earlier analogies, are we to be interpreted as arguing that the spectator cheers for a team he does not want to win? Or that the well-wisher sends a get-well card to someone she would prefer to have die? Not at all. The point is rather that the notion of "want" is itself unclear. The crucial question is whether the sorts of considerations that weigh in choosing which team to cheer for are the same as those that weigh in deciding how to invest one's savings or, more particularly, whether various relevant considerations are differentially significant in the two settings. For example, whether or not to send a card to a friend one knows to be dying involves quite a different set of issues from the question of whether or not to put that friend out of his misery if it happened to be in one's power to do so. In the former case, one is unlikely to wish one's friend a speedy death – even though, in the latter case, one might well pull the plug of the life-support system. When one is genuinely decisive – when one actually has the power to determine the outcome – different considerations are brought to bear.

It is perhaps worth emphasizing in this connection the presumptions that underlie the revealed preference tradition in economic theory. For many economists, the only clearly authoritative information about consumer preferences is that derived from the observation of actual choice behavior: Information provided by questionnaires, interviews with potential customers, and the like are either regarded with extreme skepticism or simply ignored. If the economist's judgment about the authority of alternative data sources is to be in any way coherent, it must be believed that questionnaires and interview responses are likely to diverge from observations of actual choice behavior: Otherwise there could be no grounds for preferring the latter. The argument normally offered for such divergence is precisely that only actual choice behavior is subject to the discipline of opportunity cost. For a respondent to say that she would take *A* rather than *B* at such and such a price does not involve actually taking *A* and forgoing *B:* The respondent does not have to live with the consequences of her statement of preference. The close analogy between questionnaire response and voting in this respect is clear: The individual is nondecisive in both settings. Accordingly, a predominant theme in mainstream economics carries a clear implication that we ought to expect electoral and market preference to diverge. To claim that there is no presumption against pseudorational voting is equivalent to reinstating the questionnaire and the interview as sources of information with the full authority of observed behavior, and to reject thereby an important element in the revealed preference tradition.

In fact, the revealed preference tradition, although quite emphatic about the significance of real choice in disciplining behavior, is somewhat coy about the reasons why this is so. And to our knowledge there is very little serious empirical study of the divergence between questionnaire responses and actual behavior. Moreover, the fact that market research makes considerable use of information gleaned from questionnaires – as well as from actual market trials – suggests that the revealed preference tradition may somewhat overstate the case; for in its most extreme form, the economist's claim seems to be not just that "action speaks louder than words" (as it were), but that mere words do not "speak" at all. Even in more modest variants, however, the basic point seems clear: The logic of the behaviorist tradition in economics establishes a presumption in favor of the belief that decisiveness in expressing preferences matters – that the preferences revealed in contexts where the chooser is decisive are likely to differ from those revealed in contexts (such as questionnaire responses, personnel interviews, and, crucially, voting) where the expression of preference is substantially detached from the outcome.

Why might this be so? Several considerations spring immediately to mind. In the first place, there is the prospect of whimsical or fanciful behavior. Individuals can on occasion be playful, even slightly mischievous, in contexts where the consequences to them of being so are not particularly dire. This is perhaps merely a manifestation of human imaginativeness, of a certain speculative or conjectural dimension in the human mind. It can hardly be denied that such dimensions exist, and it is reasonable to suppose both that action undertaken in the absence of a disciplined environment is likely to exhibit these elements in greater measure, and that decisiveness concerning outcome provides just such a discipline.

In the second place, it may be that the determination of a genuine preference requires information gathering and serious reflection that is costly for the individual to pursue: Only the actual choice setting provides incentives to sustain such costs. Here one might have in mind not merely the cost of obtaining information about alternatives (as emphasized in the electoral context by Downs's discussion of "rational ignorance"), but also the cost of dredging about in one's mind as to what it is that one really wants. There is indeed the suggestion in some of the Austrian-subjectivist literature that it is only in the act of choosing that the individual discovers what he wants: It is as if the individual is taken to be psychologically impenetrable even to himself, as if true preferences are themselves part of the stock of inarticulable knowledge and can only be revealed in the act of choice. It is perhaps worth mentioning in this connection the well-worn joke about a postcoital conversation between two behaviorists. She says to him, "Darling, that was wonderful for you. How was it for me?" The real thrust of the joke (no pun intended) is that this is indeed how the logic of psychological behaviorism goes. If this sort of line is taken seriously, it does call into question the authority of verbal speculations about what one's true preferences might be. Being decisive over outcomes, so the argument might go, like a hanging on the morrow, wonderfully concentrates the mind.

Both the considerations examined so far indicate why the preferences that individuals reveal in actual choice over outcome on the one hand, and those revealed by speech, voting, or other "expressions of support," on the other hand, might diverge. But such considerations do not suggest anything substantive in terms of the direction of divergence. The presence of whimsy and ignorance may be predictable, but their content is not necessarily so. There are, however, several other considerations that are sometimes mentioned in the context of revealed preference that do suggest a systematic and predictable bias in the divergence between actions and words (and by extrapolation between market and electoral preference), and these considerations are of more interest in the current setting.

The first of these involves social pressure. Consider, for example, a questionnaire relating to alcohol consumption, gambling expenditure, or domestic violence – some area of activity in which community norms obtrude. In such cases, the revealing of a particular preference is not neutral with respect to the evaluative response it draws from the interviewer: In indicating a preference for wife beating, for example, the individual must recognize the possible cost to himself in terms of the interviewer's approval. Obversely, in indicating a preference for, say, the interests of children in developing countries (as in the milk-substitute controversy), the respondent is likely to elicit public approval. Clearly, much here will depend on the publicness or privacy of the response: An entirely anonymous questionnaire will not be subject to such considerations to the same extent. The bias that is involved here is clearly connected to what, in the case of divergence between speech and action, we would refer to as "hypocrisy." Hypocrisy is, so the well-known aphorism goes, the compliment that vice pays to virtue. And, to extend the aphorism somewhat, virtue is likely to be more complimented the less costly it is for the compliment to be passed. In the voting setting, voting is more likely to be influenced by general public evaluations of behavior than market choice is because voting, like speech, does not determine an outcome. This is, however, much more likely to be the case if voting is an open public act than if it is secret. (We shall examine the issue of the open ballot in Chapter 11.)

If voting is secret, public evaluation is of diminished relevance, but it does not disappear altogether. Rather, public evaluation arises in a different way. Individuals like to think well of themselves. They have reason to act in ways that reflect well on themselves even though others are not watching. People do, in short, express themselves to themselves as well as to others. Privately held norms of conduct of all kinds become relevant here. Ms. A likes to think of herself as aesthetically sensitive, for example, even though more prosaic considerations of functionality constrain her actual choices. In the questionnaire context, she can permit the aesthetic dimension to dominate. She is "expressing herself," not so much as she actually is (even if she has reason to be well informed on this score), but as she would like to be. There is hardly anything implausible in this. We all have a natural tendency to conceive of ourselves in terms that are, if not totally self-deceiving, at least moderately generous. There is for each an image of the person he would like to have been or to become. It is this somewhat romanticized doppelganger and not the all-too-real you that is likely to be activated in the nonconsequential/expressive domain. As we have mentioned in connection with market choices, projection of self-image is a relevant consideration even though the individual must, as it were, pay the full cost of that projection in terms of instrumental benefits forgone. In electoral choices, where instrumental benefits are virtually irrelevant, this sort of self-projection will predictably be much more important.

In what ways will this romanticized doppelganger diverge from the "real" person? This depends, of course, on the specific criteria of self-evaluation that the agent adopts. It seems clear, however, that one relevant aspect here will be the general principles of conduct that the agent endorses. These include, but are not exhausted by, *ethical* principles. If an agent has ethical principles that uphold the sanctity of life, for example, these principles will guide her expressive behavior. There is, however, no necessary presumption that such principles will be decisive in her decision as to whether to terminate a disastrous pregnancy. It is not uncommon for people who are against abortion in principle to "reveal a preference" for it in actual behavior, or for people who believe in the importance of marital fidelity in principle to reveal a preference for adultery in their personal conduct; or for people who believe in racial integration in principle to reveal a preference for racial homogeneity in their choice of neighborhood; and so on. Because such ethical and ideological sympathies are unlikely to be unique to the agent, but rather reflective of broad areas of popular opinion, they are also suggestive of the nature of political argument – of the sort of territory on which electoral battles will be fought. Parties/candidates/policies will tend to be oriented toward presenting those principles with which voters are likely to sympathize – principles that articulate what the voter might like to become or that reflect the terms in which the voter might wish to see himself. Political symbols that seem likely to stimulate a sympathetic response in voters – that generate expressive returns – will become the very stuff of democratic politics.

It should not be thought that all this implies that self-interest will be irrelevant at the polls. There are good reasons to believe that interests will play some role (though a small one) directly via instrumental considerations, and also that the voter's interests and her "principles" may over some range converge. Why this is likely to be so is a matter we shall take up later in this chapter. At this point there seems to be some advantage in offering two extended examples of the way in which expressive considerations enter electoral politics, so as to flesh out the general remarks offered so far.

An extended example: income redistribution

Income redistribution is a major activity of governments. Most public interventions – whether taxes and expenditures, or regulations of various sorts – change relative prices and serve thereby to redistribute income away from some groups and toward others. Indeed, within conventional public choice theory such redistributions are seen as the central driving force of political process. Policies such as macroeconomic stabilization or the provision of Samuelsonian "public goods" that conventional welfare economics has interpreted as being motivated by quite other considerations are typically explained in public choice theory by the redistributions to which they give rise. Here, rather than attending to the whole range of public policies, virtually all of which have distributional consequences, we shall direct attention to that subset of policies that are avowedly redistributive – namely, the array of so-called welfare policies that purport to transfer income (or goods and services) from richer to poorer citizens.

There seem to be several different explanations as to why governments seek to redistribute in this way. One – the most common in policy discussions – rests on nothing more than the ethical claims of obligation to the poor and needy. Government is conceived as a benevolent despot and considerations of noblesse oblige are construed to motivate the agents of government. That is, all attention is focused on the purely ethical dimensions of transfer policy (including the question of how to achieve the relevant distributional goals most "efficiently"), as if the ethical advice proffered will indeed turn out to be compelling for the agents of the state.

This standard approach to welfare policy has been the object of some scorn from public choice analysts. A purely normative account fails to explain how democratic politics operates to create political pressure for redistribution from rich to poor (if indeed it does). Indeed, there is an implicit assumption that apolitical institutions are irrelevant to the determination of policy outcomes. Whether some institutional defense of the standard model might be mounted within a broad theory of democratic politics is a matter that has had inadequate attention. There are, however, two sorts of models of distributive politics that have had some currency in recent literature, and we shall examine them briefly here.

Income redistribution as a public good

The first possible explanation of public welfare expenditure involves the proposition that individuals have reasons to desire public redistribution even if they do not turn out to be, themselves, direct recipients. The reasons in question may involve altruistic motives of various kinds, the desire for insurance against the risk of one's own becoming poor, or, conceivably, a more direct self-interested desire to keep the poor politically passive, less disease ridden, or less inclined to criminal activity. Such motives are not, of course, mutually exclusive, but they do not, even together, amount to a case for public transfer programs unless public provision is generally deemed to be more efficient than private alternatives for securing the same ends. For example, public insurance, to the extent that it involves subsidization of bad risks (i.e., those more than usually likely to be poor, unemployed, etc.) seems unlikely to be more attractive to the general populace than is privately provided insurance (unless there is, in addition, some pure benevolence in the populace at large). Furthermore, not all forms of benevolence will be relevant to general redistribution of the state welfare variety. An individual's altruistic concern for his extended family, local football team, or alma mater does not seem to be widely enough based to justify public involvement. The case for government welfare distribution seems stronger where the altruism in question spreads broadly across the society's "poor." In this case, each altruist may not be prepared to give up most of his income to make a negligible contribution to alleviating the suffering of the masses, but all altruists acting together could, at modest cost to each, have substantial impact on the lot of the poor. All altruists are made better off by the transfer scheme (and, hence, in the standard account will vote for it) even though each would not be prepared to make any transfers unilaterally.

The claim that income redistribution may have certain publicness qualities and, hence, that generalized efficiency arguments may justify public transfer is not totally implausible. Much depends on the proportion of claimants, z, in the population since the cost per taxpayer of a dollar increase in the income of the claimant group is $z/(1 - z)$ dollars. If the claimant group is, for example, 1% of the population, each taxpayer has to give up barely more than a cent to increase the transfer level by one dollar, and it seems likely that many taxpayer-voters will prefer that the scheme proceed. Let the claimant class rise to, say, 20%, and the cost per taxpayer of a dollar's public transfer is twenty-five cents – enough, perhaps, to obliterate effective demand from all except the most benevolent. There is, after all, some reasonable doubt as to whether the objects of individuals' altruistic concerns extend as broadly as society at large. That is, we might reasonably postulate (following Adam Smith,[6] among others) that the degree of altruistic concern declines as the distance (somehow measured) between the potential donor and the potential recipient increases. Whether public redistribution of the scale we observe can be justified merely on public goods grounds seems somewhat doubtful. Moreover, there is a puzzle of sorts in this account; for, although the Smithian argument suggests a higher concern for domestic than for foreign poor, that argument does not seem consistent with a major discontinuous change once national borders are reached. Yet comparing foreign aid to domestic welfare programs in most democratic regimes, foreign aid (particularly when shorn of the military component) emerges as a negligible proportion of the domestic welfare budget. In summary, altruistic concern for the poor (at least as typically formulated), though doubtless present, does not seem sufficient to explain salient features of public welfare programs: neither their magnitude nor their coincidence with national political boundaries.

Income redistribution as political spoils

In order to explain both the magnitude and geographic focus of welfare expenditures, some reference to the political power of recipient groups seems obligatory. A simple account might begin by observing that the distributions of political power and market power differ, that political power through the franchise is more evenly distributed than is market power, and hence that one would expect the existence of government's powers to tax and transfer to lead to greater equality in the income distribution. Whether this is so or not in a more fully articulated public choice model is, however, far from clear. As it happens, public choice models have not attended much to the issue of the distributional effects of majoritarian politics. The major focus of normative concern has been the relative *efficiency* of political as compared to market outcomes.[7] However, because distributional considerations weigh heavily in public choice analysis, the normative evaluation of majoritarian politics from a distributional viewpoint falls readily enough out of the public choice literature. In this connection, three general results are worth citing:

1. If the simple median-voter model applies and the tax system is roughly proportional, the magnitude and direction of transfers depend on the relation between median and mean income. Transfers will go from rich to poor if median income is less than mean income (i.e., if the income

---

[6] See, in particular, 1982, Bk. III, chap. 3, sec. 4.

[7] For work that does attend explicitly to distributional matters within a public choice framework, see Meltzer and Richard (1981), Brennan and Buchanan (1985), and Buchanan (1975).

distribution is skewed toward the bottom end, which it is in most societies), and the magnitude of transfers will depend on the magnitude of the difference between median and mean income. This model presents several interesting comparative static results, such as the conclusion that deterioration in the lot of the poorest – other things being equal – will reduce the extent of transfers (because median income will remain constant while mean income declines).[8]

2. Since the conditions under which the median-voter result applies seem to be extremely restrictive, it is more natural for public choice analysts to describe the distributive properties of majority rule in terms of inherently unstable political equilibria. That is, any policy change that receives majority support will typically involve a redistribution from some minority to some majority, but neither the direction nor magnitude of the resultant transfer can be predicted, because coalitions will be continually shifting. On average, the poor can expect to share about equally in the spoils from this lottery and, in that sense, are made better off in an expected sense by the process. But at any point in the kaleidoscope of shifting coalitions, it is as likely as not that transfers will go from poor to rich rather than rich to poor.

3. In the case where cycling prevails, there may be scope for a strategic agenda setter to ensure the emergence of outcomes the agenda setter prefers (see McKelvey, 1976). If the agenda setter's preferences are included in the efficiency calculus, there is nothing necessarily *inefficient* about the resultant outcomes – any more than there is anything directly inefficient about genuine dictatorship (benevolent or otherwise). But dictatorship is surely objectionable – at least presumptively – on distributional grounds, and the fact that majority rule would, in this model, lead to an effective dictatorship, with public revenues available for disbursement at the agenda setter's discretion, is a distributive consequence of note.

The public choice models from which these results are derived all take as a basic assumption the proposition that individuals vote their interests. In Chapter 5 we shall examine such standard models in greater detail with an eye to the more general question of how our own theory of electoral preferences bears on public choice orthodoxy. At this point, we should note only two slightly puzzling features of the cycling model of distributive politics. First, one prevailing fact about contemporary Western democracies is the universal presence of "welfare transfers" that remain more or less intact over the sequence of electoral periods. Although the fortunes of the poorest and the magnitude of the welfare budget do change from time to time, it is virtually never the case that transfers are explicitly undertaken from poor to rich. Without denying that some of the policies governments implement have that effect (e.g., subsidized higher education, building covenants, exemption of imputed rent on owner-occupied housing under income tax arrangements, etc.), it remains to be explained why the rich, when they comprise the decisive majority, do

---

[8] To our knowledge, no serious attempt has been made to test this hypothesis econometrically.

not abandon all welfare payments instantly and institute a system of income subsidies to secure transfers in their own direction. Second, to the extent that the agenda-setter story is valid, the implication would surely be that political agents would directly appropriate a significant proportion of the public budget: Politicians ought on this reckoning to be far and away the richest members of the community. Even a modest 10% share of total tax revenue would amount to a mammoth personal fortune for each parliamentarian/congressman – a fortune sufficiently large that it would be impossible to hide it from public attention. Yet majoritarian democracy, as opposed to monarchical/dictatorial political arrangements, seems on the face of things to be substantially exempt from such political fortune making. Although bribes are doubtless paid, there does not appear to be systematic manipulation of electoral outcomes on the scale that the agenda-setter model would suggest.

Income redistribution and expressive returns

The expressive model of electoral preference we have outlined suggests a rather different theory of political transfers. The results are, on the face of things, not so different from the "income redistribution as a public good" model, though as we shall see there are detectable differences. The central notion is that individuals derive direct satisfaction from expressing support for the poor. The needy make claims on moral attention and do so even in cases where there are simply no prospects for providing succor. The spectacle of a drowning man appalls the watcher on the shore even though (perhaps precisely because) the watcher can do nothing to aid the drowning man. The expression of support for such a person is almost instinctive: It needs no bolstering from any prospect that the spectator's urgings may spur the swimmer on to greater efforts.

What, then, is more natural than the suggestion that individuals might seek to express such support at the ballot box? There need be no implication that individuals in their private behavior will find it utility maximizing to make transfers to the needy, nor even that the sum of their valuations of the transfer program should exceed the cost of implementing it. Instrumental aspects of their votes are not relevant, beyond the general requirement that the transfer program is an articulation of concern for the poor. What is relevant is the acceptance merely of the principle that one should support the poor.

A more detailed account of the voter's calculus in terms of the payoff matrix introduced in Chapter 2 is useful here. Suppose that there is a proposal to implement a transfer program that would cost the representative taxpayer-voter a sum of $100. Let us further suppose that she would derive a benefit of $35 from this program, in terms of the value the taxpayer-voter places on its implementation (supposing that this could be somehow known). That is, the voter if decisive would not implement the program, preferring to spend her $100 in another way – even though she would benefit somewhat from the program by virtue of her modified benevolent inclinations. We also suppose that the voter derives a benefit, say of $5, from expressive support for the poor in this way. Then the payoff matrix that confronts the

Table 3.1. *The expressive altruism game*

Each	All other voters			Expected return
	Vote for program, probability q	Vote against program, probability p	Tie, probability h	
Support the poor	40	105	40	$40q + 105p + 40h$
Don't support the poor	35	100	100	$35q + 100p + 100h$

individual is as shown in Table 3.1. Here, we treat the *defeat* of the program as benefiting the voter by $100, the taxes that she does not have to pay. The expected net return from voting for the program is V, where V is given by

$$V = (40 - 35)q + (105 - 100)(1 - q - h) + h(40 - 100),$$
$$= 5(1 - h) - 60h,$$
$$> 0 \text{ if the probability of a tie is less than } 1/13.$$

Clearly, if the electorate is at all large, the probability of a tie will be considerably less than $1/13$, and possibly quite negligible – in which case the voter's dilemma is revealed. Each voter is led to vote for the program, even though all (donors) would be better off if the policy did not proceed, even allowing for the altruistic benefit.

The point will, perhaps, be made that in those cases where the voter's action is most unlikely to make any difference, where her action is of "least consequence," then the voter is self-deluding to feel any moral self-satisfaction at a gesture toward the poor and, hence, is not much likely to vote for the program. But this is to construe the voter's behavior as instrumentally rather than naturally expressive. One does not need to feel any sort of righteous glow from contemplating one's own behavior in order to suffer from the spectacle of a starving Ethiopian, any more than one needs to feel pride about weeping through the soppy parts of a film in order to motivate the weeping. Of course, one's evaluation of the behavior may enter into a decision as to whether to let that behavior have full rein or whether to try to suppress it, and what others will think of one may well weigh in one's evaluation of actions, as well as one's choice of context in which the behavior will be expressed. But the motive for voting for the program does not require any such deliberation.

It is of some interest to note what Adam Smith has to say on the subject of benevolence in a passage, parts of which are well known. We here provide the passage in its entirety because it is often cited to suggest a belief on Smith's part that inclinations toward benevolence are irrelevant, since concern for others is overweighed by any "paltry misfortune" of one's own. Instead, the thrust of the passage seems to be that altruistic behavior is not driven by consequentialist concern for others, but rather a deontological commitment to principles: "It is reason, principle, conscience." And it is such principles that the agent can be taken to express naturally at the polls, where the costs of his expressing them are virtually negligible:

Let us suppose that the great empire of China, with all its myriads of inhabitants, was suddenly swallowed up by an earthquake, and let us consider how a man of humanity in Europe, who had no sort of connection with that part of the world, would be affected upon receiving intelligence of this dreadful calamity. He would, I imagine, first of all, express very strongly his sorrow for the misfortune of that unhappy people, he would make many melancholy reflections upon the precariousness of human life, and the vanity of all the labours of man, which could thus be annihilated in a moment. He would too, perhaps if he was a man of speculation, enter into many reasonings concerning the effects which this disaster might produce upon the commerce of Europe, and the trade and business of the world in general. And when all this fine philosophy was over, when all these humane sentiments had been once fairly expressed, he would pursue his business or his pleasure, take his repose or his diversion, with the same ease and tranquility, as if no such accident had happened. The most frivolous disaster which could befall himself would occasion a more real disturbance. If he was to lose his little finger tomorrow, he would not sleep tonight; but, provided he never saw them, he will snore with the most profound security over the ruin of a hundred millions of his brethren, and the destruction of that immense multitude seems plainly an object less interesting to him, than this paltry misfortune of his own. To prevent, therefore, this paltry misfortune to himself, would a man of humanity be willing to sacrifice the lives of a hundred millions of his brethren, provided he had never seen them? Human nature startles with horror at the thought, and the world, in its greatest depravity and corruption, never produced such a villain as could be capable of entertaining it. But what makes this difference? When our passive feelings are almost always so sordid and so selfish, how comes it that our active principles should often be so generous and so noble? When we are always so much more deeply affected by whatever concerns ourselves, than by whatever concerns other men; what is it which prompts the generous, upon all occasions, and the mean upon many, to sacrifice their own interests to the greater interests of others? It is not the soft power of humanity, it is not that feeble spark of benevolence which Nature has lighted up in the human heart, that is thus capable of counteracting the strongest impulses of self-love. It is a stronger power, a more forcible motive, which exerts itself upon such occasions. It is reason, principle, conscience, the inhabitant of the breast, the man within, the great judge and arbiter of our conduct. It is he who, whenever we are about to act so as to affect the happiness of others, calls to us, with a voice capable of astonishing the most presumptuous of our passions, that we are but one of the multitude, in no respect better than any other in it; and that when we prefer ourselves so shamefully and so blindly to others we become the proper objects of resentment, abhorrence, and execration. It is from him only that we learn the real littleness of ourselves, and of whatever relates to ourselves, and the natural misrepresentations of self-love can be corrected only by the eye of this impartial spectator. It is he who shows us the propriety of generosity and the deformity of injustice; the propriety of resigning the greatest interests of our own, for the yet greater interests of others, and the deformity of doing the smallest injury to another, in order to obtain the greatest benefit to ourselves. It is not the love of our neighbor, it is not the love of mankind, which upon many occasions prompts us to the practice of those divine virtues. It is a stronger love, a more powerful affection, which generally takes place upon occasions; the love of what is honorable and noble, of the grandeur, and dignity, and superiority of our own characters. (1982, 1.i.1.3)

It might readily be concluded, from our reference to Smith's theory of *moral* sentiments, that the expressions that individual voters will be inclined to make at the ballot box will be those exclusively of moral principle. Here certainly, the inclination to express support for the poor may well be seen as having a benign

Table 3.2. *The expressive envy game*

| Each | All other voters | | |
	Majority for soaking	Majority against soaking	Tie
Soak the rich	15	105	15
Don't soak the rich	10	100	100

consequence. And, more generally, the consequences of permitting individuals to act in accord with moral principles without being distracted by considerations of where their own narrow interests lie may seem to represent a major advantage of electoral politics over other forms of decision making. Whether or not this is so is an issue we take up directly in later chapters. Here, it is relevant to foreshadow one aspect of the discussion there, dealing with the political role of malice and envy, for it is worth pointing out that rather similar distributional outcomes can emerge from the expression of antipathy to the rich as of support for the poor. And such antipathy may well, like benevolence, be costly to pursue through private action – either because of the risk of retaliation or for more direct ''economic'' reasons. The bigot who refuses to serve blacks in his shop forgoes the profit he might have made from their custom; the anti-Semite who will not work with Jews is constrained in his choice of jobs and may well have to knock back one she would otherwise have accepted. To express such antipathy at the ballot box involves neither threat of retaliation nor any significant personal cost. The cost to the voter of legislating blacks out of certain occupations or of consigning Jews to concentration camps may well exceed the ''benefits'' he enjoys from inflicting harm on the sufferers. Yet the calculus of the voter may well lead him to vote for the policies in question. Nor is this in any way out of line with Smithian psychology: As Smith points out, ''sympathy,'' the central Smithian concept, ''may be made use of to denote our fellow feelings with any passion whatever.''

In the current setting, it is worth emphasizing that much redistributive rhetoric seems as much concerned with antipathy toward the rich as compassion for the poor. Accordingly, we might reformulate Table 3.1 as Table 3.2. Here, the expressive return originates from a ''principle'' or sentiment that the rich should be brought low: The relevant expressive preference is for ''soaking the rich.'' Once again, provided the electorate size is plausibly large and the probability of being decisive correspondingly small, then each is led to vote rationally for soaking the rich even though the costs to each of having that policy enacted may be very considerable.

The significant difference between this case and the altruism case depicted in Table 3.1 is that in the altruism case the principle expressed would seem to require that full account be taken of the negative effects of transfers on the size of what is to be transferred. If policy *A*, by ensuring a larger pie, enables the poor to be made better off than under policy *B*, which involves more progressive tax rate scales but smaller effective redistribution, a principled compassion would provide reason for support of policy *A*. But no such limits exist in the "soak the rich" model. It would be in no sense inconsistent with the negative sentiments that a vote expresses to vote for taxes on the rich that cost more to administer than they return in revenue, or to push the rates of tax on upper incomes to levels where they raise less revenue than might have been raised at lower rates.

Conventional public choice models have some difficulty in explaining how it can come about that any polity could be on the "wrong" part of the Laffer curve, and have therefore been critical of supply-side recipes for increased public revenues except in the long term.[9] In the light of Table 3.2, however, we conjecture that tax rates on higher income levels may well be pushed to "excessive" levels. In fact, it is a well-known proposition in optimal tax theory that revenue would be increased if the tax rate structure at the very top end were regressive, and it is therefore a challenge for conventional theories (of either the public choice type or the rival normative orthodoxy) to explain why this is a phenomenon that is never observed. Indeed, extraordinarily high rates of tax have been imposed on the income of the rich at various times in living memory (e.g., in the United Kingdom through the early seventies, rates of up to 93% were imposed on investment income at the top end). It is surely not too far-fetched to suggest that such tax rate structures serve a *symbolic* rather than a genuinely distributive function – that they pander primarily to the envy that many ordinary voters feel toward the rich.

Of course, both propoor and antirich sentiments can exist side by side and be simultaneously operative in electoral politics. But an important implication is that it may be a mistake to see all aspects of transfer policy as parts of a single political objective, captured under the "redistribution" rubric. Welfare payments may cater to a set of expressive preferences different from those to which progressive taxation caters, even though the redistributive consequences may be similar over a considerable range. In this sense, a theory of electoral preference that focuses on the expressive dimension to voting seems capable of explaining pieces of the policy landscape that the orthodox public choice model cannot.

The case of war

The object of the somewhat extended discussion of redistributional policy in the preceding section has been, first, to provide some additional evidence for the proposition that individuals may have reason to express preferences that they would not choose to activate if decisive (i.e., that expressive preference and interests may diverge); second, to show that this divergence is of some possible policy significance; and third, to indicate the implications of our model of electoral preference for one area of politics that is of some account in its own right.

We now turn to a further example – that of war. It seems easy enough to explain the existence of war in predemocratic days. Megalomaniacal dictators could pursue

---

[9] See Brennan and Buchanan (1985), chap. 6, and Buchanan and Lee (1982) for more detailed discussion.

glory, empire, and a place in history at the expense of their own treasuries, their own citizenry, and certainly at the expense of the citizens of other countries. But with the extension of the franchise, there are fewer citizens, one would have thought, available for exploitation. Of course, it is true that wars involve substantial gains for some parties – even some on the losing side. Nevertheless, it could hardly be denied that wars – particularly those on the scale experienced in this most "democratic" of centuries – involve very substantial net negative returns to all the combatant nations. It is difficult to see how a community of rational voters could have sufficiently large expected returns from belligerence to vote for a program that would lead to war. A conventional public choice explanation would presumably have to make appeal to the fact that many of those who stand to suffer the greatest cost (namely young men of military age) are disenfranchised – and that their parents and enfranchised friends are not sufficiently concerned about them to defend their interests – or make appeal to a claim that the established political elite are sufficiently powerful to be able to defend the current institutional order (and expand its influence) whatever the state of electoral enthusiasms. But neither of these explanations can account for the historical fact that there seems to have been enormous widespread support (on all relevant sides) for pursuing the belligerent course in most of the major wars of our time – and this despite the fact that there were spectacular gains possible to all parties from reaching an accommodation. Surely no proper cost–benefit analysis of any of the significant military confrontations of this century could establish that total benefits outweighed total costs – that the whole business was an "efficient undertaking" in the standard economic sense. Indeed, this is almost surely so even if we restrict attention to the victorious; "success" in war is merely a matter only of the least bad of dread alternatives.

How is it, then, that such mammoth exercises in irrationality seem to have been pursued so vigorously and with such popular enthusiasm in this most democratic of ages? The voters' dilemma provides a possible explanation. Consider the individual voter contemplating a vote between competing political candidates in a setting where international relations are tense. One candidate offers a policy of appeasement, recognizing the enormous cost in lives and resources that any antagonistic stance might involve. The other candidate stands for national integrity – "By God, we are not going to be pushed around by these bastards." We might well presume that few voters, making a careful calculation of the costs and benefits to themselves and those they care about, would actually opt for war. Just as individuals, in situations of interpersonal strain, will often swallow their pride, shrug their shoulders, and stroll off rather than commit themselves to an all-out fight (particularly one that might imply someone's death), so the interests of most voters would be better served by drawing back from the belligerent course. Yet a careful reflective computation of the costs and benefits of alternative outcomes to herself (and those others relevant to her concerns) is precisely what the voter does not entertain: Any such computation is essentially irrelevant. What is relevant, we might suppose, is the opportunity to show one's patriotism, one's antipathy to servility, one's strength of national purpose. Accordingly, it is by no means implausible to postulate that each voter confronts a payoff matrix as in Table 3.3.

Table 3.3. *The expressive belligerence game*

Each	All other voters		
	Majority for appeasement	Majority for tough line	Tie
Appeasement	100	10	100
Tough line	105	15	15

Each voter quite rationally prefers the *outcome* of no war, but equally votes for the tough line policy; and it is not too difficult to see how, if both combatant polities are afflicted with the same sort of voters' dilemma, both will be led to pursue a course of which war is the likely outcome.

We do not, of course, claim that this model provides a complete account of how war comes about or of the political mechanisms that are relevant to decision making on such matters. Neither do we claim that expressive preferences will always be revealed for war: They may equally be recorded for peace. But in either case, it will be the *symbolic power of the policy* rather than the costs and benefits the policy scatters on particular voters that will be most relevant. And the war example seems to be one in which, on any reckoning, the assumption of voter "rationality" seems particularly strained. What our discussion shows is that individual voters may, each of them, be entirely rational in voting for war – even where no one of them would, if decisive, take that course. And the prevalence of war in postdemocratic times provides a reason to believe that, on occasion, expressive preferences may well take the particular bellicose form that Table 3.3 reflects.

The role of interests

The argument in this chapter is devoted to an attempt to spell out something of the likely nature of expressive preferences. So far, much of our discussion has been oriented toward defending our overall line of reasoning against the claim that expressive and instrumental preferences are highly correlated; If this claim were valid, then even if the *logic* of our argument were accepted, there would be no empirical significance in our critique of public choice orthodoxy. Accordingly, we have tried to argue that there are cases – and ones of substance – in which expressive preferences may diverge sharply from interests and, hence, in which electorally chosen outcomes will be different from those that individuals could be said to truly prefer, using the notion of preference standard in utility theory.

At this point we must attempt to balance the account. There are reasons – we think good ones – to believe that voters' expressive preferences will reflect their interests much of the time. The presence of this relation will tend to moderate any systematic possibilities for electoral pathogeny. However, we emphasize that nothing we shall say can entirely rule out the prospect of perverse electoral outcomes.

We should begin by noting that at least some of those cases in which expressive preferences diverge systematically from preferences over outcomes are cases of either *akrasia* (weakness of the will) or hypocrisy – that is, where the individual expresses views (or votes) that are at variance with his ordinary behavior. Neither *akrasia* nor hypocrisy are commonly regarded as entirely neutral characteristics. Hypocrisy may be the compliment vice pays to virtue and, in that sense, may be construed as a display of minimal decency among the vicious, but the charge of being a hypocrite is hardly one of approbation and awareness of being a hypocrite hardly a source of pride. The moral force of the charge of hypocrisy does, then, imply the desirability of congruence between expressive and instrumental behavior. And though we might *explain* why it is that expressive and instrumental behavior tend to diverge in certain settings, we do not normally regard such explanations as entirely exculpatory. Consider, for example, the individual who explains why his behavior was in violation of his expressed principles by observing that it is in his own interest in expressing those principles that people should think well of him. No such explanation can allow him to avoid opprobrium. In the same way, *akrasia,* although it has never had as bad a press as hypocrisy, is nevertheless commonly regarded as a character flaw. The one who acknowledges the force of particular principles, but can endorse them only by words and not action, is a moral weakling and is to be deplored. In short, the internal moral and external social forces encouraging congruence between expression and action are strong – and the one who lives with substantial lack of congruence must suffer some moral discomfort and some public disdain.

We leave it as an open question as to how such dissonance is commonly resolved. It may be that action is constrained by principle; or it may be that principles themselves adjust, as the actor comes to develop ethically acceptable rationalizations for his actions. In either way, however, there is pressure for such resolution to occur – pressure that makes for a measure of consistency between electoral and market behavior.

Examples of such consistency abound. It would hardly be surprising if academics generally turned out to vote for policies or candidates who support higher education. Such voting behavior may well be seen as self-serving, but it need not be motivated by self-interest. Individuals choose jobs on the basis of their general principles, and among academics' principles (we hope) is a belief in the importance of, and an affection for, academic values. Equally, someone who finds herself on the path to an academic career may well find it privately profitable to internalize academic culture. In the same way, support for tariff protection for a particular industry will tend to come from those who believe the industry to be important – and this belief is likely to predominate among workers in that industry possibly because they see their own work as significant. Support for defense expenditure would be expected particularly from those who have already evinced their belief in the importance of defense by working in defense-related industries, and so on. Whether values lead job choice, or vice versa, is immaterial for our argument here. All we need note is that there are forces that encourage convergence.

Moreover, I am more likely to look with affection on a candidate who has already demonstrated an affection for *me*. And it is, after all, not unfamiliar for one who desires the affection of another to shower the object of his desire with gifts.

Such gifts are to be construed as an *expression* of affection for the recipient, not as payment for affection received or promised. The gift giving alerts the recipient to the interests and affections of the other; the acceptance of the gift may even create some obligation of response on the part of the recipient. But his is not the same obligation as lies on the person who is party to an agreed exchange; the activity may be in some ways reciprocal, but the reciprocity does not make it trade.

In this sense one may think of politicians ''wooing'' votes by the choice of particular policies in the same way as a prospective lover woos her beloved. The transactions are, on both sides, primarily expressive or symbolic, designed to express the favor of the candidate and the fact that the candidate and the voter have a common concern – namely, the interest of the voter. But this is not the same as ''buying'' votes and cannot be so construed without doing much violence to the language. There is no trade and no commitment on the voter's part to deliver on some bargain. There is a tendency for the vote-wooing process to elicit policies that are in the interests of electorally crucial groups of voters, because each voter is more likely to support a candidate who has shown the good taste to take an interest in that voter's welfare. The politician is in the game of winning friends and influencing people, and how better to do this than by being generous toward and concerned about potential supporters?

In summary, then, because of the voter's natural affection for his own, and because of the pressure for him to render expressive and purposeful behavior congruent, the voter's interests will come to occupy some amount of political territory. But this is so only to the extent that the voter's interests mirror his expressive preferences over candidates and policies. This relation between interests and expressive preferences may apply some – possibly much – of the time, for the reasons we have here outlined. But as we have also been concerned to point out, expressive preferences and interests will diverge systematically in some cases. It would be an error of method to assume whenever electoral behavior is consistent with the self-interest hypothesis that citizens vote in order to further self-interest. And it is an error of logic to assume that rational agents will, purely as a matter of course, vote in a self-interested manner.

4   The analytics of decisiveness

Rational choice modellers will be able to explain voting and non-voting as soon as they can solve the problem of why people salute the flag when they know that nobody is looking.

                                                    Grofman, "Models of Voter Turnout"

Introduction

In the foregoing chapters, we have developed a theory of electoral preference which exploits the fact that electoral "choice" by a single individual is intrinsically non-decisive. For expositional purposes we have at times talked as if the probability of being decisive in large-number electorates is quite negligible. Nevertheless, in the fomulation of our central proposition (Proposition 1 in Chapter 2) we were careful to emphasize that the underlying logic does not depend on the particular *value* of the probability of being decisive, given only that that value is significantly less than one. Clearly, however, the probability of being decisive is an important parameter in the whole argument, and it is therefore important for us to devote some attention to its value. Interestingly, this is a matter on which there is some disagreement. Some writers claim that, under most reasonable assumptions, the probability of being decisive is virtually infinitesimal (see, e.g., Meehl, 1977). Others, such as Beck (1975), argue that it is, though small, by no means negligible. And yet others – most conspicuously Palfrey and Rosenthal (1983) – claim that it may be re-markably high, and certainly large enough to provide an interest-based explanation of the turnouts that are actually observed in Western democratic experience.

In what follows, we shall survey the main lines of reasoning and attempt to iso-late what is at stake in each. Some scaffolding first. We shall, except where oth-erwise stated, assume that there are only two electoral options – which can be conceived either as parties or candidates or explicit policy positions. These we shall denote *a* and *b*, and except in the section on the mandate model, we shall take those options to be exogenously determined. Further, we shall take it that the only cir-cumstance under which a voter can be properly described as decisive occurs when the electoral outcome would have been different if the voter under consideration had voted differently. Where the number of voters is odd and is fixed, the voter is decisive if and only if the margin of victory is exactly one vote. In this event, of course, *every* voter in the minimal majority is decisive. Where the number of voters is even, the voter will be decisive if she *creates* a tie (rather than breaks one) in which event all voters are decisive. In the case where the voter can vote for either candidate or not vote at all, then she may be "decisive" either by creating or by breaking a tie among all other voters. In all cases where there is a tie, there is a question raised about what electoral outcome will prevail. In some of the literature, this issue is finessed by assuming the number of voters to be odd, so that ties are

54

impossible. It is clearly a useful simplification to make this assumption, and nothing of analytic significance is necessarily lost. Accordingly, we shall make this assumption everywhere in what follows, except where we explicitly note otherwise.

The focus on the probability of a tie among other voters implicitly involves setting aside an alternative model of electoral process – one that we might term the "mandate model." In its extreme form, the mandate model postulates that electoral outcomes depend solely on the size (and not at all on the direction) of the majority. Because each voter contributes, either positively or negatively, to the size of the majority, each is *always* decisive. Even in less extreme versions where both the direction and the size of the majority matter, it will remain the case that each voter is decisive in determining the mandate. However, as we shall show, the mandate model does not change the logic of our argument; it merely requires us to modify the formulation, in an essentially minor way.

The binomial formulation

Recall that, for the most part, public choice writers have been interested in the probability of being decisive because its value is relevant to whether self-interest can explain electoral turnouts of the magnitude actually observed. The turnout issue thus provides the major focus for discussing decisiveness probabilities. In that context, it is reasonable to take the number of voters as given and ask what expectation of being decisive any arbitrarily selected voter may reasonably hold, as a function of that number of voters. Accordingly, we take the number of voters[1] to be $(2n + 1)$ – taken to be odd so as to suppress the issue of how to resolve ties. The probability of any arbitrarily selected voter being decisive is then the probability that exactly n of the $2n$ other voters cast their votes for a. The most common method of determining this probability is to treat each voter as an independent "trial," rather like the toss of a coin.[2] That is, each voter is conceptualized in terms of exercising the *same* stochastic choice – in which she votes for a with some exogenously determined probability, p (and hence for b with probability $(1 - p)$). The option of not voting is ruled out by the structure of the problem: The number of voters is given as part of the parametric structure. The electoral outcome is then taken to be determined as the aggregation of the outcome of this sequence of independent random trials. The number of votes cast for a, denoted N_a, is thus a random variable drawn from a binomial distribution with mean $p \cdot 2n$ and a variance of $p(1 - p)2n$. The probability of being decisive is the probability that N_a will take the specific value n.

Consider, for example, the case in which p is one-half. In this case, each voter is conceived as deciding whether to vote for a or b by tossing a fair coin. The probability of an exact tie among all other voters is then the ratio of the number of ways in which $2n$ votes can be arranged among the two options so that exactly n vote for a, to the *total* number of ways in which those can be arranged among the two

---

[1] This is the number of actual voters, not the number of enfranchised persons.
[2] The standard exposition here is Beck (1975). See also Margolis (1977) and Thompson (1983).

options. The former number is depicted $\binom{2n}{n}$ and is given by $2n!/(n!n!)$; the latter is 2^{2n}. The probability of a tie is then

$$h = \frac{\binom{2n}{n}}{2^{2n}}.$$ (4.1)

In the more general case where the probability that each voter votes for a is not one-half but simply p, the relevant formula is

$$h = \binom{2n}{n} p^n (1 - p)^n.$$ (4.2)

It is useful to express (4.2) in terms of (4.1) by defining a parameter t by the relation

$$p \equiv (\tfrac{1}{2} + t).$$ (4.3)

This parameter, t, shows the divergence of p from a fair coin toss and clearly can take values from $-\tfrac{1}{2}$ to $+\tfrac{1}{2}$. Then we can express (4.2) as

$$h = \frac{\binom{2n}{n}}{2^{2n}} (1 + 2t)^n (1 - 2t)^n,$$

that is,

$$h = \frac{\binom{2n}{n}}{2^{2n}} (1 - 4t^2)^n.$$ (4.4)

Stirling's formula allows us to approximate the value of the first term. That is,

$$\frac{\binom{2n}{n}}{2^{2n}} \approx \frac{1}{\sqrt{\pi n}}$$ (4.5)

or

$$h \approx \frac{1}{\sqrt{\pi n}} (1 - 4t^2)^n.$$ (4.6)

A convenient way of depicting the voter's calculus for our purposes here is to ask the question: How large would the return to having one's preference over electoral outcomes prevail have to be – that is, how large would the instrumental return need to be – in order for the *expected* return to casting such a vote be one dollar? This is given by the inverse of h.

On this basis we can show various values of this threshold instrumental return – which we denote V – for different values of electorate size and the parameter t. This we do in Table 4.1.

Several remarks should be made about these results. In the first place, it is notable that at least for values of p close to one-half (i.e., t close to zero), the derived

Table 4.1. *Value of instrumental return required to explain voter turnout (where cost of voting is one dollar)*

Electoral size	Value of t			
	$t = 0$	$t = .0001$	$t = .001$	$t = .01$
101				
2001	56	56	56	56
20,001	177	177	179	481
200,001	560	566	619	12.3×10^6
10 million	4,000	6,533	60,000	$\rightarrow \infty$
100 million	12,500	1.9×10^6	6×10^{25}	$\rightarrow \infty$

threshold values for instrumental returns are not particularly high. For quite substantial electorate size (say, 100 million, which is a rough approximation to that relevant for a U.S. presidential race),[3] the threshold value is only $12,500. Now, over a presidential term, $12,500 may be a plausible estimate of the difference in real income at stake for at least some voters. For example, if candidate a promises free trade while candidate b promises tariff protection for certain industries, workers in those industries may find it instrumentally profitable to vote for b even given that the turnout is expected to be 100 million or so. Of course, it is doubtful whether amounts of this size will be at stake for *all* voters: The size of turnout cannot be explained *solely* on such grounds. All the same, the probability of being decisive is not necessarily negligible even for large electorate size and may be sufficient to induce some voters to vote instrumentally.

This conclusion depends critically, however, on t being very small – that is, on the probability that any voter votes for a being very close to .5. For values of t that are anything other than negligible, the threshold value rises astronomically. Suppose, for example, there is a turnout of 1 million voters, and the probability that voters vote for a is .51, not .5. Then, as the bottom right-hand entry in Table 4.1 indicates, the amount that would have to be at stake to induce any voter to vote (instrumentally) exceeds the global GNP many times over: The probability of decisiveness is genuinely infinitesimal.

We can explore the influences of electoral size and expected closeness on V more formally by deriving elasticities for the way in which V responds to changes in N and t. Recall that

$$V = \frac{\sqrt{\pi N}}{2} (1 - 4t^2)^{N/2}. \tag{4.7}$$

We can differentiate V with respect to n and t. It is trivial to do the former when t is zero. We obtain

---

[3] Setting aside the complications involved in the stratified structure of the electoral college system.

$$\frac{\partial V}{\partial N} = \frac{1}{2} \frac{\sqrt{\pi}}{2} N^{-1/2}$$

and

$$\frac{\partial V}{\partial N} \frac{N}{V} = \frac{1}{2},$$ (4.8)

which states that the point elasticity of V with respect to N is one-half. That is, if the number of voters increases by 2%, the value of V (the inverse of the decisiveness probability) increases by 1%. Where t is nonzero it can be shown that

$$\frac{\partial V}{\partial N} = \frac{1}{2} \frac{\sqrt{\pi}}{2} N^{-1/2}(1-4t^2)^{-N/2} - \frac{1}{2} \frac{\sqrt{\pi}}{2} N^{1/2}(1-4t^2)^{-N/2} \log(1-4t^2)$$

$$= \frac{1}{2} \frac{V}{N} - \frac{1}{2} V \log(1-4t^2),$$

and

$$\frac{\partial V}{\partial N} \frac{N}{V} = \frac{1}{2} [1 - N \log(1 - 4t^2)].$$ (4.9)

Note in connection with (4.9) that, when $t = 0$, we obtain (4.8) as expected, and that for $t \neq 0$, $\log (1 - 4t^2)$ is negative, so that the elasticity implied by (4.9) cannot be less than one-half. For example, for $t = .01$ and turnout of 10,000, the elasticity is 1.4; a 1% increase in turnout increases the value of V (the inverse of h) by 1.4%. This elasticity shows how, at the margin, V responds to N. For elections expected to be very close, V increases less fast than N does: For elections expected not to be very close, V will rise rather faster than N does.

A corresponding elasticity of V with respect to t can also be estimated. We can differentiate V in (4.7) with respect to t to obtain

$$\frac{\partial V}{\partial t} = \frac{4t}{1 - 4t^2} NV$$

and

$$\frac{\partial V}{\partial t} \frac{t}{V} = \frac{4}{1 - 4t^2} N.$$ (4.10)

Clearly, this elasticity depends on t and N, but for large N and significant t, it will be quite large. For example, for $t = .01$ and $N = 10,000$, the elasticity will be 4; an increase of 1% in the value of t will lead to an increase of 4% in the value of V. In brief, V is potentially very sensitive to t when t is anything other than nonnegligible and will be more sensitive the larger is electorate size.

The elasticity of V with respect to N in (4.9) tells us that although the probability of being decisive falls as turnout increases, it does so at a diminishing rate, provided that the election is expected to be sufficiently close. Consequently, although the probability of being decisive is surprisingly high for large-number elections and where the chances of either *a* or *b* winning are 50–50, that probability does not change particularly rapidly as turnout changes. This fact lends some point to our claim in Chapter 2 that the implications of voter indecisiveness for expressive preferences remain in a less spectacular way even for small electorates, such as large committees.

A somewhat analogous test for pseudorational voting is afforded by the relation between turnout and expected closeness of election. As the elasticity of V with respect to t (as in 4.10) indicates, we would predict that V would be lower for closer elections (lower values of t), and the fact that turnout does seem to be higher for closer elections is often used as evidence for pseudorational voting. The standard reference here – at least in public choice circles – is Barzel and Silberberg (1973).[4] Interestingly, Barzel and Silberberg see their task to be that of rejecting the hypothesis that instrumental considerations are entirely irrelevant: The fact that the turnout and closeness are positively related is taken by them to provide grounds for rejecting that hypothesis. They do not, however, advance the alternative hypothesis that self-interest can explain everything. No more do Tollison and Willett (1973): On the contrary, "the role of 'socio-logical' variables as a source of benefits from voting is stressed in explaining absolute voter turnouts" (p. 50). However, turnout may be related to closeness for noninstrumental reasons as well: Just as spectators are more engaged in close games, so expressive voters may be more stimulated to express their preferences in close elections. The difficulty for the self-interest model is to explain why turnout is not *much more* responsive to closeness than it actually seems to be. Using data from U.S. state gubernatorial elections, Barzel and Silberberg find an elasticity of turnout with respect to expected majority of somewhere between .55 (for 1968) and .75 (using an aggregative sample for years 1962, 1964, 1966, and 1968). The formulation in (4.10) suggests, for example, that an increase in expected majority from 2% to 4% of the population increases V, the threshold value required to induce voting, by a factor of 40 in an electorate size as low as 100,000: It seems implausible to suggest that such a significant increase in V would reduce turnout only by 1.5% *unless factors other than self-interest play a predominant role.* Interestingly, Barzel and Silberberg also include the total size of the enfranchised population in their regressions, finding that it yields significant results and that a larger enfranchised population does diminish the proportion of the voting population that votes: "An increase of one million in voting age population tends to reduce turnout by six percent" (p. 55). Now, it is worth emphasizing here that, in any model of instrumental voting, turnout ought to be specified in terms of the absolute number of voters. There is no reason at all to expect that the size of the enfranchised population per se will exercise any influence at all on the expected instrumental benefits from casting a vote: The Nash independent-adjustment equilibrium will isolate an equilibrium number of voters for any policy options, *a* and *b*, and adding extra potential voters ought not affect that equilibrium

---

[4] Though see also Tollison and Willett (1973) and Riker and Ordeshook (1968) for relevant analysis.

in any significant way. To define "turnout" in terms of the *proportion* of eligible persons who actually vote, and to treat turnout so defined as a variable to be explained is already to have jettisoned any purely instrumental account of voting behavior. The fact that the proportion of the nominal electorate that votes declines with increasing nominal electorate does seem to imply that instrumental considerations play some role in the decision to vote – but unfortunately the Barzel and Silberberg formulation does not help us much in isolating how important a role. We shall discuss these results again in greater detail in Chapter 7. At this point, we simply note the interpretative questions the results seem to beg.

There are, however, more general, conceptual questions that arise with the binomial formulation of decisiveness. One of these involves the relation between the expected majority for one or other electoral option, on the one hand, and the probability that that option will win the election, on the other. The binomial formulation postulates a relation between these parameters that is strongly counterintuitive. An example may help here. Suppose that the expected majority for *a* is 2% of the vote – that is, that *a* will get 51% of the vote and *b*, 49%. On the face of things, this seems like a reasonably close outcome, and the possibility that *b* might after all win does not seem too remote. We naturally think of the expected majority as drawn from a prior distribution of possible majorities, which distribution has a variance of a more or less standard magnitude. However, within the binomial formulation the expected majority of 2% for *a* can only arise if the probability of (all) voters voting for *a* is .51 and the probability of all voting for *b* is .49. And in this case the possibility that *b* could win is utterly negligible. Under such conditions, with an electorate size of, say, 1 million voters, the outcome in which *b* gets one-half of the total vote is 20 standard deviations away from the expected outcome (where *b* gets 49% of the votes). So if the expected majority for *a* is 2%, a victory for *b* is impossibly remote! In short, there seems to be a totally implausible connection between expected size of majority, on the one hand, and probability of a particular outcome, on the other. This result comes about because the binomial formulation conceptualizes each voter as involved in an identical independent stochastic experiment – one in which the probability of each voter voting for *a* is equal to the proportion of votes that *a* is expected to receive. The effect is to make the variance of outcomes implausibly small. Of course, such a conceptualization is absurd as a description of voter behavior. We surely do not wish to argue that this stochastic experiment is a proper description of the decision-making calculus of all voters. To do so would, for example, imply that the probability that any voter would vote the same way in two successive elections is about one-half and the probability that any voter would vote the same way over her entire political life is extremely small. Whereas we know that many voters, and possibly a majority, vote for the same party for their entire voting histories.[5]

---

[5] In Australia, for example, the proportion of the electorate voting for the same party in every election in which they have voted has been of the order of 60% (Aitkin, 1985). Comparable figures for the United States and United Kingdom are lower, but still substantial.

It would be possible to reformulate the binomial model by making p (the probability of each voter voting for a) to be itself a random variable selected from some distribution. In this case, the expected majority for a would reflect the mean of the distribution of the ps, but the probability that b would win where that expected majority for a was positive would not necessarily be negligible: The variance of the distribution of votes for a would be increased. The effect of this modification on the probability of being decisive (and hence on the calculated threshold value, V) is a matter that seems worth investigating and seems intuitively likely to yield results that may be somewhat closer to reasoned intuitions about the connections between electoral size, expected closeness of election results, and probability of decisiveness. Moreover, there is a sense in which the simple binomial formulation is self-refuting. If the main conclusion from that model is the one we (and others) have drawn – namely that, in fact, many citizens vote for the intrinsic benefits derived from the act of voting – then we cannot rule out the prospect that some voters, recognizing that others are voting expressively or habitually, may be induced to vote instrumentally. That is, the probability of being decisive may not be entirely independent of the motives one attributes to other voters. Accordingly, we need to reformulate the derivation of the probability of being decisive in a slightly more elaborate way.

An alternative formulation

Taking the previous section as a point of departure, the genuinely rational voter will recognize that the act of voting, for a significant number of actual voters, must be explained by appeal to considerations other than instrumental maximization. He knows that there exists a group of citizens, of indeterminate size, who will vote for a with virtual certainty, and an analogous group who will vote for b with virtual certainty. And he will reckon with this fact in determining the probability that he himself will be decisive. To compare this environment with the binomial formulation, consider the following example: Suppose there are three voters in all. If, as in the preceding section, the voter under consideration can treat the two others as if they each toss a fair coin to decide how to vote, then he will calculate the probability of being decisive as .5, because in half the cases the random process will generate one vote for a and one for b. Suppose, however, that one of the voters votes for a with probability .9 and that the other votes for a with probability .1. Then the probability that the third voter will prove decisive (the probability of a tie among the other voters) is not .5, but .82.

More generally, once expressive considerations are permitted to enter the analysis at all, each voter might, in a simplified setting, be taken to compartmentalize the set of "all other voters" into four groups:

    (i) those who will vote for a with certainty, of size x;
    (ii) those who will vote for b with certainty, of size y;
    (iii) the "uncommitted" voters, who can be treated as if they vote stochastically – that is, vote for a with probability p; and
    (iv) those who abstain, of size e.

Each of the parameters can be treated as uncertain, but for each set of values, there is a probability that a tie will prevail among all the "other" $2n$ voters. Without loss of generality, suppose $x \geq y$. The number of uncommitted voters among the $2n$ others is

$$2n - (e + x + y) \equiv 2d, \tag{4.11}$$

which for simplicity we assume to be even and denote as $2d$. The probability of a tie is, then,

$$h = \frac{\binom{2d}{d+j}}{2^{2d}} (1 + 4t)^d \left| \frac{1 - 2t}{1 + 2t} \right|, \tag{4.12}$$

where j is half the majority for a among *committed* voters and t is defined as in (4.3) and is a function of p (relevant to the "uncommitted" voters). This first term on the right-hand side of (4.12) shows the number of ways in which the noncommitted voters can be arranged between a and b so as to yield a majority of $(y - x)$ for a (which will exactly offset the majority of $(x - y)$ for a among the committed voters); this is divided by the total number of ways in which the uncommitted voters can be arranged across a and b.

This modified formulation is based on what we might refer to as a "truncated binomial" model. Its essential analytic features resemble those of the binomial formulation, but there are two important differences. First, stochastic elements enter both in the way conceptualized in the binomial formulation – with some voters conceived as conducting identical random experiments – and also via the prior estimation of x, y, and e. Second, there is an element of simultaneous determination in x, y, and e with h: That is, as the probability of being decisive increases, the total number of voters $(2n - e)$ alters (not necessarily increases, as we shall see later), and the numbers who can be predicted to vote for a and b on expressive grounds can also be expected to change.

Consider a simple example to focus on the first of these matters. Suppose an electorate of 101 voters, in which x is taken to have values 35, 40, and 45 with equal probability and y is taken to have values 30, 35, and 40 with equal probability. Some relevant values of h are set out for such a case in Table 4.2, when p has the value $\frac{1}{2}$ (i.e., $t = 0$). In the example, each of the possible (x, y) combinations is equally likely, so the probability of a tie is the average of the entries in the cells. This is about 8.3%, or roughly a one-in-twelve chance – almost exactly the same as in the pure binomial setting with $t = 0$ and the same number of voters. If x and y can take values in the same range from 35 to 45 with identical probabilities, then the probability of a tie rises to about 11% – one chance in nine.

The implications of this reformulation for likely values of h are clear enough. The presence of committed voters increases the probability that a voter will be decisive, other things being equal. The parameter t plays the same role as before, but over a smaller range: Some of the work done by expected closeness in the strict binomial formulation is taken over here by the relative sizes of x and y. Clearly, if x and y are equal, the effect is simply to reduce the number of voters in the conventional binomial calculation.

Table 4.2. *The probability of decisiveness in a simple truncated bino-mial formulation*

		y	
x	30	35	40
35	.09	.14	.10
40	.03	.10	.18
45	.0016	.01	.09

The question of the mutual determination of h and x and y is also worth exploring here briefly. For this purpose, we categorize voters into two groups:

   (i) those for whom expressive and instrumental considerations indicate voting in the same direction – call this group (i);

  (ii) those for whom expressive and instrumental considerations work in opposite directions – call this group (ii).

In each group, we rank individuals according to the size of the expressive benefit they derive from exercising a vote for a over b (which will, for those voters that support b, be negative) and derive thereby a "demand" curve for votes for a based on the expressive element alone. This is shown in Figures 4.1 and 4.2 as the L curve. With individuals so identified, we can add the instrumental element, hR. There is no presumption made here that the R and L terms are positively correlated *within* the groups. The groups are, of course, defined by reference to the *sign* of the correlations, but nothing is assumed. Consequently, it seems appropriate to assume that, on average, the absolute change in demand for voting will be more or less identical for all voters. Diagrammatically, the shifts in demand are as indicated in Figures 4.1 and 4.2 for groups (i) and (ii) respectively. The effects of increasing h on turnout can then be identified in these diagrams as follows. We take two values of h; one case is that where h is zero, the other where h is positive. We hold the cost of voting constant at c throughout. Now consider the former group: Any increase in h will increase turnout. When h is zero and the cost of voting is c, x_0 votes will be registered for a and y_0 for b. When h is positive (at h'), and with R fixed, there will be x_1 voters for a and y_1 for b. The increase in turnout is $(x_1 - x_0)$ for a and $(y_1 - y_0)$ for b and is, of course, larger the larger is h, ceteris paribus. For this group, increases in h increase turnout unambiguously. Obversely, for the second group, any increase in h will *reduce* turnout. As shown in Figure 4.2, as the value of h moves from zero to some positive value, h', the number of voters is reduced from x_0' to x_1' for a, and from y_0' to y_1' for b.

The latter case is worth emphasis precisely because it is somewhat counter-intuitive. The point is that because in this case expressive and instrumental influences go in opposite directions, an increase in the probability of being decisive *reduces* the total value to each voter of a vote cast and, hence, will reduce turnout, ceteris paribus.

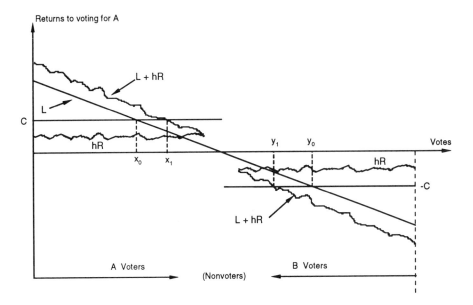

Figure 4.1

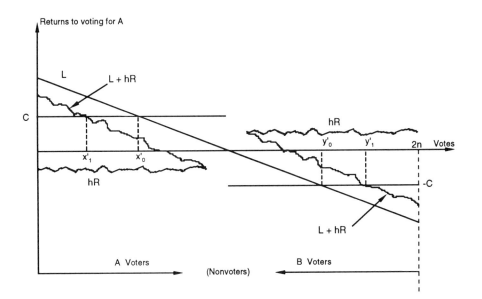

Figure 4.2

In isolating the effects of the probability of decisiveness on turnout, then, the crucial issue here is which of these two cases predominates. If there are larger numbers of voters in group (i), then the net effect of increased probability of decisiveness on turnout will be negative. Now, of course, none of this denies the technical validity of the elasticity calculation in (4.8) and (4.9), which shows the connection between turnout and probability of being decisive when expressive considerations are ignored and turnout is treated as exogenous. But we must acknowledge the influence of increased probability of decisiveness on turnout – that is, reverse the direction of causation. What we are claiming is that reductions in the probability of being decisive will not *necessarily* discourage citizens from voting. Such reductions will lead to lower turnout in general only if expressive and instrumental considerations indicate voting in the same direction more often across all voters than they indicate voting in different directions, that is, if group (i) is larger than group (ii).

It should perhaps also be emphasized that none of this calls into question the relative insignificance of instrumental benefits for most voters. It is one thing to argue that expressive benefits predominate in aggregate, and another to deny that, *at the margin,* changes in either the probability of being decisive (or for that matter in the size of expressive benefits) will leave turnout, or indeed the direction of individuals' votes, unaffected.

The possibility of a "perverse" connection between expected decisiveness (or equivalently, the size of instrumental benefit or loss) and turnout level is of interest not only in its own right, but also because it suggests an independent test of the relation between instrumental and expressive returns. If increased expected instrumental returns have little effect on turnout, this would suggest that expressive and instrumental considerations are often in conflict (or that instrumental considerations are irrelevant for most marginal voters). This suggestion is one we shall want to bear in mind in Chapter 7, where we examine the empirical record in greater detail.

The diagrammatics in Figures 4.1 and 4.2 suggest a further test of one hypothesis that enjoys some popularity in public choice circles – namely, that voters go to the polls out of civic duty but that, once there, vote their self-interest. If this were so, then voters would shift allegiance between parties without the mediation of the possibility of exit and entry into the voting population. An implication of our model, however, is that voters will rarely shift from being an *a*-voter to a *b*-voter; the relevant margins are in the neighborhood of *x* and *y* (in Fig. 4.1) and x' and y' (in Fig. 4.2), and at these margins voters move from being *a*- (or *b*-) voters to being nonvoters (and vice versa). Which of these behavior patterns predominates is a matter that has been investigated by political scientists, and we understand that the results are on the whole congenial to our own model. That is, voters are more likely to choose not to vote than to switch loyalty to the "opposition."

Palfrey and Rosenthal: a radical challenge

The general thrust of the public choice literature on the turnout issue is to argue that the probability of being decisive is nothing like large enough to explain turnouts that are observed, without appeal to something other than instrumental returns. Little of this literature attempts, however, to isolate the level of turnout in a world of purely instrumentally motivated voters. Owen and Grofman (1984) do attempt this task. They seek, that is, to isolate the Nash independent-adjustment outcome in terms of a "mixed strategy solution" for a community of voters for whom the benefits and costs of voting are identical. This Nash solution involves the choice of a probability of voting that, if chosen by all voters, will generate a mutually consistent behavior pattern. If each voter uses this probabilistic strategy, then each will rationally continue to use it. The Owen–Grofman analysis is in the spirit of the foregoing discussion: "that people must generally be induced to vote through some argument other than an interest in affecting the election outcome: no matter how close an election, it is almost inconceivable that one vote will prove decisive, and the slight probability of this event is simply not great enough to make the effort of voting worthwhile" (p. 318).

The general spirit of the Owen–Grofman results, and indeed the entire "rational abstention" literature, has, however, been challenged by Palfrey and Rosenthal (1983). In that paper, the authors claim that one cannot rule out quite high voting turnout within a community of (pseudo)rational voters. Indeed, in the limiting case turnout can approach the full enfranchised population. "Substantial voter turnout may occur even in a totally instrumental, outcome-oriented polity" (p. 8). The Nash equilibrium that Palfrey and Rosenthal develop involves a turnout of "roughly twice the size of the minority," even when the cost of voting is quite high (say, one-third of the stake at issue in the election).

The Palfrey and Rosenthal technique is to set the problem up as one of competitive teams: the M-team and the N-team. Within teams voters are identical in respect of the direction of the vote, and all voters endure the same costs of voting and the same benefit if their team proves victorious (i.e., the spoils per team member are independent of team size). Clearly voters will have an incentive to free ride on other members of their own team. However, the relation between teams is competitive in a special way. For any level of voting (or any voting strategy) adopted by members of the opposing team, the members of one's own team provide a "public good" of an extremely lumpy sort: That is, if the number of M-voters exceeds the number of N-voters by 1, then the full benefit accrues to all M-voters. Votes below and above that threshold level are entirely wasted.

Consider, then, a public good of this sort – that is, one such that

1. each (identical) individual can contribute either exactly one dollar or zero;
2. if t dollars are received, the public good is provided;
3. the dollars contributed are lost whatever happens; and
4. the number of individuals in the community is S ($>t$).

Now, it seems clear in this case that one Nash equilibrium occurs where no one contributes: If each believes that all others will contribute nothing, it is best for him to contribute nothing, and each will continue to contribute nothing while all others do. The question is whether there exists a stable Nash equilibrium in which the public good is provided.[6] Consider initially a case in which some coordinator draws (possibly at random) exactly *t* names out of a hat and appoints the nominated persons to contribute. Then if each person nominated believes that all others nominated will contribute, it is rational for him to do so provided the benefit (denoted *B*) to each exceeds the cost (*C*) to each of the contributors, taken to be one dollar in this case. The resultant equilibrium will be stable if no one makes any mistakes and *believes* that no other will make any mistakes. However, if anyone does make a mistake or believes it to be likely that others will do so, the equilibrium may prove unstable: It is, in that sense, susceptible to what in game theory circles has come to be known as the "trembling hand."

Consider alternatively the case in which each potential contributor chooses an independently rational stochastic strategy in which she contributes with probability *p*. We can derive for each citizen an independent-adjustment curve in which each chooses a probability of contributing, p_i, in the light of the probability of contributing chosen by others, denoted p_o. As p_o approaches t/S, the rational strategy for *i* involves increasing the probability of her own contribution, because it is more likely that she will tip the balance and secure the desired public good. For p_o beyond t/S, *i* recognizes that it is likely that the public good will be provided anyway – whatever she herself does. The relation between p_i and p_o is indicated in Figure 4.3: The Nash independent-adjustment equilibria are those points where the individual reaction curve cuts the 45° line. There are three such: T_1, T_2, and the origin. At these points each contributor will rationally adopt the mixed strategy required to induce all others to adopt it. The question is, however, whether the individual reaction curve will rise sufficiently to cut the 45° line. And here it is the probability of being decisive that is again crucial.

Note that any mixed strategy equilibrium involves the prospect of both under and overcontribution: The distribution of actual outcomes does have positive variance. In this respect it is quite unlike the pure strategy solution already mentioned in which a team coordinator A assigns the responsibility to contribute. In that case, if A does not contribute after being assigned to do so, the public good will not be provided. In the mixed strategy case, however, A (and all others) conduct their own private hat-drawing experiment with *Z* "contribute" tickets and (*M* − *Z*) "don't contribute" tickets. And A knows, even after drawing a "contribute" ticket, that failure to act on his emergent "instructions" will not necessarily make a difference to the actual outcome and will become increasingly negligible as the number of individuals increases. It is recognition of this fact that leads Palfrey and Rosenthal (1984) to argue that mixed strategy equilibria will tend to be "driven out": "The only equilibria which are supported by positive contribution costs for all *n* are the pure strategy equilibria: . . . all (inefficient) mixed strategy equilibria seem to disappear in large populations" (p. 178).

Recall, however, that the variance of possible outcomes here is $Sp(1 - p)$. And note that this variance vanishes as *p* tends to 1. (It also vanishes as *p* tends to zero,

---

[6] Palfrey and Rosenthal (1984) discuss a public goods problem of this kind in some detail.

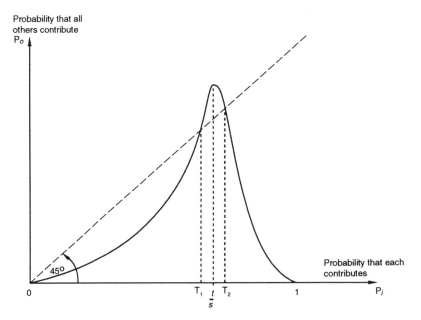

Figure 4.3

but in the current context that is not so interesting.) That is, if t is very close to S, so that the mixed strategy involves a probability of contribution very close to unity, then the probability that each will be decisive is very high. If the cost of the public good is \$99 and there are 100 potential contributors, each knows that if she fails to contribute her one dollar, the public good is very unlikely to be provided. Although not emphasized by Palfrey and Rosenthal, it is the fact that the variance of outcomes goes to zero as p tends to unity that seems to drive their conclusions. In other words, the equilibrium T_1 in Figure 4.3 is likely to emerge only if t is very close to S (in which case T_2 may not exist).

Let us return now from the particular public goods example to the voting case. As we have noted, Palfrey and Rosenthal conceptualize the turnout issue in terms of the competitive provision of a public good by each team – competitive in the sense that success for one team implies failure for the other. Can a stable equilibrium outcome emerge in such a setting in which turnout (contribution) by members of both teams is significant? Palfrey and Rosenthal argue that such a stable equilibrium is quite likely. It seems to us, however, that there is only one such stable equilibrium – that in which both teams are of equal size and all vote. Suppose such an outcome prevailed. In this case each voter will know that if all other voters behave as they did on the previous trial, then failure on one's own part to vote (and to vote for one's outcome) will lead to certain defeat. By voting, one secures a tie, with an expected benefit to oneself of $\frac{1}{2} B$. If $\frac{1}{2} B$ exceeds the cost of voting (C), then each will vote. We can, then, explain an outcome that has the following characteristics: All voters vote, and there is an exact tie among voters for the two options.

Does such an equilibrium generalize? We do not think so. Suppose, for example, that N is less than M, and that all N-members vote. There are, then, two kinds of strategies possible for the M-team, corresponding to the two arrangements we examined in the public goods example. In the "pure strategy" analogue, a team coordinator commissions exactly N-members of the M-team to vote. And each of these N-voters may plausibly find it rational to vote because the benefits of securing a tie (a 50–50 chance of B) exceeds C. But what of the nonvoting M-members? Any one of these can secure certain victory for his team by voting, and since certain victory yields a benefit of $\frac{1}{2}B$ over a tie, and since $\frac{1}{2}B$ exceeds C, any nonvoter will have an incentive to vote. Since the N-voters know this, they will not continue to vote. And so the putative equilibrium collapses.

So much Palfrey and Rosenthal seem to acknowledge. The solution they advance as plausible to deal with the case in which N and M are unequal is a "mixed:pure" strategy equilibrium of the following kind. Suppose again that M exceeds N, and that all N-voters vote. Let the M-team voters vote with probability roughly N/M. Might not such an equilibrium be stable? What must be the case is that the following conditions hold:

1. Each M-voter must be sufficiently likely either to cause a tie or break one in the M-team's favor so that voting with probability N/M is preferable to not voting;
2. each M-voter must be sufficiently unlikely to cause a tie or break one in the M-team's favor that voting with probability N/M is preferable to voting with certainty; and
3. each N-voter must be sufficiently likely to either cause a tie or break one in the N-team's favor that voting is preferable to not voting.

Now, these conditions pull in different directions. If conditions 1 and 3 are to be jointly fulfilled, then the voters must have an acceptably high chance of causing a tie. But if that is so, then condition 2 seems unlikely to be fulfilled, since in any case where causing a tie is likely, so is the likelihood than an M-voter will break a tie in M's favor. That is, those M-voters who roll their dice and get the result "don't vote" would seem to have an incentive to change their minds and vote after all. But if this is so, then the M-team will win sufficiently often for the N-members not to find it profitable to vote.

We do not deny that some equilibria of this kind may exist in some cases – though we believe the prospect unlikely. What we do deny is that the resultant equilibria much resemble those we observe in electoral practice. The most plausible Palfrey–Rosenthal case is that where *everyone* votes. Moreover, all their projected equilibria involve very close elections where ties are quite probable. But the one thing we know about elections is that not everyone does vote and that many elections are landslides. The one sort of outcome that Palfrey and Rosenthal's argument cannot seem to explain is a stable equilibrium in which between 40 and 80% of the voters vote and in which the size of actual majorities is often large. Yet that is exactly the sort of outcome that seems to be most common and that our theories have to explain.

The mandate model

> If election outcomes are not all-or-nothing (forty-nine percent is defeat) and instead influence is a monotonically increasing function of vote share, then the probability that one's vote will make a difference is unity, not some infinitesimal fraction. (Stigler, 1972, p. 104)

It is perhaps a natural query to ask what effect on our analysis would be wrought if it were cast in terms of a mandate model. The characteristic feature of the mandate model is the assumption that political outcomes are a continuous function of plurality size: The larger the plurality the more the political outcomes will reflect the orientation of the victorious party candidate. Such a model does not logically preclude elements of the alternative model of electoral choice that we have assumed throughout: It would, in other words, be possible for the voter to weigh the effects of her vote both on which of a or b prevailed and on any effects on the nature of the a and b themselves. Put another way, the mandate model does not need to assume that victory is irrelevant – the relation between plurality and political outcome need not be continuous in the neighborhood of a tie. It may be, for example, that the electoral options are parties whose policy positions differ, but which positions are also a function of the number of votes received. In Figure 4.4, we illustrate a simple example. That diagram indicates the way in which mandate and policy position might be connected: Policy position A_0 applies if the majority for party a is minimal and A_1, if the majority for party a is maximal. B_0 and B_1 are the analogous positions in policy space chosen by party b if it wins.

However, for purposes of exposition, it is useful to take the extreme if simplified case in which the policy position taken is a linear function of votes received – ranging from B_1 when b gets all the votes to A_1 when a gets all the votes and indicated by the diagonal dashed line in Figure 4.4. In all these cases, to be sure, each voter will be involved in the determination of the outcome: In that sense, each is "decisive" with probability 1. But no single voter *chooses* the plurality. Moreover, the expected instrumental return from casting a vote seems likely to be even smaller than in the more traditional "decisiveness" models. The reasons for this are twofold. The first is an arithmetic point. In the mandate model, the influence any one voter exercises is related inversely to absolute electorate size. Simple continuity and convexity restrictions suggest that either A_1 or B_1 will be the least favored position. Then the most favored position must be at least $N/2$ votes away: It will be exactly $N/2$ votes away if the voter prefers the point at which half the electorate votes for each option. Accordingly, the net value that the individual places on having his most favored position, rather than his least favored, must be at least $N/2$ dollars in order for the value of a vote cast to be worth one dollar, since the individual voter can only change the number of votes by one. In a U.S. presidential election, assuming a turnout of 100 million, this sum would be $50 million as compared with a sum possibly as low as a mere $12,500 in the binomial case discussed earlier.

Second, the voter has an additional dimension of uncertainty to reckon with in casting his vote – one that does not arise in the decisiveness model. Specifically, he must estimate the number of votes cast for a by others in order to decide how to

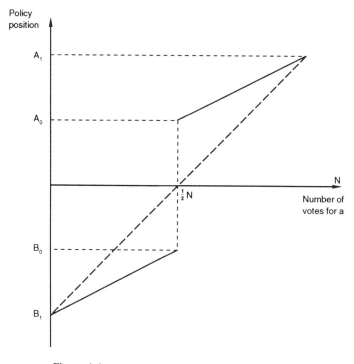

Figure 4.4

cast his own vote: There is, in particular, a positive probability that he will cast a vote in the wrong direction. Suppose, for example, that the policy position preferred by some voter, *i*, is that which would prevail if 60% of the electorate voted for candidate/party *a*. Then *i* must predict whether more or fewer voters than that will vote for *a* in deciding whether he should vote for *a* or *b*. If he decided that the probability that fewer than 60% will vote for *a* is, say, .7, then there is a .3 probability that, in voting for *a*, he will shift the electoral outcome away from his preferred position. That is, the instrumental value to him of a vote for *a* is in the linear case:

$$V_a = (r - w) \frac{V_{max} - V_{min}}{|N(V_{max}) - N(V_{min})|} \qquad (4.13)$$

where *r* is the probability of voting in the right direction, *w* is the probability of voting in the wrong direction, $N(V_{max})$ is the number of voters voting for *a* at the point most preferred, and $N(V_{min})$ is the number of voters voting for *a* at the point least preferred.

It seems quite clear that V_a so defined will in many (perhaps most) plausible instances be less than the expected instrumental value of a vote for *a* in the decisiveness models examined earlier. Accordingly, expressive considerations will be no less significant in the mandate model than in the model outlined in Chapter 2 and will almost certainly be more so. Compared with a market choice in which the chooser is genuinely decisive, expressive preferences will tend to predominate, whether there are mandate effects or not.

Stigler's (1972) brief discussion can be used to good effect here. Stigler draws an analogy between the effect of a vote and the effect of consumer search on automobile quality. Stigler observes:

Presumably the individual buyer communicates some small message by the type of automobile he chooses from the existing variety, at a definite cost in search and experiment with new goods. It is presumably often rational for the buyer to make a search intended to influence future production . . . that is, to undertake a larger amount of search than would be undertaken if the variety of automobiles was fixed forever. (p. 104, n. 22)

The issue, however, is not whether it can be rational to undertake more search if quality is endogenous, but rather how significant this motive is likely to be in explaining search activity. To extend the analogy, suppose a consumer decidedly prefers car A to car B, but firm B is more "sensitive" to the market and is likely to adjust car quality in the future, if the buyer signals her preference for B's model K over model T. How heavily will a rational consumer weigh this latter aspect in her current choice among cars? Not much. It is implausible that the one buyer can exert so much influence that it would be worth her while to forgo her current, certain preference for A in return for the effects her purchases might have on firm B's future production plans.

Of course, to the extent that mandate effects exist, some modification to the language and style of the basic argument will be required. It will, for example, be potentially misleading to talk of "decisiveness," as if having *some* influence, however small, were the crucial issue. However, the central propositions of our analysis remain entirely unaffected. Within the mandate model, expressive considerations continue to weigh disproportionately – and indeed, are likely to weigh even more heavily than in the case where only electoral victory is relevant.

Summary

The voter's expectation that she will exercise an influence on the outcome of an election is clearly a critical parameter in her electoral decision making, and accordingly a critical parameter in any theory of voter choice. The standard approach to theorizing about such voter expectations is to postulate

1. that the voter exercises an influence if and only if she is decisive;
2. that she is decisive if and only if she makes or breaks a tie; and
3. that the probability of a tie among all other voters (or a tie minus one vote) is properly determined by postulating that each voter is engaged in an independent stochastic experiment of voting for a given option with a certain probability.

Under the latter formulation, the probability of a tie is inversely related to the square root of turnout and is, hence, nonnegligible even for large turnout provided the election is very close. The probability of a tie may be as high as one in twelve thousand for a turnout of 100 million. However, this probability is extremely sensitive to expected closeness and becomes infinitesimal for even quite small values of the expected majority.

Other formulations of voting can be explored, but none of them seem to do serious violence to the conviction that, in most plausible cases, any one individual's vote is very unlikely to change the electoral outcome. Within the mandate model, for example, one individual's vote may "exercise an influence," but the influence thereby exercised is surely negligible. And within the competitive-teams model offered by Palfrey and Rosenthal, although a stable equilibrium with large turnout may be possible, the conditions for stability seem to us to be extremely unlikely to prevail in practice and the equilibrium thus identified to be rather unlike anything we actually observe.

Even on the rendering least congenial to our own position, it seems clear that the probability of decisiveness is likely to be quite small. And this conclusion is, of course, borne out by electoral history. Claims that particular elections have, in fact, been "decided by a single vote" usually dissolve on inspection to a much weaker claim – namely, that the outcome in some one electoral district was decided by one vote, and perhaps that congressional/parliamentary majority also turned out to be by one. But this is not enough for a proper calculation of ex ante probabilities, for although in such cases it may be possible to identify some set of allegedly decisive voters, the critical question is this: How many citizens could have changed their vote without the electoral outcome changing? Only if the answer is none do we have a case of genuine ex ante decisiveness, because only in such a case can the arbitrary voter be sure that it will be she who is decisive.

In determining how the probability of being decisive should properly be calculated, there are some puzzles; and these are puzzles we have not been able to fully resolve. However, we do not believe that any plausible resolution could seriously affect the general thrust of the argument in this book. On any reading, the probability of any one voter's being decisive (or more generally the extent of any individual voter's influence on electoral outcomes) is bound to be small, and the role of expressive considerations in electoral choice correspondingly magnified compared with conventional market choice.

5 The theory of electoral outcomes: implications for public choice theory

The term "free-trade," like "virginity," refers to one condition only, whereas "protection" covers a multitude, as does "sin." This book is an investigation into the morphology of the sin of protection, not into conditions of a fall from grace.
J. J. Pincus, Pressure Groups and Politics in Antebellum Tariffs

Introduction

In the preceding three chapters, we have attempted to spell out our theory of electoral preference, derived from the standard axioms of rational actor theory. This theory is one part of a general rational actor theory of politics – and an important and much neglected part – but it is not the whole story. To develop a theory of electoral politics out of a theory of electoral preference requires us to connect electoral outcomes to voter preference in some way. It is necessary, in other words, to show how the interactions of individual voters operating within the institutional structure of electoral political process serve to generate political outcomes. In fact, orthodox public choice models have focused almost exclusively on this latter issue: In technical terms they have been primarily concerned with the properties of majority rule as an aggregation device. What these models have shown is that the connection between electoral outcomes and (revealed) voter preferences is, under the most plausible assumptions, complex and potentially perverse – perverse in the sense that majority rule can lead to electoral outcomes that no voter would desire, even if revealed electoral preferences were identical with the voters' true preferences over electoral outcomes.

Because these orthodox models depend on little more than the internal logic of majority rule and are relevant under what seem to be very general assumptions about voter preferences, it is tempting to think of such models as dealing with a dimension of electoral politics that is quite independent of the one our theory addresses. We might, in other words, conceptualize the connection between electoral outcome and voters' preferences in two steps: one that deals with the relation between voters' preferences over electoral outcomes and their votes; the other that deals with the connection between votes and the electoral outcomes themselves. Potential "slippage" might occur at either step. Our theory could be seen to deal with the former, conventional public choice with the latter. The orthodox treatment can be interpreted as demonstrating a divergence between electoral outcomes and voters' preferences, even if electoral preferences are unproblematic, while our discussion is seen to demonstrate a divergence between electoral outcomes and true electoral preferences, even if *majority rule* were unproblematic.

This simple division of the relevant territory is appealing, but it does not quite work – and this for two reasons. First, we have not yet *shown* that electoral outcomes will not reflect true electoral preferences when standard majoritarian cycling problems are absent. It is possible that although there is no systematic relation between voter preferences over outcomes and votes cast taking all voters as a group, the electoral outcome may nevertheless reflect voter preferences. It is a characteristic feature of electoral politics that significant numbers of voters can alter their votes and indulge all sorts of eccentric inclinations without electoral outcomes changing in any way. For example, suppose most of the electorate votes entirely randomly, but that a small critical mass of voters vote their interests. Then the law of large numbers will ensure that the random voters will roughly cancel one another out, and the only *systematic* feature of electoral process will be attributable to those voters who vote in a self-interested way. Competing parties/candidates cannot influence random voters, but they can compete for the votes of the self-interested minority and will rationally do so. If that minority is representative of the community as a whole (i.e., if the self-interested voters are a random sample of the polity), then electoral outcomes will be the same as if *all* voters voted their interests. In this event, any test of the relation between interests and individual voting behavior will show that interests "explain" voting behavior very poorly; and yet it will still be the case that standard public choice models will work quite well in explaining electoral outcomes. On average, electoral outcomes will be explicable by assuming voters vote, say, on a simple wealth-maximizing basis, even though we may know that most voters do not.

Note that this is one way in which political and market processes are different. In the market, all individuals' preferences count in determining the aggregate outcome. The indulgence of random choice would alter the market equilibrium in predictable ways. Politics is not analogous. In one sense, this difference is the aggregative version of our general individual indecisiveness point; and it seems that this aggregate version may work in favor of standard public choice models rather than against them. In order to establish whether that is so, we must explore the construction of electoral equilibria with an eye to showing exactly how and to what extent the predominance of expressive elements in electoral choice affects electoral outcomes. To focus on the issues at hand, we shall begin by investigating the role of expressive preferences in a context where majority rule as an aggregation device is relatively unproblematic. Specifically, we shall begin with a "median-voter" model of the simplest kind, where there are two competing parties and all preferences are single peaked. This investigation occupies the next section.

It could, of course, be argued that the simple median-voter model, though it produces results that show majority rule in a good light, is in fact implausible. Consequently, while our argument in the next section may perform the useful function of isolating a distinct source of potential "political failure," it may be viewed as being somewhat beside the point. Moreover, since public choice orthodoxy has already conclusively shown that there are major problems with majority rule in general, tracing out additional independent sources of political failure may seem to be entirely redundant – a little like shooting (as opposed to flogging) a dead horse.

However, we believe that the simple median-voter model is of some interest – and this because the empirical relevance of the more general spatial equilibrium models, with their striking result that majority rule generates the global instability, seems quite dubious. Those more general models offer a picture of electoral politics characterized by perpetually changing coalitions and an omnipotent agenda setter; and it is by no means obvious that this is what we observe. There appears to be a problem here for public choice orthodoxy – specifically, why it is that there is so much stability in political life. Interestingly, expressive voting may suggest something of an answer, which brings us to the other reason why questions of preference and questions of majority rule cannot be rigidly compartmentalized. This reason is that although majoritarian cycling can in principle arise with almost any set of preferences, the nature of the preferences to be aggregated does bear, if not on the logical possibility of cycling, then at least on the empirical likelihood. In the upcoming section on cycling and expressive preferences, therefore, we shall explore the implications of the expressive preference theory for conventional majority-disequilibrium models.

There is finally a more general question about how much of conventional public choice theory we might "rescue." It is at least conceivable that much of that theory might stand if its scope and domain were properly understood. Having indicated why a strict logical separation between expressive voting theory and majority-rule analytics is not possible, we may nevertheless be able to suggest a division of the intellectual territory along different lines that preserves a role for standard public choice models in an appropriately modified context. We shall explore this issue in the last section of the chapter.

The median-voter model and expressive preferences

The median-voter model has had a distinguished history in public choice theory. One of the first contributions to public choice analysis in modern economics was a paper in the median-voter tradition by Howard Bowen, entitled (conspicuously for our purposes) "The Interpretation of Voting in the Allocation of Resources" (1943). This paper represents a suitable focus for our discussion here. Although it is an early paper, it has attained something of the status of a classic and has become the foundation (explicitly or implicitly) both for an important tradition of empirical investigation (notably Borcherding and Deacon, 1972, and Bergstrom and Goodman, 1973) and for public finance theory with a public choice orientation (see, e.g., Buchanan, 1967, and Brennan, Bohanen, and Carter, 1984). The central thrust of the Bowen thesis is that one can induce the median-voter's preferences for public policies from the policies that actually emerge under majority rule. This induction exercise requires both that electoral competition generates the outcome voted for by the median voter and that that outcome is indeed the one that the median voter truly prefers.

The simplified model that Bowen presents is one in which there is a single public good to be provided by proportional taxation. Each individual can be presumed to have preferences for the public good that obey conventional convexity properties (i.e., the demand curve is downward sloping over the entire range). Each faces a tax price for the public good equal to the ratio of his tax base to total tax base. For expositional purposes, the tax base can be thought of as income, so that the tax price is equivalent (more or less) to income share. The postulated demand curve and tax price together define for each taxpayer an ideally preferred level of public goods output, and any change in output that takes the taxpayer further from his preferred level (in the same direction) necessarily leaves that taxpayer worse off. Arraying the taxpayers in order of their ideal points, there is a "median" voter so defined. Electoral competition between two parties under majority rule will tend to settle on this median level, given that each party wishes to maximize its chance of election. Individuals will, by assumption, vote for a more preferred over a less preferred level of public goods supply, and levels of supply "close" to the median (in terms of the numbers of voter-taxpayers) are preferred by more taxpayers than are levels of supply that are "further away."

The attractions of a model of this kind to the economist are clear. For one thing, the model generates a determinate political equilibrium, in contrast with models of the sort we shall examine in the next section. Relatedly, the model is capable of generating reasonably sharp predictions using the conventional apparatus of demand theory. And it meshes nicely with the theory of public goods on which the economist's theory of the state is largely based.

Yet it is clear, if our earlier analysis of voting behavior is accepted, that the model is fundamentally misconceived. The "demands" for public goods that individuals exhibit via their voting behavior do not bear the required relation to the individuals' utility functions (defined over public and private goods): They do not properly justify the ascription of "demands." Even if political parties knew the various agents' *true* marginal evaluations for public goods and could derive the median level for any given tax regime, those parties would have no incentive to locate at that median level. Suppose, for example, that we were at this median level, as determined by the true demands for the public good. Suppose further that by reducing the level of public goods supply by one dollar, a party could generate expressive benefits for a majority of voters. In a proper utilitarian or cost–benefit calculation, the expressive benefits would not justify the departure from the initial point. But given the relative magnification of expressive benefits that the electoral process involves, the expressive benefits will tend to dominate in determining the positions rational parties take. Consider, for example, the calculus of a party making a choice between spending one dollar on some project A, which by hypothesis is calculated to return $100 worth of total benefit, and spending that dollar on some other project B that generates little consumption benefit but that has considerable symbolic value and generates significant expressive returns. The party will, under plausible assumptions about the size of the community, choose the latter project. The ulilitarian cost–benefit calculation becomes essentially irrelevant: Given that voters vote with an eye mainly to expressive returns, competitive parties will choose policies on the same basis.

It may be tempting to reinterpret the Bowen diagram in a way that shows *electoral* demands for the public good in question as opposed to "true" demand. For example, in a simple three-person community let rr_i be the ith individual's instrumental demand for G, and ee_i be the corresponding "expressive demand." Then the

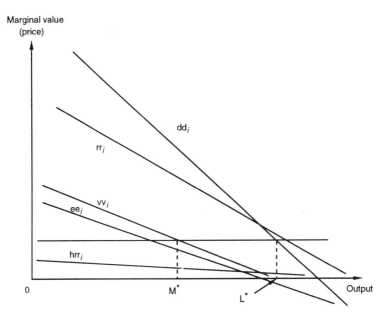

Figure 5.1

vertical sum of rr_i and ee_i could be thought of as the Bowen demand curve, dd_i; while the "distorted" sum, $ee_i + hrr_i$ (where h is the probability of decisiveness, and significantly less than unity – here, one-half reflecting the stylized three-voter setting) is the electorally revealed demand curve, $v_i v_i$. It can then be recognized that, in general, the median-voter outcome, M in Figure 5.1, will diverge from the median of the truly *preferred* outcomes, depicted as L^* in Figure 5.1.

The diagrammatics of Figure 5.1 provide a *suggestive* way to reinterpret the Bowen discussion. They can, however, be greatly misleading, for that formulation implies a form of opportunity cost calculation on the "supply" side that is inappropriate. That is, the dd_i curve shows the benefits of providing the public good by reference to private goods benefits forgone. To place the ee_i curve in the same plane suggests that voters evaluate public goods in terms of their expressive benefits measured in the same dollar units of private goods forgone. Not so. If the object of the Bowen analysis is to describe electoral "choice" over alternative levels of some public activity, then the expressive benefits of the public activity undertaken must be compared with the *expressive* benefits of private alternatives forgone. The standard, instrumentally based calculation is substantially irrelevant on *both* the benefit and the costs side.

An appropriate formulation of voter choice requires us to determine for each voter a *net* demand for any public project with respect to the instrumental and expressive elements. That is, we derive in Figure 5.2 RR_i, which is rr_i minus the individual's tax price; and we form EE_i, which is the *net* marginal expressive benefit of the public project pursued at various levels. Then we can add RR_i to EE_i to de-

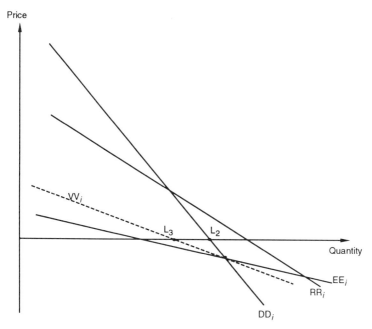

Figure 5.2

termine the net Bowen demand curve, DD_i. And we form the "distorted" vertical sum, VV_i, $EE_i + hRR_i$. The median voter in our three-person community will, on this basis, choose output level L_3 – as distinct from the Bowen equilibrium, L_2. In the diagram as drawn, the "distortion" due to expressive preferences appears modest. More generally, and acknowledging fully the arguments presented in Chapter 3 concerning the possible concord of expressive and instrumental returns, there seems no reason why those goods that generate large net expressive returns will always be those that generate large net instrumental returns. We should expect that the *domain* of public activity no less than the *level* will be profoundly affected by the predominance of expressive considerations.

The difference between the formulation in Figures 5.1 and 5.2 is not merely one of analytic nicety. In Figure 5.1, changes in tax arrangements can, by virtue of changing cost shares, alter electoral outcomes in predictable ways. This is the central insight in the tax-price/cost-share tradition (as represented, e.g., in Buchanan, 1967, and Brennan, Bohanen, and Carter, 1984). Provided the influence of expressive returns can be restricted to the *demand* side of the political equilibration process, then the standard results emerging from that sort of tax-price analysis will hold. However, expressive considerations cannot be so restricted. Tax-price considerations relate only to the instrumental part of the electoral model; accordingly, recognition of the predominance of expressive considerations *undermines* the "taxes-as-cost-shares" tradition in fiscal theory. Ironically perhaps, the conventional normative (apolitical) tradition in public finance theory, a tradition that emphasizes the differential fairness and efficiency of alternative tax instruments, may be more relevant electorally than the standard public choice account, for all that the latter account has attempted to deal explicitly with the role that tax instruments play as elements in political process. "Fairness" and "efficiency" are potentially potent political symbols, capable of capturing the expressive sympathies of voters: Although fairness and efficiency also influence the tax prices that voters must pay for public benefits, their role at this level is entirely instrumental and, consequently, of relatively little electoral significance.

At this point, it is appropriate to take up the conjecture offered in the Introduction: Is it conceivable that the median-voter model as conventionally interpreted might apply in certain cases? What conditions would be necessary and/or sufficient to resurrect the basic results? How likely is it that such conditions will prevail? To answer these questions, it may be useful to appeal to the "mixed" model of voter choice introduced in the second section of Chapter 4. The central feature of that model was that though most voters vote according to expressive considerations, it may be that the probability of being decisive is high enough that some citizens for whom expressive returns are very low will actually vote. This group represents a set of voters for whom instrumental considerations are relatively significant. Suppose expressive voters are drawn randomly from the voting population in the sense that half would vote for more public good than the median (of the *true* preferences) and the other half of the expressive voters would vote for less than that median. Then expressive voters become irrelevant: They cancel one another out. Electoral competition will, in this case, focus on the smaller set of voters who vote their interests. Since this latter group is a random sample of the population with respect to true demands for the public good, then the median-voter analysis can be held to apply: The process of electoral competition among the smaller set would generate the same level of public goods supply and the same comparative static results with respect to electoral equilibrium as for the larger set.

It is, therefore, conceivable that the median-voter model may survive in an "as if" role – conceivable, but highly implausible. Why is it, after all, that electoral competition should focus on one margin of notional calculus that is tens-of-thousands less significant than another? After all, any change in policy has to be worth $12,500 or so to be the equivalent of one dollar to the instrumental voter; an expressive voter seems intrinsically a cheaper proposition. And even if the relevance of self-interest for some voters at the margin were established, the requirement that these voters be a random sample of the electorate seems more than a little strained. It may be, of course, that there are really two margins of political competition that are relevant – one symbolic and expressive, the other relevant to interests. This is a possibility we take up in the last section of this chapter. But the conventional median-voter model, with its characteristic interpretation of electoral preferences in terms of standard demand curves for public goods, must be jettisoned. One cannot induce preferences over electoral outcomes from voting behavior, so all the normative properties of the model must be abandoned. And any comparative static analysis involving the predicted effects of changes on the tax side is simply misconceived. An appropriately modified median-voter model

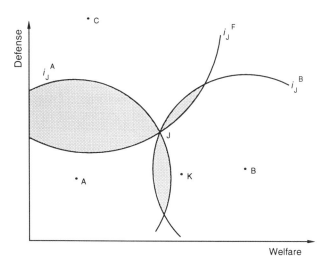

Figure 5.3

may serve some useful purposes, but the results would have to be interpreted with extreme care. And for our part, we cannot see what those "useful purposes" might be.

Cycling and expressive preferences

Some years ago, the editor of the journal *Public Choice*, Gordon Tullock (1981), posed in the title of a notable contribution the question: "Why So Much Stability?" It is a fair question. A central proposition in public choice orthodoxy is that except under what seem like very stringent assumptions, majority rule does not generate a stable outcome. That is, there is no outcome that cannot be defeated by some majority of voters. The picture of democratic politics that this fact suggests is one of continual policy change as the composition of the decisive coalition alters – there will be an endless kaleidoscope of shifting majorities as each faction (and in the limit each individual) joins coalitions with others to secure the outcome best for itself.

Although generalized proofs of the instability proposition are rather fancy technically, the essential features of the problem can be easily presented by appeal to a simple diagrammatic example. Suppose A, B and C are voters casting their votes over a policy set that consists of two issues – say, defense and welfare spending. The preferred positions of the three voters are indicated by the points *A, B,* and *C* in Figure 5.3. Each voter prefers points closer to her ideal point, with "closeness' defined in the natural way as the length of the line connecting her ideal point to the actual policy option. Preferences for each voter can on this basis be represented by a set of circular indifference curves, with the ideal point as the center and the level of utility declining as the radius of the circle expands.

In our diagrammatic example, A prefers low levels of spending on both defense and welfare, B prefers high welfare spending but low defense spending, C prefers a high level of defense spending but very low welfare spending. In the standard account, these voter preferences are taken to be an accurate reflection of the voters' "true" preferences, and voters are assumed to vote for the policy package that they prefer, in any pairwise comparison. The precise location of such preferences will depend of course not only on tastes for defense and welfare, but also on the manner in which the cost of the expenditures is allocated across taxpayer-citizens. The construction of Figure 5.3 presumes that tax arrangements are given and fixed in such a way that the cost-sharing arrangements are known by taxpayers.

Consider now any point space – say, the point J. The set of points that are preferred by A to J is the set within the indifference circle i_J^A; the set of points preferred by B to J is the set within indifference curve i_J^B; the set of points preferred by C to J, the set within i_J^C.

Clearly, any two of these three sets must have a nonempty intersection. This shows that a coalition of any two voters prefers some other points to J and will vote for any of these points in a pairwise comparison with J: For *any* point in policy space, there is some set of points preferred by a majority to that point. For the point J the majority-preferred set is indicated by the various shaded areas; that is, any point selected from the shaded area would defeat J in a simple majority election.[1]

The general result here is McKelvey's (1976): that one can get from any point in policy space to any other by a sequence of moves each of which is approved by a majority of voters. The requirement that any move must be approved by a majority is, in itself, then not sufficient to constrain policy outcomes *at all* in the long run. A commitment to majoritarianism seems to represent a commitment to a random walk through policy space – with even quite disastrous outcomes permitted. McKelvey himself, however, raises an alternative possibility – that the person who sets the agenda possesses the ability to secure any outcome she desires. By an appropriate selection of options, the agenda setter can arrange for any outcome at all to emerge: If she is rational the emergent outcome will be the agenda setter's own ideal point. If the agenda setter's preferences are included as part of the relevant normative calculus (and the onus of argument would seem to lie with those who would seek to exclude her), then the resultant outcome is "efficient" in the standard economist's sense: Any move away from the equilibrium would make the agenda setter worse off. But the prospect of instability and gross inefficiency is set aside only by appeal to the possibility of dictatorial outcomes.[2]

This, then, is the standard account of majoritarian democracy as it appears in public choice orthodoxy. It is a story either of endless cycling and outcome inde-

---

[1] Some of the areas in Figure 5.3 may be empty. If we were at K, along the straight line connecting a with b, then there would be no policy arrangement that is simultaneously preferred to K by both A and B. However, there are points simultaneously preferred by A and C, and points simultaneously preferred by both B and C. By appropriate choice of policies, we could, as it were, shrink the size of any one of the three arms of the "propeller" depicted in Figure 5.3, but only by increasing the area of the other two arms.

[2] It might be remarked, at this point, that it is a feature of the Paretian efficiency norm that rational dictatorship is always "efficient."

terminacy, on the one hand, or of (ultimate) electoral irrelevance and lavish dictatorial power, on the other. And at least to the untutored eye, it is a story that strains credulity. Over successive electoral periods, one hardly observes the degree of instability that the standard analysis seems to suggest: Welfare and defense spending may vary somewhat from period to period, but hardly with the degree of volatility the model requires. We should note, moreover, that since the ideal arrangement for each decisive coalition would presumably be one in which the members pay negligible taxes and receive mammoth transfers, we ought to expect fairly substantial swings in the magnitude and direction of transfers and in the nature of tax arrangements, as the composition of the decisive majority (and disadvantaged minority) changes. At the same time, the structure of policy outcomes does not exhibit the sort of fixity that suggests that we are at a dictator's optimum; nor do political agents (either politicians or bureaucrats) seem to enjoy that level of opulence that seems to be consistent with the possession of such extreme dictatorial power. Hence, Tullock's question.

Various explanations of the apparent relative stability of political outcomes have been offered by public choice theorists (including Tullock himself). And practitioners have been ready enough to point out that elements of a majority-cycling pattern can be discerned in political process, though in a very much more muted way than public choice orthodoxy would suggest. It would perhaps be surprising if things were otherwise: The central propositions of public choice theory derive from the simple arithmetic of majority rule. Consequently, unless voters' preferences all happen naturally to lie along some straight line in policy space,[3] or the operation of majority rule is very highly constrained within a structure of institutional rules, then cycling seems a necessary logical concomitant of majority rule (and indeed of any decision-making rule that falls short of unanimity).

The question of how institutional rules might constrain the operation of majority rule so as to ensure "single-peakedness" is an interesting one, but we shall not pursue it at this point.[4] Our object here is rather to explore the connection between majoritarian cycling and the theory of voter choice developed in earlier chapters. Specifically, are there reasons to believe that the predominance of expressive elements in voting behavior may moderate cycling and/or the scope for agenda-setting manipulation?

We believe that there are such reasons – that there is a connection between the logic of majoritarian cycling and the notion of interest-based voting. Consider first of all the agenda-setting possibility. Let us emphasize, first of all, that the central element in the cycling logic is the prospect of redistributing from a minority to a majority. Continuous such redistributions are what permit the agenda setter to obtain profits. Again, to take a simple example, we show in Table 5.1 a sequence of policies, each preferred in pairwise comparison to the previous one and each

---

[3] See Plott (1967) for an early formulization and Enelow and Hinich (1984) for an extended discussion of such questions exploiting spatial voting models of the kind illustrated in Figure 5.3.
[4] See, however, Chapter 11 for a general discussion of the institutional implications of our own argument and for a brief discussion of how those implications differ from those that emerge under a more traditional public choice view.

Table 5.1. *The transfer spiral under majority rule*

| | Payoff to | | | |
Policy	Voter A (shares)	Voter B (shares)	Voter C (shares)	Agenda setter[a] (shares)
x	1,000	1,000	1,000	(0)
y	1,200	1,200	0	(600)
z	1,400	0	200	(1,400)
w	0	200	400	(2,400)
v	100	300	0	(2,600)

[a]The agenda setter does not vote in this simple example.

leaving the agenda setter with higher rents. That is, *z* defeats *y*, *y* defeats *x*, and so on. Now, policy *y* defeats policy *x* *because*, in the move from *x* to *y*, the agenda setter has redistributed from voter C to voters A and B; moreover, in the process the agenda setter is able to pocket the major share of that which is redistributed.

The scope for such moves depends both on the voters A and B being sensitive to relatively small changes in their private payoffs and on the relation between policy choice and payoff being reasonably transparent to the agenda setter. Even under a minimally modified interest-based theory of voting behavior, these assumptions are somewhat at risk, and they become decidedly more dubious in the expressive voting model. Specifically, rational ignorance of the Downsian kind implies that the costs and benefits of various policies are likely to be perceived only dimly by voters – and if, as seems plausible, the probability of noticing a difference in payoffs under alternative policies is dependent on the size of that difference, then it well may be that the number of votes lost in taking $\$a$ from minority members will exceed the number of votes gained in giving $\$(a − s)$ to majority members – the number of minority members who are induced to vote against the policy may be greater than the number of majority members induced to vote for it. Of course, if this is the case then there will be expected electoral gains from taking $\$a$ from the majority members and giving the proceeds to a minority – the sort of redistribution that is taken to be electorally advantageous in the private interest theory of regulation and tariffs.[5] In either case, however, potential returns to any strategic agenda setter will be squeezed. In the limiting case where the probability of voting for policy *a* over *b* is taken to be a linear function of the differences in payoffs from *a* and *b* over the relevant range, then there are simply no potential rents for the agenda setter to appropriate.

In our model of expressive voting, similar problems emerge. The agenda setter can no longer be sure that any policy that is in voter A's interests will secure voter

[5] This tension between the presumptions about electoral equilibrium in the "special-interest" theories of regulation and in the conventional majoritarian cycle models is not often remarked upon but seems to amount to exactly opposite assumptions about the shape of the relation between size of payoff and probability of voting for policies that have higher payoffs.

A's support. Even accepting that interests and expressive returns will often move in the same direction, a policy that makes A better off can only be presumed to increase the probability that A will vote for it. In such an environment, competitive parties may be led to adopt *centrist* policies.

To maximize the expectation of victory, parties will offer policies that tend to equalize returns across voters, provided that the probability of a voter voting for a party is related to that voter's net benefit from the party's victory in an appropriately convex manner. In fact, as Coughlin and Nitzan (1981) show, under reasonably plausible assumptions electoral competition will lead to the Nash social welfare maximum (i.e., the maximum of the product of voters' net utility levels), a characteristic feature of which is that the distribution of individuals' gains tends to be fairly equal.

Of course, the appeal of the Coughlin–Nitzan model depends on the idea that voters' *interests* are transparent, but their *expressive* preferences totally opaque. Parties are assumed to determine policies according to voter interests, despite the fact that the connection between interests and voter choice is so loose. This assumption seems unnecessarily restrictive. Parties may not be able to rely on a simple deductive incidence analysis of alternative policy packages to predict voter support, but they are not bereft of other sources of information. Trial and error, to say nothing of general political nous, questionnaire information, voter polls, and the like, will enable parties to discern what there is of regularity in voter behavior. Parties will come to know what principles voters support and what policies generate expressive returns to various voter groups.

At first sight, it seems as if, since such information is available, the prospect of cycling will reemerge no less strongly in the context of expressive voting as in the conventional interest-based case. There is no reason to suppose, for example, that expressive preferences will not exhibit the same properties as do instrumental ones. The preference structure in Figure 5.3 could, after all, simply be interpreted as reflecting expressive considerations. But there are important differences between an account of cycling in terms of expressive preferences and the standard account in terms of instrumental ones. Note, for example, that in the standard account, a rational party will be continually changing the constituency from which it draws support. To do otherwise is to be predictable, and predictability guarantees defeat: The other party can always offer a subset of any predictable constituency a better deal.[6] But the recognition of expressive voting modifies this account considerably. A party will have to exhibit "integrity" to attract support, and this requirement translates into some basic historical continuity over policies and policy attitudes. Any excessive political opportunism, whoring after the "swinging voter," or betrayal of traditional supporters is likely to lose more votes than it gains. In the standard interest-based account, there is little logical room for categories such as "loyalty," "party principle," "ideological tradition," "consistency," and the like. In the expressive voting account, by contrast, these categories emerge as the stuff of

---

[6] This is one of the strong propositions in the Downsian account (Downs, 1957, chap. 10): The party that announces its policies first always gets beaten.

electoral competition. And to import such categories is to impose major constraints on the possibility of cycling. We do not here wish to deny that the problems of instability that cycling theory implies may arise.[7] We simply want to deny that cycling instability is the *central* problem in large-scale majoritarian electoral politics. It may not even be a *major* problem.

What can public choice orthodoxy explain?

Given the theory of expressive voting developed in earlier chapters and having explored its (essentially negative) implications for public choice orthodoxy, it seems reasonable to ask how much of the orthodoxy remains. After all, that politicians are primarily self-serving, that voters are sensitive to their hip-pocket nerves, and that catering to special interests makes up an important part of political life – these are claims within public choice orthodoxy that have some considerable echo in ordinary observation. How much of this is really overturned by expressive voting? Even if the analytics of majoritarian cycling are in doubt and the cost-share theory of taxation is undermined, at least some flavor of public choice analysis may remain without egoistic voting.

Consider politicians' behavior, first of all. There is, of course, nothing in our theory that would rule out egoistic or otherwise self-interested *motives* on the part of politicians: Political agents can, and should, be modeled just as in standard economic theory. However, politicians may be induced to *behave* ethically, in the interests of securing electoral support. That is, they may embrace ethical principles of one sort or another because such principles are among the things likely to engage voters' expressive support. It is, for example, a notable feature of ordinary politics that sexual and personal scandals are often enormously costly electorally. In the 1988 Democratic primaries, to take an example that is current at the time of writing, one candidate has more or less destroyed his chances through marital infidelity, another by plagiarizing his speeches and falsifying his academic credentials, and a third by confessing that he had smoked marijuana in college some decades previously. It is difficult to explain how such things could possibly be relevant within the orthodox public choice account of electoral behavior: A politician's personal lifestyle does not obviously impinge on the ability to deliver goodies to self-interested voters. Within the expressive theory of voting, however, the sort of persona that a politician projects becomes electorally significant. If it is the case that politicians are punished electorally for involvement in personal scandal (or obversely are rewarded for presenting an attractive and/or principled public face), it follows not only that politicians will have an incentive to live impeccable lives and develop an aura of personal integrity and responsibility, but also that persons who

---

[7] The conspicuous instability of coalition governments in multiparty systems is instructive here. The small number of parties, all with an obvious interest in being part of a "government," means that party-politicians' interests are more likely to be a significant motive in parties' behavior. But even here parties must be tolerably faithful to their traditional electoral support – to voters who vote for expressive reasons – and so are constrained in the policies they can be seen to endorse. There tends to be instability, to be sure. But coalitions do emerge and are often stable over long periods (at least outside Italy).

possess such characteristics naturally will tend to have a comparative advantage in electoral politics. There are, in other words, reasons to believe that politicians as a group may be more respectable and more principled (say) than others who enjoy equivalent positions in public life (such as corporate executives or pop singers).

Care must be taken here not to paint too heroic a picture. Expressive voting also rewards charm, grace, articulateness, and good appearance – and these filters may well be much more significant than respectability and/or integrity. But alternative theories are to be distinguished as much by what they *reject* as by what they predict. And it is in this that the implications of expressive voting for behavior are most notable. Consider, for example, the predicament of the statesman under the two rival theories. (For the exercise here, a ''statesman'' is to be defined as one who is faithful to some political principle – and is to be contrasted with the political opportunist.) Can the statesman survive? Within public choice orthodoxy, it is difficult to see how. To be principled is to be predictable, and predictable along nonexpedient lines: A politician or party that adopts a statesman-like stance will court defeat at the hands of someone who offers a better deal to some strategically calculated majority of voters. Within the expressive theory, however, the statesman may well survive. He will be vulnerable, to be sure, to attack from those who are more eloquent, better looking, or otherwise capable of mobilizing electoral support, and who are more expedient and less scrupulous. But the statesman's scruples are not by any means a total liability: And hence, his demise is not a foregone conclusion. There is, of course, a reverse side to this observation. The same considerations that allow the statesman to survive will also tend to encourage the doctrinaire – even the fanatic. The general point is that expressive considerations in voting modify our understanding of what characteristics in electoral politics are rewarded and what are punished; and though the theory does not say anything directly about politicians' behavior, it does bear *indirectly,* because it offers a distinctive picture of politicians' incentives and of the kinds of persons best fitted for political careers.

So much for politicians. At a more general level, it has been suggested that the expressive theory of voting implies that the relative costs of alternative programs will become entirely irrelevant in public decision making. The reasoning is that since voters rationally discount the costs of programs in electoral decisions, politicians will be led to do so in deciding on policy packages. To take a specific case, a recent study by Faith and Tollison compares welfare expenditure across U.S. states and shows that such welfare spending is essentially unrelated to the proportion of the population that is below the poverty line. The authors then conclude that the apparent relevance of ''cost considerations'' is evidence *against* the expressive voting model. But it is difficult to see how such a claim can be sustained. Provided only that higher taxes per se are of negative expressive value at the margin, itself a very weak assumption, fiscal resources will always be scarce: A dollar spent on one program will be a dollar not spent on another. And though *voters* may not reckon on such opportunity costs, politicians surely will. Policy packages will be constructed so as to give the biggest expressive bang for each buck. It is, therefore, entirely predictable that in those polities (states) where making a gesture toward the poor costs more in terms of other gestures forgone, the gesture toward the poor will tend to be more modest. Indeed, the evidence that Anderson, Faith, and Tollison amass seems rather to raise doubts about orthodox public choice voting models. Those orthodox models might have been thought to predict larger welfare expenditure both in toto and per recipient in states where there are larger numbers of poor voters, on the grounds that those larger numbers of poor voters can be relied on to vote their interests.

The general point here is that expressive voting does not obliterate relative costs in explaining policy outcomes – even though these relative costs are not directly relevant to voters, and even where political parties/candidates are totally constrained by electoral competition. This point is sufficiently important to merit emphasis. The relative costs of alternative programs in tax dollars necessarily remains a central ingredient in any theory of politics based on expressive voting. The total level of fiscal activity will be pushed to the point where the expressive benefit of the marginal expenditure program terms is equal to the expressive cost of the marginal tax levy. Within the resultant budget, each expenditure program will be pushed to the point where the marginal expressive benefit is equalized, and those areas in which it costs more to generate expressive returns will be relatively underexpanded. If politics is dominated by rhetoric and posturing, this is in large measure because such activities are cheap – more or less as orthodox public choice theory would have it. But what orthodox public choice theory cannot explain is why the rhetoric and posturing have any place in electoral politics at all: On an interests-only view, such things are simply not demanded, however cheap they may be to produce. (The nature and scope of political rhetoric is a matter we take up in greater detail in the next chapter.)

What then can orthodox public choice theory explain? Not, it seems, the motivational structure of politicians, nor the style of electoral politics. But in the analysis of policy outcomes, where public choice has always focused, it can explain those aspects of policy that depend on relative costs. Specifically, in cross-sectional studies it can explain those variations in policies (across the polities compared) that are attributable to differential costs; and in time-series/comparative static analysis, it can explain those changes attributable to cost changes. It can explain these things because the relative cost element in analysis is essentially unaffected by expressive considerations, and because it may be reasonable (depending on the cross-section or time period taken) to assume that expressive returns remain unchanged. What the orthodox treatment cannot explain is the "demand" side of electoral politics, and hence it cannot explain the general shape of the budget – why governments spend on A and not on B, or why overall policy is what it is.

Having said this, we do not wish to deny a second-order role to interest-based politics. When it comes to the *detail* of particular policies, interests are more likely to emerge as relevant, and this for two reasons: first, because lobbying activity as well as voting is relevant to the determination of policy, and lobbying is often more relevant to details of policy; second, because expressive returns are generally a matter of the overall symbolic aura of policy and not details of execution.

The two reasons are not unrelated. Lobbying tends to be reflected in policy detail rather than in the general sweep precisely *because* electoral (i.e., expressive) considerations are less relevant at the level of detail. Moreover, even setting lobbying aside, interests will tend to obtrude at the electoral level when expressive elements are secondary: The interests of voters may not be particularly significant electorally in toto, but politicians will rationally take voter interests into account in policy design wherever those voter interests promise to return any votes at all (and they will promise to return some votes from voters for whom the stakes are unusually high in contexts where expressive considerations are insignificant).

What emerges from all this is a dual-level theory of electoral politics. At the macrolevel, where the broad sweep of policy is determined, interest-based voting is unlikely to be able to explain much of what we observe. At a more micro level, where policy details are determined, interests are more likely to be relevant – though they operate within a rather narrow domain constrained by expressive considerations. That is, interests cannot, we would argue, explain the level of defense spending or the shape of foreign policy: They may, however, explain where the army base is located or who gets the contract. Equally, voters' interests cannot explain the level of welfare payments, but they may explain some of the administrative details. Voters' interests cannot explain the nature and extent of conservationist policies, but they may explain which tracts are assigned to be national parks, or whether regulations or taxes are used for pollution control. Voters' interests cannot explain whether a government is for or against free trade: But they may be able to explain something of the pattern of tariffs. As Jonathan Pincus puts it in the epigraph to this chapter, to explain the *pattern* of tariffs rather than the *fact* of them is a task that orthodox public choice can reasonably attempt. The modesty of Pincus's object is appropriate in our view. Interest-based theories of political behavior may be able to tell us something about some matters – but they will do so best if their limited role is properly understood, and specifically if the crucial role of central expressive considerations in electoral behavior is borne in mind.

6   From anecdote to analysis

Economic theory must be more than a structure of tautologies if it is to be able to predict and not merely describe the consequences of action: if it is to be something different from disguised mathematics.
         Milton Friedman, "The Methodology of Positive Economics"

Introduction

In this chapter and the next, we consider directly the question of empirical warrant. Does the expressive theory of voting developed in the foregoing pages explain what we observe better than does the homo economicus alternative? Does it provide new hypotheses that the data do not reject? Does the alternative view of voting behavior it offers actually fit the facts?

These questions are not so easily answered, partly because the facts that have to be explained are various and are themselves theoretically constructed, partly because homo economicus is a very slippery customer, partly because the expressive theory may often enough map the self-interest account, and partly because it is not entirely clear what the expressive theory predicts. We do not, therefore, see ourselves as unveiling some single millennial event that will constitute final and definitive refutation of the standard interpretation of pseudorational actor political theory, or even some series of events that will conclusively establish the expressive account of voting as a preferred alternative. The picture of confirmation and rejection of theories as a swashbuckling drama of bold conjectures lance to lance with mortal refutations does not strike us as descriptive in fact or even worthy in aspiration. Confirmation–rejection is much more a matter of patiently building up *presumptions,* one way or the other. Accordingly, what we aim to do in these next two chapters is to provide evidence on our side: to point to the anomalies that the homo economicus account finds difficulty in explaining, to argue that our account provides a plausible explanation for some of these anomalies, and to show that our account explains more of what we observe than does the homo economicus alternative. We think that the balance of evidence is pretty clearly on our side, but we do not deny the ambiguities.

Those who have a romantic notion of Popperian empiricism may find this ambiguity irritating. They may also find our treatment of the "empirical record" a little fast and loose. We do not take it, for example, that the world is describable exhaustively by numbers or that broad brush descriptions of the political landscape have nothing of relevance to contribute to the collection of evidence. The economist's quip that a historian is one who believes that the plural of anecdote is data leaves us undeterred: Anecdote does in our view have a role to play, and a good feel for the whole story is a crucial prerequisite for proper empirical judgment. Accordingly, in this chapter, we shall offer what we see as important general facts about politics, and accounts of several areas of policy in which we see the expressive dimension most clearly in evidence. We shall reserve for the next chapter the exercise of grappling with the numbers, an exercise that some would take to be the only authoritative key to the real world.

We should, at the outset, reemphasize the point made in Chapter 2 that no theory can be a contender for acceptability if its internal logic is in disarray. We believe we have shown that the public choice model[1] of voting behavior is victim of a kind of internal contradiction; for economics holds that changes in relative prices are critical to understanding changes in behavior, yet it assumes that the change in relative prices between input- and outcome-oriented elements in preference expression involved in moving from markets to elections is of no significance. And public choice cannot claim that input-oriented (expressive) elements do not exist, since otherwise it can provide no account of why voters vote in the numbers they do. Public choice can argue, coherently, that the voter derives expressive benefits solely from the *act* of voting, and not at all from voting one way rather than another. But this claim is a very strong one, is prima facie implausible, and would need a great deal in the way of empirical support to make it credible. Moreover, this result would make the nature of voting behavior a contingent, not a decision-theoretic, matter. If proponents of the public choice model of self-interested, outcome-oriented voting are able, after running a suitable number of regressions, to show that there is a tolerable fit between that model and the numbers, they would still be obliged to give an account of why interest-based outcomes emerge. A rigorously positivistic insistence that predictive power is the sine qua non of good theory does not entitle us to conclude that good predictions are *all* that is required. The Copernican astronomical theory firmly supplanted its geocentric, epicycle-clogged predecessor despite the latter's historically demonstrated ability to generate an impressive retinue of predictions and despite its continued ability in the seventeenth century and later to match the Copernican account prediction for prediction. More than "fitting the facts" is required of a theory; it must also genuinely *explain,* in the sense of rendering intelligible, the facts it fits. Otherwise one may have an undeniably handy mnemonic device for drawing inferences but still lack anything that can be called an "explanatory theory." "Explanations" of behavior that lack internal coherence are incapable of explaining anything.

However, the expressive theory of voting would hardly be a very interesting construct if it yielded the same predictions as the homo economicus alternative virtually all the time. We would, to be sure, have to reconstruct the public choice orthodoxy along expressive lines – get the grammar right, as it were. But such reconstruction does not present enormous difficulties. The public choice theorist can, for example, argue that interests mirror expressive preferences much of the time, and there seem to be good reasons (discussed in Chapter 3) as to why this might be

---

[1] Or rather, public choice theory's assumptions about voting behavior, since those assumptions are not necessarily to be dignified with the status of a "model."

so. Alternatively, it might be held that although many voters vote expressively, expressive considerations more or less cancel one another out, and one is left with interests as the relevant determinant of electoral *outcomes*. If expressive voting does not translate itself into political results, then although it may do quite well as a theory of voting behavior, it will not contribute anything much to political analysis more broadly. As another possible response, public choice scholars may prefer to emphasize the role of nonelectoral considerations (lobby groups, campaign contributions, bribes, or various bureaucratic imperatives) in explaining political outcomes. All these maneuvers do have their empirical side effects, but they all serve to maintain as central the connection between political outcomes and particular citizen interests. And of course, the very fact that such maneuvers are so easy makes it difficult to isolate sharp differences between the orthodox and expressive account. Some sharp differences can, we think, be found (and we shall discuss them), but we concede that the evidence is not entirely conclusive. And that is as we should expect, because interests clearly do play a role in politics, and our voting model predicts that they will. It is just that interests play a lesser role and a different kind of role than public choice orthodoxy claims. They play, specifically, a lesser role than in market behavior.

Which "facts"?

With all this as background, it may be useful to lay out at greater length what "facts" about the political world a theory of voting might seek to explain, or better put, the domain of various possible hypotheses that we might seek to confront with the facts. Three such domains present themselves: The first deals with voting behavior per se, the second with the nature of political outcomes, the third with the nature of political *process*. Consider them seriatim.

Voting behavior

The orthodox public choice account and our expressive alternative offer potentially rival accounts of voting behavior as such. The public choice account states that individuals vote for the outcome they prefer, and that voters preferences are largely reducible to simple income/wealth maximization. There are, in fact, two hypotheses at stake here: first, that voters are pseudorational in the sense defined in Chapter 2; and second, that utility functions include only (or predominantly) private goods consumed by the individual voters themselves. The latter assumption is clearly critical. If agents have preferences over other agents' consumption levels (of either a benevolent or malicious kind), or over alternative states of the world that bear negligibly on their own wealth levels, then much of the predictive power of the rational actor account of voting behavior is lost. As Buchanan (1979b) persuasively argues, the "science" of choice requires a specification of the arguments in utility functions; the "logic" of choice requires only that there *be* a utility function (or more weakly, a relevant preference ordering). The homo economicus construction used in public choice analysis is just such a specification of the utility function, and not a particularly plausible one at that.[2] It is, however, important to recognize that our critique is not just one of the particular utility function that public choice theorists assume. Public choice economists may be wrong to assert that individuals are rational egoists *in their market roles:* We are inclined, in fact, to think public choice economists are wrong on this matter (or at least that they greatly overstate the case). The claim that the evidence is overwhelmingly in favor of the self-interest postulate (egoistically interpreted) – a claim made most eloquently in recent times by George Stigler (1981) – usually ignores the fact that convincing tests of the hypothesis are few and far between, and that much contrary evidence is ignored.[3] But although the claim that homo economicus is an implausible model of human motivation is one possible line of criticism against public choice orthodoxy (and may be a persuasive line), it is not our line. Our point is that, more or less *whatever* the utility function chosen, market and electoral choices will predictably differ. It is therefore simply impermissible to use evidence from individuals' voting behavior to induce their "true preferences" (as decision theorists would understand that term) and equally impermissible to extrapolate from revealed market behavior to the electoral context. For purposes of empirical testing, however, it is helpful for us to treat the matter of market behavior as uncontested; so we shall take it that market behavior does indicate predominant egoism. To be sure, such a move makes life easier for us, for it will then be sufficient to show that nonegoistic considerations get significant play in the electoral context. It will, for example, be sufficient to show that the distributional consequences of particular policies constitute a relatively poor explanation of the pattern of voting. And here it will not be enough to show that the *probability* of voting for a policy is marginally higher for voters whose incomes are increased by its implementation than for voters whose incomes are reduced. The challenge for the public choice account is to explain why those whose incomes are increased do not *all* vote for the policy. In this connection, some slippage can presumably be traced to random errors: But if there is reason to believe that "something else" is going on (such as the influences of party loyalty, ideology, or the like), then we consider this fact to be reasonable grounds for holding that the public choice account is inadequate.

Of course, whether individuals vote on a wealth-maximizing basis is essentially an empirical matter and one that is amenable to direct confrontation with the numbers. We shall therefore postpone it to the next chapter. But as we note there, public choice scholars themselves have not been much concerned to examine voting behavior directly. To the extent that there has been any defense of public choice orthodoxy in this area at all, it has proceeded more by the *indirect* method of examining the effects on turnout of various changes in relevant parameters – the size of the enfranchised group or the expected closeness of the election. We shall review that literature also in Chapter 7.

[2] As many critics are inclined to argue with varying degrees of vigor. For an interesting and highly readable critique of economics from this viewpoint, see Sen (1987) and Etzioni (1988).
[3] Sen (1987) makes precisely this point in relation to Stigler's Tanner Lectures, and we mean to follow Sen here.

Political outcomes

We have already noted (in Chapter 5 and briefly in the introduction to this chapter) that even where virtually all voters vote for reasons other than self-interest, political outcomes may nevertheless reflect voter interests in much the way that public choice theory predicts that they will. There are several different ways in which this kind of slippage may come about. The first possibility is that, in a choice between given alternatives, expressive voters may cancel each other out, leaving self-interest as the determinative factor. A simple example may remind us of the possibilities here. On offer are political options *a* and *b*, which involve an income-equivalent benefit to groups A and B respectively. Most members of A and B vote expressively: A few in each group vote their self-interest. Let that few be, say, 10% of each group. Then 10% of group A will vote systematically for *a*, 10% of group B will vote for *b*, and the remaining voters will vote expressively over *a* and *b* and will (we assume) split about evenly between the two options. Then, in group A about 55 % will vote for *a;* in B, 55% for *b*. And if group A exceeds group B, then *a* will win, and the interests theory of politics is vindicated, more or less. That is, the probability that the voter will vote for the policy that defends his interests is greater than one-half, and that is all we need to get some explanatory power out of the interests story.

To some extent, however, this "vindication" is a result of the fact that interests are relatively salient and easily identifiable, whereas expressive considerations are, like tastes for jam, relatively obscure. It is also an artifact of the example, where the electoral options themselves are given. If one focused on some equivalently transparent, analogously simple characteristic of electoral options and voters – for example, party loyalty or ideological identification – our prediction is that that characteristic would explain at least as much of electoral behavior and resultant political outcome as does the self-interest account. And if the political options themselves are part of the explanatory agenda, then it needs to be explained why the options on offer are what they are; and that explanation must fit the account provided of how voters vote. It is, as we have argued, plausible to argue that interests will play a much larger role in deciding where to locate a military installation or a public university than in deciding whether it is defense and education or direct transfers that are to be provided. In other words, in choosing what is to be explained in such a way that expressive and symbolic dimensions are minimized, one can give a disproportionately favorable cast to the interest-based story. But what then needs to be accounted for is why the political options on offer are not of the kind, transfer $x from every blue-eyed to every brown-eyed person (or from everyone whose name begins with J to everyone whose name begins with K). If politics is about voters' interests, why are taxes as general as they are, and why are expenditures so obscurely related to identifiable interests in so many cases?

There is a second way in which interests may be relevant to political outcomes without their being anything like as relevant to individual voting behavior. Suppose voters do not vote their own individual interests, but rather the interests of some group (or faction) with which they identify. Again, a policy may harm many members of some such group, and yet those members may continue to vote the group interest, as they perceive it. In this case, the self-interest theory of voting behavior may perform relatively poorly, in that many voters are voting contrary to their own interests much of the time. But there may be enough correlation between individuals' interests and the interests of the factions to which they belong for individual interests to play a critical role in explaining political outcomes. The analytics of much of orthodox public choice theory could proceed unscathed in this kind of case, except that the relevant "political actors" would be the groups to which individuals give their allegiance rather than the individuals themselves. A critical question for public choice theory in this account is to explain why *those* groups of individuals and not some other coalition that may reflect its members' interests better are relevant and, indeed, why the optimal group size for each individual is not one. If expressive considerations work at the level of providing reasons for individuals to identify with some groups rather than others and *group* interests are what determine electoral outcomes, then there will be some (and conceivably much) explanatory power in the individual interests story as applied to electoral *outcomes,* but no individually instrumental account of group membership will be available, and the individual interests account of individual voting behavior may perform relatively badly.

Note that any "public interest" account of voting behavior (such as that set out as a possible civic ideal in Chapter 10) can be viewed as an extreme form of the group interest story. If the group with which voters identify is the nation state, then political outcomes will reflect voters' interests on average, even though the prediction that individuals vote their self-interest will perform fairly poorly. The problem with this account for the public choice theorist is then not that the electoral outcomes that prevail cannot be explained by voters' interests, but that particular electoral outcomes that would reflect any subset of voters' interests *better* do not receive those voters' votes (and in particular that an option that better reflects a *majority's* interests does not defeat an option that reflects that majority's interests less well).

There is a third possible source of slippage between a theory of electoral behavior and a theory of political outcomes, perhaps the most obvious possibility of the three we canvass here. This is that political outcomes are largely independent of electoral considerations altogether, that political outcomes are mainly determined in arenas other than the electoral one and by reference to nonelectoral dimensions of political reality. We have already noted the possibility of a model of politics as dominated by lobbying, supported by direct payments of one kind or another to political decision makers. Alternatively, policies may be determined largely by bureaucratic imperatives. Bureaucrats, as privileged suppliers of "expert" policy advice and with monopoly access to critical sources of information, may have the capacity to set most of the dimensions of public policy, leaving electoral politics a substantially epiphenomenal role. Or it may be that the relevant decisions are taken by elected politicians, but on the basis of their own judgments and interests and with little direct reference to the policy preferences of the electorate per se. Some proponents of representative democracy, for example, see the primary function of elections as being not to reflect the citizens' preferences over policy outcomes, but simply to constitute a more or less representative body that will make relevant decisions on policy matters. In an interesting version of this line, John Burnheim (1985) in his *Is Democracy Possible?* offers the suggestion of determining representatives not by election but by well-ordered lottery, and some may see current electoral procedures as not far removed from the lottery analogy. If so, however, it would be an entirely contingent matter as to whether the policy outcomes chosen by politicians would reflect citizens' interests or not. The populist complaint that, whoever you vote for, a politician always gets elected and the increasing popularity of devices like the citizens' initiative attest to some anxiety as to whether politicians will be reliable protectors of citizen interests.

For our purposes, such possibilities greatly muddy the waters. On the one hand, if the public choice account of demand-side electoral factors does not predict well, it is always possible to appeal to supply-side considerations (e.g., bureaucratic imperatives or politicians' preferences). Equally, however, if the interest-based account "works," it is open to us to point to these alternative mechanisms as explanatory (lobby group "bribes," or the decisions of a roughly representative assembly in which it is the members' direct interests and not electoral constraints that drive the outcomes). It is, therefore, simply not possible to conclude, on the basis of a few simple tests, precisely what the nature of the demand-side influences is, and specifically whether or not electoral considerations force interests-oriented outcomes in the way public choice orthodoxy maintains. Ideology may appear as a relevant factor in politicians' decisions (as in the work of Rubin and Kau and Kalt and Zupan, to be discussed in the next chapter) either because politicians' own preferences are ideologically cast or because citizens' electoral preferences are. The "facts" do not necessarily speak for themselves.

The general point we want to make here is that we do not claim that in many instances a tolerable empirical fit cannot be found between the interests of some group of voters and the electoral outcomes that prevail – or indeed that an interest-based account cannot predict with fair success which policies are most likely to gain electoral success. What we do claim is that this interest-based account performs rather less well in many cases than a rival "expressive" account. In this chapter's section on the domain of politics, we shall offer several instances of policy in which we think the expressive story does rather better, and some in which we think the interests account is in real trouble. Most of the examples we consider are ones that we have mentioned in passing along the way in preceding chapters – transfers to the poor, the U.S. Social Security system, pollution abatement, general research, sumptuary taxation, and so on. But in that discussion we will be focusing on the explanation of the policy *outcomes.* It seems to us important to consider as well some critical aspects of political process, aspects that may or may not be reflected in policy choices but that demand some attention in their own right. We shall confront these "aspects of political process" first, before turning to the examples of public policy we want to discuss.

The nature of political rhetoric

It is difficult to deny that politics has a distinctive rhetoric. Public choice theorists may claim that the moralizing and ideologizing that characterize much political discourse is epiphenomenal, a kind of noise screen to hide the real play of competitive interests underneath; but those theorists do not, we think, deny that the "noise" is there. At this point in the argument, we can leave it as an open question whether or not moral and ideological considerations have any influence on political decisions. It might be argued that the repertoire of morally and ideologically charged language is so vast that its use imposes no constraint at all on political action – that the supply of ethical rationalizations lying on the shelf is sufficient to accommodate virtually anything. But here we set such claims temporarily aside: We do not seek to explore so much how politicians are influenced by their use of what is on the shelf as why they bother to pick things up from it at all, or why what is on the shelf is as it is.

The orthodox public choice account sees political rhetoric, with its moral and ideological appeal, as a form of political advertising more or less analogous to the use of bikini-clad girls and sporting celebrities to sell cars, cigarettes, and beer in the marketplace. Just as in market advertising the seller seeks to provide an association between the product and some attractive image, so the political advertiser makes appeal to relevant images in order to attract votes. Of course, as we have claimed in Chapter 3, to argue thus is to concede all the soil that we need in which to plant our general decision-theoretic argument. Here, however, we want to emphasize the distinctiveness of the political case.

If the standard public choice account were true – that is, if voters voted for policy packages according to how they affected their own individual incomes – then one would expect that a significant part of the terrain in political advertising would be taken up in explaining why policy A would deliver more goodies to voter group G than policy B does, more or less in the way that cash-management accounts advertise their current rates of interest, or property trusts their records of capital growth. Yet *that* kind of advertising is almost entirely absent from politics, and politicians who are too readily identified as "trying to buy votes" are rarely successful. Of course, much market advertising is also heavier on appeal to affective symbols than to information – but even here, the character of the appeal is different. No private firm, not even a health spa, offers its customers "nothing but blood, sweat, and tears." The catch cry "Ask not what IBM can do for you; ask rather what you can do for IBM" strikes one as preposterous. Yet such slogans used politically have considerable potency, as history has amply demonstrated.

Indeed, if our expressive account of electoral behavior has any validity, it is doubtful whether the characterization of political rhetoric as advertising is at all adequate. After all, no one believes that market advertising is itself the product that people buy: If there were no product at all to be purchased, there would be no advertising. If, as we have postulated, electoral politics is to be construed as a participatory spectacle in which voters identify themselves by association with rival teams much as they do in national sports, then the manner in which those teams

identify *themselves* is a critical piece of the whole procedure. What voters are doing in large measure is locating themselves in political space, and the positions of
candidates in that space provide a necessary means to that end.

Political rhetoric deals then much more in terms of rival conceptions of political
"good" than in well-articulated specifications of which set of rival interests one is
catering to. The provision of a conception of the political good is, on this view,
precisely what electoral competition is all about. Those politicians who are good at
articulating some such conception, or perhaps even creating one that voters can
"identify with," will be successful, while those who are poor at this task will not
be. The processes of political competition will promote the survival of affective
political rhetoric (and rhetoricians) and the demise of the nonaffective. Indeed, if
human traits of moral conviction have evolved in such a way as to make mimicry
difficult (as Robert Frank [1988] argues in his *Passions within Reason*) or if, for
whatever reason, we tend to be reasonably transparent to each other, it may even be
that effective politicians will turn out to be those who actually believe the moral
and ideological rhetoric they spout. Or at least, clear and honest identification with
popular moral and ideological principle will be one among a number of relevant
assets for any aspiring senator/parliamentarian. The claim that politicians are typically *believers* is not, of course, necessary to our general argument and may strain
the credulity of all political cynics (among whom we have been inclined in the past
to count ourselves). However, it is a plausible claim and perhaps offers some explanation of why the extent of political corruption is as limited as it is, given the
apparent capacity to take bribes with relatively small fear of detection and the vast
amounts that are at stake in many public decisions.

It is, we reckon, precisely the fact that political parties/candidates offer rival
conceptions of political "good" for expressive consumption that has fed the benevolent despot image of politics and that accounts for the counterintuitive thrust of
much public choice orthodoxy. In other words, it is the nature of political *rhetoric*
that has encouraged the romantic view of politics as the quest for the morally good
or the "true." We do not, of course, take the existence of such rhetoric to imply
that democratic politics can be relied on to promote the public interest. Politicians
may believe their own rhetoric, but political theorists do not have to. And, of
course, the potential perversity of expressive politics is, in fact, of major concern
to us. The *normative* apparatus of public choice – its instrumental conception of
political institutions, its appeal to contractarian forms of evaluation, and so on –
can be accepted without conceding that the description of political process that
public choice offers is even halfway satisfactory. The expressive theory, we believe,
offers a much more persuasive account of political rhetoric, both of its nature and
the amount of space it occupies.

On this latter question of space, it is worth noting the account that democracy
itself gives of the *role* of its talk. The tradition of parliamentary debate, for example, is often understood as a central feature of democracy, even though in most
cases there seems virtually no prospect that that debate might persuade anyone on
the floor of the chamber to change her mind. Public choice theorists may, of
course, see the inconsequential nature of this parliamentary talk as grist for their

mill. In the face of the heroic vision of representatives arguing their way to a common mind under "ideal speech conditions" – an ideal often associated with the Athenian prototype, Rousseau's romantic notions of the "general will," and, in these days, with the democratic theory of Jurgen Habermas – parliamentary debate in any system where party discipline is at all strong seems a total charade. If there is any political debate remotely like the Habermas ideal, it takes place in the party room, usually behind closed doors: What goes on in the public arena is, on this reading, simply a farce. Even conceived as some liturgical rite symbolizing a kind of discourse that is presumed to take place in the wider community, parliamentary debate is surely more likely to *undermine* the principles of serious political engagement within the community than to uphold them. Is it, after all, the case that parliamentary debate is simply a smokescreen for the interplay of interests that constitutes real politics, exactly as the public choice afficianado might have it?

We think not. We think that an account can be given of parliamentary processes that is in line with the expressive theory of politics. Conceive the parliamentary debate not as an attempt to persuade other representatives on the floor to change their minds, or indeed to engage those other representatives in any serious way at all. Think of the object rather as that of persuading the citizenry at large, of instantiating and adumbrating a particular political position, in its various dimensions, in such a way that voters will come to want to associate themselves with that position. The parliamentary debate is, in this sense, like a forensics exercise – like a debating competition – with the *audience* (in this case, the electorate at large) the object of persuasion. No one expects in a debating competition to persuade the members of the opposing *team:* One might hope to persuade the audience and perhaps the adjudicators.

Does this description of parliamentary talk amount simply to an admission that it is, after all, merely a form of political advertising? We think not. We suggest that the extent and the apparent centrality of parliamentary talk in democracy's self-conception seem to suggest that something more is at stake. Part of what that more is, is the self-disciplining nature of political rhetoric. Not *any* policy will do – only those that are consistent with the political and ethical position the party identifies with. In other words, the politician is, we maintain, constrained by the conception of the political good that he endorses and is the more constrained by the requirement that he publicly articulate and defend the particular policies his party advances. On this account, then, parliamentary debate is a critical piece of the whole democratic process, not because it instantiates the ideal of the forum, but because it structures and supports the crucial expressive aspects of community evaluation and political participation.

We should emphasize that our object at this point is primarily to describe and explain parliamentary debate, not to justify it. We do not argue that what commands expressive support, what can engage and mobilize the moral and ideological enthusiasms of the electorate, will itself always be ethically defensible. What we do argue is that the whole political process itself is encased in a moral and ideological frame that cannot be removed without losing the capacity to understand what is going on.

The domain of politics

Orthodox public choice analysis offers, among other things, a picture of the domain of politics. In constructing any majority coalition of special interests, a party/candidate will provide: first, for the maximal redistribution to coalition members, executed in the most efficient way; and second, for the provision of the public and quasi-public goods that those coalition members value, provided in the most efficient manner. The "efficiency" in both these dimensions should be uncontroversial: If there are potential gains from exchange, these can be mobilized to increase benefits for the coalition members (or possibly to increase surplus accruing to political agents). The process itself may not be efficient, in that any individual may lose more from being in a minority than she gains from being in a majority: All citizens may, at the constitutional level, prefer that the redistributions from minorities to majorities be curtailed or inhibited in some fashion. But at the in-period level, the majority will predictably seek its best deal.[4]

Accordingly, the domain of politics will be constituted by offers of rival packages. Just what public goods will be valued by any particular majority is, of course, a somewhat open question on which economics qua economics does not purport to throw much light, but there is some presumption that law and order, defense, pollution control, "public" health (the draining of malarial swamps has become a classical example), public infrastructure, macroeconomic "management," and perhaps some subsidization of education would make up most of the territory. The remainder of the political agenda will be oriented toward effecting maximal transfers to the current majority – either via the tax transfer system directly or through a slew of special interest subsidies, tariffs, regulations, and the like.

The expressive theory of politics offers its own distinctive picture of the political domain – one in which merit goods rather than public goods predominate[5] and where the practice of interparty competition is as much concerned with rival positions on major symbolic or ethical-ideological issues as with the redistribution of income among special interests. In Chapter 3 we discussed two examples of policy decision with an eye to the expressive account: war and income redistribution. There we argued that the interest-based explanation of war – at least within democratic polities – is implausible, and that an expressive account leaves much more room for the kind of large-scale Pareto "pessimal" moves that war manifestly involves. We also argued that the public choice model of redistribution as "political spoils" takes inadequate account of the simple fact that most of the explicit redistribution that occurs goes from richer to poorer – a fact that suggests that abstract considerations of "distributive justice" (ones that are nonetheless largely dormant in arenas where the "donor" is decisive) play a critical role in distributive politics.

An additional – in our view, instructive – instance of the expressive account of the domain of politics is provided by the progress of the abortion dispute in the

---

[4] The distinction between constitutional and in-period efficiency is familiar from the work of Buchanan. The distinction is particularly clearly set out in Buchanan and Tullock (1962).
[5] See specifically our discussion in Chapter 9.

United States in recent years. Before the seminal Supreme Court *Roe v. Wade* decision of 1973, a gradual tendency for states to liberalize their abortion laws was under way; yet abortion policy was, especially at the federal level, a peripheral issue in the political arena. It entered, for example, hardly at all into the 1972 presidential campaign. However, once the Supreme Court performed the delivery, the abortion issue took on a political life of its own, entering into races for all kinds of offices, from the presidency to the city council and irrespective of the extent to which an officeholder could be expected to influence abortion policy matters. Quite clearly, the much enhanced politicization of abortion was not a function of officeholders having more scope after 1973 to determine abortion policy; due to the Supreme Court's entrance into the political question, officeholders at all levels had demonstrably less sway. Nor is it plausible to suppose that narrow cost considerations had been substantially altered so that opponents and proponents of a liberal abortion policy had more to lose by adverse legislation. In fact, no purely interest-based account of the abortion issue seems possible: Those whose interests were imperiled (the as-yet unborn) were not there to defend their interests. And it strains usage to cast abortion decisions as providing some kind of "public consumption." Without a capacity to include in one's model of human motivations a significant matter of *principle*, it is difficult to see how an account of the abortion question could be provided. More to the point here, however, is the rise of that question to salience in the political arena and its emergence as a kind of touchstone for political identification and as a source of potent political expression. Our claim is that, with abortion policy crystallized post-1973 in a manner that readily captured public attention, far greater expressive returns, both positive and negative, became available to politicians in virtue of how they positioned themselves on this issue. The evidence that this is so does not follow from "reading minds" of voters or from public opinion surveys; it is induced from the behavior of political candidates themselves. It is apparent that they have learned, in the period since *Roe v. Wade*, to treat abortion as an issue charged with electoral significance.

And what of the rhetoric that accompanies the abortion issue? "Right to Life," "Freedom of Choice": These are terms laden with moral significance and thus are the stuff of which expressive voting is made. Although the wealth distribution is doubtless affected by abortion legislation in force, narrowly economic magnitudes are ludicrously disproportionate to the intensity of the political struggle and hardly merit mention in the debate. It would be simply grotesque for an erstwhile back-alley operator to argue for more restrictive abortion legislation on the grounds that otherwise his business will go to pot. Even to support legal abortion on the grounds that one might oneself *one day* want one seems insensitive to the issues – and this although deciding one's position on such grounds does not obviously generate inappropriate judgments from an ethical point of view. The demands of political rhetoric do not readily admit this kind of argument: better the broad sweep of abstract principle.

It is also worth noting the progressive *inflation* of rhetoric on the abortion issue over its political history and the corresponding inflation in the demands put forth on both sides. Before 1973, for example, opponents of abortion seemed to be entirely satisfied with the criminalization of abortion – but not that abortion be brought under the rubric of homicide. Now, however, the Right to Life wing center their case on full legal recognition of the fetus as a person, with the concomitant definition of abortion as murder. We know of no orthodox public choice analysis that even makes a beginning at explaining the political potency of the abortion dispute, its explosive growth since 1973, the nature of the rhetoric that has accompanied it, and the degree of response that has been observed in political actors. When, however, voting is viewed as fundamentally an expressive activity and when attention is paid to the impact of external circumstances on the tendency to invoke principles of different sorts, the significance of abortion in the U.S. political arena during this period is rendered at least comprehensible – and possibly even predictable.

The same sort of argument might be mounted around the civil rights legislation that had been stimulated some two decades earlier by the 1954 Supreme Court decision for school integration in *Brown v. Board of Education*, with the Freedom Rides, and the unleashing of police dogs on peaceful demonstrations. The psychological immediacy of these events to a large public, rather than any sudden transformation in the cost–benefit calculus of racial discrimination, explains, we believe, the relative rapidity of subsequent political response (as against the glacial pace of the previous half century).

The generalization we intend to point up here is that expressively charged issues tend to drive out the merely interest-laden ones from the political arena. Issues that are interest laden will, we suggest, only play center stage on the electoral agenda to the extent that they resonate, or can be made to resonate, with expressive considerations. An example of some salience here is the U.S. Social Security system.

The Social Security game

In recent decades the U.S. Social Security system has been a fount of periodic fiscal crises, each more severe than the previous one. While there is no shortage of proposals for the radical reform or restructuring of the system, what seems most conspicuous about such proposals is their political irrelevance. Despite grave intonations in professional literature and the popular media, there seems to be no constituency whatsoever for anything more than tinkering with current arrangements. Politicians have uniformly recognized that, to recommend abolition, even to raise the question of whether an alternative means of providing retirement income might be preferable, is to commit political suicide. Approval of Social Security appears to be effectively unanimous at the political level.

Why this should be so, given standard theories of political acceptability, is mysterious. The retirement provisions of Social Security are essentially an intergenerational transfer mechanism redistributing income from the young to the old. (We do not deny the existence of other significant transfer effects, notably from upper to lower income groups and from males to females, but the intergenerational aspect is the crucial one.) It is not at all surprising that the current group of elderly supports the provisions of the system; but we need some explanation as to why others are either supportive of Social Security, or antagonistic, or indifferent to its removal. The financial burden on those who are net losers is by no means trivial; more than one-third of all households in the United States pay more in Social Security taxes than they do in federal income tax. This then is not a case in which small impositions are spread out across a large number of persons for each of whom the burden is too slight to cross the threshold of awareness. Nor is it the case that support by the young for Social Security is explicable in virtue of a conviction on their part that the present value of their lifetime payments into the system is exceeded by the present value of the benefits they expect to receive. Private pensions offer to the current younger generation (in contrast to the situation in their parents' generation) a higher rate of return than does Social Security. Even more significant is the expressed skepticism by the young concerning their eventual status as pension recipients. For example, a CBS/*New York Times* Poll in mid-1982, a time coincident with one of the system's periodic fiscal crises, asked, "Do you think the Social Security system will have the money available to provide the benefits you expect for your retirement?" Of those respondents expressing an opinion, 80% of those aged 18–29 and 76% of those aged 30–34 responded in the negative. Even for those aged 45–54, a small majority answered no. Surveys conducted on different dates and with variously worded questions have elicited similar responses. These facts appear to be a prescription for intergenerational warfare, the young assaulting the foundations of Social Security and the old resolutely defending. But no such battle has commenced, nor are there signs of one in the offing. Those young persons who express pessimism concerning their own future pensions simultaneously declare support for the maintenance of the system. It is surely to the point to ask why.

Were there actually a latent constituency for the abolition or radical revision of Social Security, one would surely expect political entrepreneurs to seize the opportunity to mobilize it. Conversely, in the absence of attempts by political entrepreneurs to build a political coalition around a platform of opposition to Social Security, one can only conclude that no such constituency exists. Even if there were a "hands-off conspiracy" among federal politicians, one might expect some popular antagonism among the young or others disadvantaged by the system. But no. No relevant political voice sounds. And what requires explanation is why it does not – why Social Security is politically untouchable. Various hypotheses have been suggested to explain why economic interest is not reflected in political opposition to the system: fiscal illusion, public goods aspects of Social Security, informational-communication failures, naiveté. And it has regularly been predicted that although no significant opposition has *yet* surfaced, it is brewing and will soon erupt.[6]

We believe that the political status of Social Security represents as clear a test case as one is likely to encounter between the orthodox theory and the expressive alternative. Pecuniary stakes are high, net gainers and net losers are distinguishable with a tolerably high degree of precision. The dividing point does, of course, shift with changed legislative provisions and with variance in economic and

---

[6] See, e.g., Browning (1975), Campbell (1979), Patton (1977), Mitchell (1977), and Weaver (1982).

demographic factors. We do not assert that the average voter will know the economic impact on his lifetime income of the Social Security system, but most can make a fair estimate. Vast quantities of information – as well as some misinformation – are available, and the system has operated in its current form for several decades,[7] long enough, one would think, for nascent opposition to have coalesced into a politically potent coalition.

By way of contrast, attention to expressive factors is illuminating. Obligations toward the elderly are acknowledged by most persons. These are typically backed not only by abstract principles mandating concern for the aged, but also by emotionally intense personal relationships. The United States is a country in which Mother's Day and Father's Day are sacred festivals within the civic religion, in which grown children are expected to make the welfare of parents and grandparents a primary concern, and in which conspicuous failure to do so is grounds for opprobrium. The controls on behavior are not exclusively, or even primarily, external; obligations toward the elderly, especially those who are near kin, are internalized constraints. Individuals who perceive themselves as neglectful are apt to incur unpleasant feelings of guilt and remorse. Because emotional distress is itself a cost, rational individuals will attempt to minimize it.

In societies where the extended family household is the norm, it can be expected that the urge to express concern for the elderly will largely find an outlet in private activity within the family. But in a mobile society where children typically live apart from aged parents, opportunities to express regard for the old are not thrust upon individuals as an inevitable corollary of social arrangements. It then becomes a live option to discharge feelings of concern through public rather than private means.

To send monthly remittances to an aged parent or to provide living quarters within one's domicile decreases personal consumption. But voting for policies that transfer resources to the elderly imposes negligible expected cost on the voter yet provides, we conjecture, considerable expressive returns. "I'm not neglecting the interests of the old," one can say sincerely. Whether such votes when aggregated generate voters' dilemmas or not is a separate issue and irrelevant to the rationality of voting for the continued existence of Social Security benefits, of responding to national surveys by declaring one's fealty to the system, and so on.

It should not be supposed that expressive returns are available only to the young. Older voters too can – and, as is evident, in fact do – avail themselves of *principled* reasons to back Social Security: They have *earned* the benefits that they now (or soon will) receive through their previous payments into the system; everyone has a *right* to a decent retirement income; they do not want to be a *burden* on their own children. Note that each of these purported justifications explicitly invokes some moral principle, and note how natural and familiar is the application of each to discussion of Social Security. Dismissal of all such rhetorical data as "epiphe-

---

[7] The Social Security Act of 1935 created a funded pension system. Amendments in 1939 began the transformation to the current pay-as-you-go scheme. Given these circumstances, continued reliance on ad hoc explanatory devices seems especially unsatisfactory.

nomenal'' requires a leap of faith inconsistent, we would have thought, with the self-professed ''tough minded'' attitude of empirically oriented behavioral scientists. We have reason here to accept the expressed moral principle as explanatory rather than to search for ingenious auxiliary hypotheses that might explain such principles away. Of course, those who have reached or soon will reach retirement age do have an ''economic stake'' in the continued existence of the system, but it does not follow that expressive factors do not explain political support even among this group. At most, one can conclude that such support is overdetermined.

We do not intend to assume here the role of experts on voter psychology. But it is surely reasonable to look to the behavior of professional politicians, those whose business it is to appraise correctly which motivations can be elicited from voters. It will be observed that, virtually without exception, politicians not only support the continued existence of Social Security but *couch their support in terms calculated to capitalize on expressive motivations.* Moralistic proclamations are the common currency of their public remarks on Social Security, with dispassionate discussion of the system's fiscal implications running far behind. It is entirely consonant with the methodological foundations of orthodox public choice theory to maintain that political entrepreneurs supply the brand of rhetoric that voters demand. If voters demand opportunities to gain expressive returns through their votes, then politicians will comply. It misses the point to accuse politicians of demagoguery when they profess unyielding support for a system whose unfunded liabilities they simultaneously allow to grow to astronomical levels (current estimates run at some 7 trillion dollars). Politicians are merely acting in their own self-interest when they govern their activity in accord with constraints of majority-rule institutions that strongly encourage expressive voting.[8]

We have claimed that feelings surrounding the Social Security program run high, that they are unusually concentrated on one side of the issue, and that the dynamics of majority-rule institutions display a tendency to magnify the political potency of such expressive factors over repeated electoral runs. If these assumptions are correct, then the expressive theory of voting provides an explanation of the otherwise puzzling fact that there exists no politically meaningful opposition to Social Security. Importantly, it also provides a basis for *prediction* concerning the conditions under which significant opposition would emerge.

Increased payroll taxation to ensure the continuation of benefits has not resulted in noticeably diminished support for the system; nor will it, we predict, tend to do so. Higher taxation slightly increases the expected payoff to an instrumental vote against the system, but because the probability of being decisive is so minute, the dominant factor for most voters will continue to be the expressive return to an affirmative vote. Survey results previously cited reveal that young voters already are skeptical of promises that they will receive benefits upon reaching retirement age, but that they also generally support continuation of the current system. We have argued that these results are not paradoxical. Rather, younger voters can be expected rationally to persist in their support of the system even as their losses grow.

---

[8] They cite racial issues, including busing, and attitudes to energy shortages.

Any decrease in *expressive* returns would, however, critically alter the voter calculus. Principles concerning distributive justice are among those that can provide motivation for expressive activity. The voter who perceives herself as endorsing through her vote an *equitable* distribution of resources thereby receives a direct expressive return. If individuals came to believe that Social Security in its present form is *unfair*, that it dispenses benefits and burdens in a capricious and morally arbitrary manner, then expressive support predictably would diminish. Individuals would in such a case have an incentive to reap expressive returns by casting a ballot against practices perceived to be unfair, and politicians' incentives to mobilize a coalition promoting fairness in the distribution of wealth would come into play.

Increased attention to the long-term financial precariousness of Social Security can contribute to such an apprehension, but that result is by no means assured. One element of a moral indictment of the system is the demonstration that younger taxpayers are unlikely to receive retirement benefits commensurate with those enjoyed by current retirees, but this in itself is not enough. What must be added, if serious political opposition is to crystallize, is persuasive argument that the disparity in returns constitutes objectionable *unfairness*, that such disparities are not merely due to actuarial miscalculation, shifting demographic patterns, a temporary downturn in the economy, or some other impersonal event for which no one is to blame, but rather are attributable to explicitly self-serving behavior by some people at others' expense. One would not expect outpourings of expressive activity in response to revised actuarial projections: What would be required is the identification of actual culprits. Accordingly, if charges that Social Security is a version of the chain-letter swindle assume prominence in public forums, if special interests are represented as cynically conniving to bring about unjust transfers, then we predict that substantial expressive voting against Social Security will be generated.

One significant dimension of our prediction here (one exhibiting the separation between the expressive and orthodox theories) is that it will not only be the young who are induced to respond in this manner. If net gainers from Social Security become convinced that they are the beneficiaries of an unjust system, they too will be in a position to realize expressive gains by voting against the continued existence of Social Security or by voting for its radical modification. It would become rational for each of the aged to vote to abolish a system that no one of them, were he decisive, would choose to eliminate.

As we have argued previously, it is not only *moral* principles that can motivate expressive votes. If younger voters perceive themselves to be the dupes of a social policy that favors the old, they may come in increasing numbers to feel resentment or envy toward those profiting at their expense. Whenever resentment exists, its expression is a consumption good. Indulging such resentment in the private arenas comes at a price. Resentful behavior is generally grounds for disapproval and especially so when it is focused at a respected individual or group: Older persons will respond in damaging ways, relations with older persons to whom one has special ties will become strained, and so on. Accordingly, it seems more likely that resentment occasioned by perceptions of Social Security as unjust will be channeled predominantly into political activity.

In short, the rise and current stability of the U.S. Social Security system is, in our view, best explained by reference to expressive factors. So is the possibility of any demise of that system. In all this, of course, interests play a role: If the system were not seen to be in the interests of the elderly, then the expressive support could not be delivered. But the demonstration that the system is not in the community's interests overall, or not in the interests of the young, is not itself enough either to mobilize the young against it or to induce the public spirited to establish a political coalition against it. Interests are not, in themselves, significant grounds for political action. That is our point.

Conclusions

It would be possible to continue the accumulation of/expressive accounts of particular policies, or areas of policy, to the point of tediousness. Perhaps we have already reached that point. There are, after all, other examples that are, obviously, relatively congenial to our general argument. We could, for example, offer a brief history of the prohibition movement in the United States, and its less striking but more stable manifestation in sumptuary taxation. The "nuclear freeze" movement and the politics of foreign policy would surely repay investigation. We shall, in Chapter 9, pursue the significance of public provision of global antipollution strategies and of fundamental research as "merit goods": Both these are goods for which purely national interest would best be served by a strategy of free riding on other countries and yet for which public activity is already extensive and increasing.

We do not deny that interests play a role in politics. We do not deny that the expressive theory is somewhat looser and more open ended in empirical application than the wealth maximization alternative – though it is notable how quickly economists will retreat from wealth maximization to utility maximization when the going gets tough, and utility maximization is at least as open ended as the expressive benefits story in most applications. What we are convinced of is that students of electoral politics must be content to "trawl in the data" to see what is there, and to do so with an open mind. And we include as relevant data one's general sense of the world and of political history. Induction, not deduction, is the procedure that seems best suited for electoral analysis. What deductive methods can do is tell us what to look for and what prejudices to set aside. The interest-based theory of electoral preference is, in our view, just such a prejudice. And the broad brush of general anecdote supports us, we think, in that view.

7   Interpreting the numbers

. . . fantastic rather than rigorous, enthusiastic rather than scientifically exact.
Comment about Condorcet, quoted in Duncan Black,
Theory of Committees and Elections

Introduction

Some commentators will presumably find the evidence for the expressive theory of voting offered in the preceding chapter excessively anecdotal in character, with all the negative connotations that the anecdote carries in properly acculturated econometric circles. As we have made clear, we do not totally deprecate the anecdote as a source of information; but we concede the need to examine the relevant numbers in a systematic way, without retreat into "adhocery," and that is a prime object of this chapter.

The most obvious source of relevant data here is that available on the voting behavior of individual voters. Does that evidence offer genuine support for the use of homo economicus as an appropriate behavioral abstraction in electoral politics? Does it offer any support for our expressive voter alternative? Beyond this evidence, is there any other information of a systematic kind that is relevant? What, for example, can we say about the behavior of politicians? In particular, is there econometrically respectable evidence indicating, *pace* public choice orthodoxy, that politicians may to some extent internalize the ethical/ideological principles that expressive voting suggests will be an important element in electoral contests? And what are we to make of the indirect evidence that has often been taken to lend support to the instrumental theory of voting? We have in mind particularly the literature on voter turnout and the tests of whether (and to what extent) voter turnout responds to expected closeness.

In this chapter, we seek to answer these questions. The chapter has a further purpose, however. In addition to interrogating the numbers, we need to acknowledge those aspects of political reality that seem to argue *against* the expressive voting account or at least represent something of a puzzle for that account. Consideration of these puzzles will occupy the penultimate section of this chapter. In the section immediately following, we examine the direct numerical evidence on voter behavior. In the subsequent sections, we shall consider the evidence (such as it is) on *politicians'* behavior, briefly survey the literature on the turnout issue, and inquire whether the facts do square with the interest-based account of voter conduct. The penultimate section examines two residual puzzles, and the last section offers a brief summary, attempting to draw together some appropriately guarded conclusions.

Voter behavior

There is, needless to say, an enormous literature in conventional political science that addresses the question of why voters vote in the way they do. Some of this literature is directly focused on testing public choice orthodoxy, but not much – partly one suspects because the idea that voters systematically vote their interests has never been one that automatically suggested itself from the data; also partly because political science has typically been involved much more in induction than in the sort of empirical testing of rival abstract hypotheses that characterizes most empirical work in economics.

The locus classicus in political science for the empirical analysis of voting behavior in the United States seems to be Survey Research Center (SRC) work issuing from the University of Michigan – notably Campbell, Converse, Miller and Stokes's *The American Voter* (1964) and the work in that tradition (Campbell, 1964; Stokes, 1966; Converse et al., 1969; Margolis, 1977; Sears et al., 1980; Miller et al., 1986). The data used in this work consists, as the Center's name implies, of questionnaire responses from a representative sample of voters. These responses have now been gathered in a more or less comparable form for well over two decades. On the rival hand, there is the work firmly in the public choice tradition, of which Frohlich et al. (1978) and Popkin et al. (1976) are two of the earlier notable examples.

Part of the difficulty involved in unraveling this literature is that there is some lack of clarity as to what hypotheses exactly are being tested. The Frohlich et al. paper is instructive in this connection. In following Downs quite closely, the authors expose the extreme lack of specificity in Downs's own formulation. On the basis of "rational ignorance," for example, Downs (1957) acknowledges that voters may vote habitually (p. 85) or on the basis of ideology (p. 100). Downs rejects any excessively narrow interpretation of voter interest – "There can be no simple identification of 'acting for one's own greatest benefit' with selfishness in the narrow sense, because self-denying charity is often a great source of benefit to oneself. Thus, our model leaves room for altruism" (p. 37). For Frohlich et al., the appropriate operationalization of the Downsian conception comes down to an amalgam of issue-based, financial, and modified party identification to form a "party differential" that is then used to predict voting behavior. This procedure is found to predict correctly the voters' preferences in 86% of cases, as compared with the 57.4% of cases that a random method would correctly predict (using the 1964 SRC voting survey data).

Several aspects of the Frohlich et al. procedure are noteworthy. First and most obviously, the idea that homo economicus as standardly defined might be a useful behavioral abstraction at the ballot box is jettisoned at the outset and with no discussion. Interest (i.e., wealth maximization) *alone* is not considered. Apparently, the authors do not believe that individual voting behavior can be explained by wealth maximization, despite the fact that, for many observers (both friendly and otherwise, and both expert and not), the homo economicus postulate is seen as a defining characteristic of the public choice approach. Second, the direct inclusion of "party identification" as part of the explanatory variable (even when moderated by information considerations) seems more than a trifle suspicious: The connection between individual votes and party identification is surely bound to be systematically positive. It would have been instructive, perhaps, to indicate the explanatory power of the various component parts of the composite explanatory variable that Frohlich et al. use; at the least, the role of personal financial interest should be discernible independently. Frohlich et al. do, however, compare their predictions with those of the SRC model, the central feature of which they take to be encapsulated in the focus on the "immediate psychological influences on the voting act" (Campbell et al., 1964, p. 13). Thus, the SRC model focuses on voters' attitudes to the candidates as people, as well as to particular issues (domestic, foreign, and general management). Possibly unsurprisingly, Frohlich et al. are obliged to conclude that "both the SRC model and the Downsian model are good predictors of the party preferences of individuals; there is little to choose between them in this regard" (1978, p. 185). This conclusion emerges, however, primarily because the tests undertaken are not well focused on distinguishing the models: "The six additional factors of the SRC model are actually surrogates for the components of the Downsian model," so that "the SRC model's success in the tests described above constitutes further support for explanations of voting behaviour based on the assumption of rationality" (p. 156)! Frohlich et al. do not indicate what evidence would be decisive evidence *against* the Downsian model, but it does seem as if their conception of that model, and of what rational voting entails more generally, is sufficiently loose that the theory will not be easy to reject empirically; looseness of this kind seems to be a *problem* for theory, rather than a virtue.

For our purposes, the relative importance of direct financial interest (on the public choice side) and candidate personality (on the expressive voting side) emerges as a naturally salient question. On a Frohlich et al. reading, voting on the basis of issues, party identification, and general ideological posture would all be entirely consistent with both pseudorational and expressive voting, and on balance we are inclined to agree. That is, "political issues" can proxy as much for principles that voters might wish to support as for outcomes that voters might wish to promote. Ideology can represent the *content* of voters' expressions as well as the rule of thumb for discerning their interests. But the voter's narrow financial interest is probably not, on balance, likely to predominate in expressive concerns. And the candidate's physiognomy, personality, and/or charisma are not likely to be of any relevance to promoting electoral outcomes that maximize the voter's wealth. Accordingly, focusing on these two variables in explaining voting behavior is likely to be quite helpful in deciding the issue between expressive and instrumental conceptions of voting.

Now, there is a substantial literature (including notably Kramer, 1971; Stigler 1973; Fair, 1978; and more recently Kinder and Kiewiet, 1979, 1981; and Markus, 1988) which relates electoral success of parties to overall economic conditions. The general finding has been that good overall economic circumstances – high employment, low inflation, and the like – are congenial to the electoral success of the incumbent party, although the effect is by no means unquestioned (see, e.g., Stigler,

1973). This connection between macroeconomic and electoral success is sometimes referred to as the "hip-pocket effect," implying that voters are responding to the influence that the government's economic management policies have on their particular incomes. Now, as various authors have emphasized (Tufte, 1975, and Kinder and Kiewiet, 1979, among others) one certainly cannot induce individual behavior from a relation between aggregate economic conditions and aggregate voting, though this evidence is sometimes cited as support for the public choice view. Indeed, as a matter of simple economics, any connection between aggregate economic performance and a particular individual's well-being is likely to vary profoundly from voter to voter. That is, unemployment tends to make a minority of voters worse off but, arguably, the employed majority better off; inflation likewise redistributes from lenders to debtors, and among assetholders according to the nature of their portfolios. Public choice logic might well lead one to predict a *negative* relation between employment levels (or price stability) and electoral popularity on such grounds or, as Stigler (1973) argues, no relation at all, because the "rational" voter will not typically hold the incumbent party responsible for economic problems or will not necessarily reckon that the alternative party will do any better. In other words, the public choice prediction as to electoral implications of "poor" macroeconomic performance must be unclear. What is needed is an analysis that will isolate two distinct effects of economic conditions on electoral behavior: one operating via general perceptions of collective well-being; the other operating via voters' individual interest. Such an exercise is, for example, precisely the object of the Kinder and Kiewiet 1979 paper: "Our intention . . . is to examine two competing interpretations of the relationship between economic conditions and congressional voting: personal economic grievances vs. collective economic judgements" (p. 499). Using the SRC questionnaire data, they find virtually no association between *individual* experience of unemployment and political preference: "Economic discontent and political judgements inhabit separate mental domains" (p. 523). The evident *aggregative* association must, therefore, be attributable to a generalized judgement by individual voters as to overall macropolicy. As Kinder and Kiewiet put it:

Candidates of the incumbent party suffer when the economy sputters not because voters punish them for their private misfortunes. Candidates suffer because voters perceive the party they represent as failing to cope adequately with national economic problems. . . . Voters are not egocentric – they do not vote their *own* pocketbooks. Rather, their preferences follow a more collective reckoning. (pp. 523–4)

And in a footnote that for our purposes is significant, they remark:

Our findings add to a growing literature demonstrating the importance of a "symbolic politics." The distinction between personal experience on the one hand and symbolic, more general political attitudes on the other has proven crucial in several recent analyses.[1] Each time, symbolic discontent was surprisingly independent of grievances anchored in personal experience. And each time, it was the symbolic form of discontent, not the personal, that was the more significant politically. (p. 528, n. 20)

[1] They cite racial issues, including busing, and attitudes to energy shortages.

Other investigations along similar lines yield conclusions that although somewhat more guarded than Kinder and Kiewiet's (in that they do not deny a role for self-interest), seem to support a role for *some* non-self-interest effects. Thus, for example, Markus (1988), using pooled cross-section and time-series data, finds elements of *both* personal/economic interest and general concern: "Personal economic circumstances are moderately influential, but . . . consistent with the 'socio-tropic' thesis, a reliable effect of national economic conditions on the individual vote decision was also detected, even with perceived personal economic circumstances held constant" (p. 151).

The authority of the Kinder and Kiewiet and related evidence on this issue must however be a matter of some dispute. There is in particular a distinct possibility that the discrepancy between individual and aggregated data is merely a statistical artifact, a possibility presented forcefully by Kramer (1983). Because variations in individuals' incomes are attributable to a wide variety of factors – of which government macropolicy is probably one of the less significant – any correlation between the change in an individual's economic position over the electoral period and support for a party's policy (in a rational self-interested voter model) would be predictably small and could well be negative. The Kramer conclusion on the issue of concern here is, therefore, a nihilistic one: "There is simply no way of determining on the basis of this kind of evidence whether the observable relationships between economic variables and voting were ultimately generated by sociotropic or self-interested behaviour or by some combination of the two" (p. 106).

If any headway is to be made in distinguishing individual interest from expressive considerations we will need to focus on some political issue other than macroeconomic conditions. We require, instead, an issue that is overtly distributional and in which the gains and losses are likely to be quite considerable. One obvious contender here is tax policy, which is the subject of a recent study by Hawthorn and Jackson (1987). They conclude:

Individual preferences [in relation to] tax policies are greatly affected by attitudes towards collective issues and are not merely a rationalization for their own economic interests. . . . Many individuals with equivalent incomes have very different views on whether the poor should pay lower taxes and whether income should be transferred from the rich to the poor. (pp. 757, 572)

In a somewhat similar context, J. Smith (1975) analyzes voting for tax equalization across intermediate education districts in Oregon: Voters are postulated to vote for equalization if it lowers their tax burden and against equalization if it raises their tax burden. As Smith observes, since the only issue at stake in the election is the equalization of tax burdens across districts and since the amounts involved are "often substantial," the data offer what seems to be a good basis for testing the self-interested voter hypothesis. Smith divides districts into four categories: those that make large gains from equalization, those that make small gains, those that make small losses, and those that make large losses. He finds that the percentage that vote in favor of equalization in each of these groups is, respectively, 61%, 53%, 46%, and 33%: Clearly, voters are more likely to vote for equalization if they benefit by it, and this is seen by Smith to provide clear evidence for the private interest hypothesis. Yet his test for "clear evidence" is somewhat unambitious: As he puts it, "Rational models of voting behaviour are not dependent on total rationality among all participants. Rational models are useful if they predict the behaviour of significant groups of actors in the political arena" (p. 66). Smith's results are similar to those derived by Bloom (1979) in connection with the 1970 and 1978 referenda on property tax classification in Massachusetts. Bloom found that in 1978, for each $100 increase in tax savings, the proportion of home owners in a municipality who voted for the classification scheme decreased by 7.0 to 8.0%, whereas there was virtually no such increase for renters. However, in the less well publicized 1970 referendum, there was no difference in renter and home owner voting patterns and no response to owner tax savings. Even where results appear to favor the hypothesis of self-interested voting, an important question of interpretation arises. Mueller's (1987) remarks on the Smith–Bloom findings strike us as very much to the point. As Mueller puts it: "Caution should be exercised in generalizing from these results: in Smith's study, over 40 percent of the population voted effectively to raise their own tax rates, ceteris paribus. Some factors beyond private interest must have influenced the voting of this substantial fraction of citizens" (1987, p. 95).

At the other end of the issue spectrum, there are analyses of cases in which self-interest seems a much less relevant consideration and in which expressive dimensions are likely to predominate. For example, Sears et al. (1980) attempt to distinguish between self-interested as distinct from "symbolic" considerations in influencing the voting behavior of the U.S. electorate with respect to four "controversial" issues – unemployment, national health insurance, school busing, and crime policy. "Generally speaking, we found self-interest to have little effect on voters' policy preferences, while symbolic attitudes (party identification, liberal/conservative ideology, and racial prejudice) have major effects" (p. 673). And on the race issue specifically, the authors refer confidently to "common" and "well-documented . . . inconsistencies between expressing high levels of prejudice at a symbolic level and displaying tolerant behaviour towards minority individuals in private life" and cite Schuman and Johnson (1976) specifically to this effect. They also refer to various other work that has found "self-interest to have little effect on policy attitudes (and voting behaviour) on such issues as the economy, civil rights, the Vietnam War, busing and the energy crisis" and cite inter alia, Gatlin, Giles, and Cataldo (1978) and Sears et al. (1978, 1979).

Overall, and notwithstanding the considerable statistical and interpretative problems associated with the analysis (often, it seems, not fully sensed by the analysts themselves), it does seem safe to conclude that the evidence for homo economicus at the ballot box is rather weak. It would clearly be too extravagant to say that there is no evidence at all for any egoistic behavior, nor would that have been our claim (see Chapter 3). But the idea that voters can be satisfactorily modeled as simple wealth maximizers is not one that is borne out by the empirical evidence.

The other side of the evidential coin revolves around the role of the personal characteristics of candidates. At least on the face of things, it is difficult to see how candidates' personal characteristics would weigh at all significantly in a "rational-egoist" model of voter behavior. One doesn't choose one's stockbroker on the basis of his beauty. Party affiliation and ideological position (along some national liberal–conservative spectrum, for example) might well proxy for a voter's long-term, dimly perceived, economic interest, but it is not easy to see how candidate personality can plausibly do so. Again, however, the tradition in mainstream political science has always afforded a major, perhaps predominant, role to this consideration in voter calculus. In the classic Stokes analysis of the SRC data (e.g., 1966), the author's claim was that personality effects played a stronger role in U.S. presidential voting than either party affiliation or "issues"; and in a more extended appraisal, Miller et al. (1986) conclude that "perceptions of candidates are generally focused on 'personality' characteristics rather than on issue concerns or partisan group connections (including party)" (p. 521). Interestingly, Miller et al. are at pains to argue that this focus on personal characteristics is by no means inconsistent with an instrumentalist account of voting. They explicitly reject the prevailing interpretation of personality-based evaluation as being "emotional, irrational and lacking in political relevance" and emphasize that more than half of the comments on personality characteristics that voters make relate to categories like "competence," "integrity," and "reliability" that bear on the candidate's capacity "to deal competently with the nation's problems in an honest and even-handed manner" (p. 536). One should also concede, for the purposes at hand, that competence, integrity, and reliability will also bear on the candidates' likelihood of delivering on campaign promises to specific voter groups. However, it is to be emphasized that a significant group of voters (typically around one-third of those who focus on personality considerations, and about 15% of voters overall) register themselves as mainly concerned with such candidate characteristics as charisma, appearance, sense of humor, dignity, and so on – characteristics that seem unlikely to bear on candidates' capacities and/or inclinations to deliver goodies to those who vote for them. It seems perfectly clear that, just as politicians themselves seem to believe, the creation of a generally attractive image is an important part of the electoral enterprise: Voters are influenced by a variety of candidate attributes that seem to bear only marginally if at all on voters' *interests.*

Politicians' behavior

To the extent that political agents (either politicians or bureaucrats) are constrained by electoral considerations, the behavior of those political agents will tend to reflect the nature of voter choices. An indirect test, then, of the individual interests account can be obtained by examining the behavior of politicians. The test is asymmetrically powerful. If politicians can be shown to act so as to promote constituents' interests, then whatever the logic of rational choice tells us, the interest theory of voting can proceed as a satisfactory "as if" model of electoral choice. If, however, politicians do not so act, this might be either because electoral constraints are nonbinding or because electoral constraints are binding but induce politicians' behavior that is at variance with that which the interests theory would suggest. It is only in the latter case that we would have positive evidence against homo economicus in politics. To separate these latter two possibilities, we should be alert to systematic aspects of politician behavior that cannot plausibly be reconciled with direct utility maximization on the part of politicians themselves, and such aspects may not be easily identified.

Kau and Rubin (1982), for example, in their study of congressional voting take it as given that representatives who are elected ''are those who have been successful in coming up with the optimal strategy'' (p. 33) – so that electoral constraints (including optimal response to potential campaign contributors) are taken to be totally binding. Kau and Rubin draw an explicit analogy between their assumption and the Alchian (1950) theory of the firm – namely, that the competitive process (whether electoral or market) filters out nonoptimizers. This means, specifically, that the role of ideology in congressional voting, which turns out to be the predominant influence, is to be attributed to electoral and internal political considerations and not merely to the eccentric tastes of the politicians themselves. Whatever one makes of this assumption, Kau and Rubin's (1982) basic conclusion from the data ''is that ideology appears to be *the* explanation for much of the new (regulatory) legislation. . . . In all cases, the ideological variable is by far the strongest and most significant variable in explaining congressional voting, even after numerous attempts to adjust statistically for the economic interests of constituents and campaign contributions'' (p. 123) (and, we should add, for the possibility of log rolling among representatives). The economic interests of constituents, as for example captured by the level of government spending in congressional districts, do not appear to be significant. However, ''one aspect of constituent characteristics, the liberalism or conservatism of voters . . . is highly significant in explaining voting by members of Congress'' (pp. 122–3).

In a similar study focused mainly on U.S. Senate voting on coal strip mining, Kalt and Zupan (1984) conclude both that ideology plays a predominant role in explaining representative voting and that a significant part of that ideological influence is to be explained as utility-maximizing behavior on the part of the representatives (what Kalt and Zupan term ''ideological shirking'') rather than as a reflection of electoral constraints per se. Kalt and Zupan are sensitive to the Peltzman (1984) charge that ideology in voting may proxy for constituent interests, and make extensive allowance (arguably excessive) for this possibility in attempting to isolate a pure ideological residual to be attributed to politicians' utility maximization. For our purposes, of course, the greater the amount of ideological influence attributed to representatives' tastes, the smaller the amount to be attributed to the ballot box.

In order to distinguish whether ideological influences are attributable to candidates' preferences or to electoral influence, Kalt and Zupan investigate whether the role of ideology decreases as senators come up for reelection. They show that ideological influences are more significant the *further* the senator is from reelection and conclude on this basis that ideological effects reflect candidates' preferences. Even if this is accepted, there remains the issue (for economists, at least) as to why representatives' shirking takes the form of ideological self-indulgence rather than some more typical form of wealth/consumption maximization. Kalt and Zupan canvass several possibilities:

. . . non-ideological shirking on floor votes (for example, taking bribes, failing to be informed or missing roll calls in favour of office parties) is comparatively costly as a result of institutional penalties, while a legislator does not face expulsion or censure for voting his or her "conscience."

. . . to the extent the individual legislator can rationally take the fate on the floor of any particular piece of legislation as given, the legislator's vote becomes valueless to any constituent [the legislative floor analogue of the argument advanced in this book more generally].

. . . a self-selection process that attracts individuals with relatively intense demands for ideology to the political sector. (p. 284)

Two observations on this list seem called for. The first point is that one reason why ideological shirking is relatively cheap compared to other forms of shirking may be that ideological shirking is not particularly costly *electorally*. The second is that the selection process that ensures that ideologically oriented persons tend to be successful politicians need not be an entirely demand-driven one: If ideological commitment is an electoral asset, as we have argued may well be the case, then supply-side considerations will tend to ensure that politicians are ideologically motivated. No one who cannot present a vibrant ideological profile will be elected, even if other matters are also relevant to election (such as being seen to "look after constituent interest"). And as we have noted in connection with the Kinder–Kiewiet analysis, such concern with constituent interests may itself be collective and symbolic rather than a result of voters voting their individual interests.

Other hypotheses might, of course, account for representatives' behavior. One possibility is that voting behavior is oriented not toward general electoral constraints but to internal party-political ones. An individual prior to election must be "preselected," which requires commitment to the party machine in the constituency rather than the constituency at large. Moreover, once elected to office, progression within the political hierarchy partly depends on forming coalitions, often of an ideological kind, with other representatives. It is, in other words, not necessarily to be assumed that rents created by slack in electoral constraints are available to the individual politician: Such rents may be mainly appropriated by the party machine.

In this connection, one small piece of evidence is worth noting, namely the Bennett and Di Lorenzo (1982) discovery of a connection between politicians' political philosophies in collective decision making and their personal conduct. In the Bennett–Di Lorenzo study, the authors examined the proportion of the government's "free" allocation of funds for congressional staff that is returned to the Treasury. They hypothesized that "conservatives who publicly eschew 'excessive' government spending would return a larger amount than would 'free-spending liberals.' " Four measures of conservatism were employed, but the empirical results were generally invariant to the indicator of political philosophy. As Bennett and Di Lorenzo put it, senators who are conservative in making collective decisions are also fiscally conservative in spending public funds under their direct control: "An ultra-conservative would spend about 22 per cent less on staff than an ultra-liberal" (p. 1160). Since facts on staff expenditures are not widely known, it would be difficult to rationalize this result as a form of political advertising: It seems more natural to interpret it as evidence in favor of the Kalt–Zupan "internalization-of-ideological-values" line.

Voter turnout and instrumental voting

The relation between voter turnout and expected closeness of electoral outcome has often been taken to constitute an important indirect test of the outcome-oriented theory of voter behavior, of which public choice orthodoxy is one variant. If more voters go to the polls when the outcome is expected to be close, it indicates – so the argument goes – that voters are voting in order to influence outcomes. Relevant discussions include the early contribution by Riker and Ordeshook (1968) and subsequent work by Silver (1973), Barzel and Silberberg (1973), Kau and Rubin (1976), and Ashenfelter and Kelly (1975) among others. An extremely useful survey of this work is provided by Mueller (1987). In Chapter 4 in our discussion of the probability of being decisive, we mentioned the arguments involved, and we shall here reiterate the claims made there and indicate how we think the evidence should be interpreted.

As we emphasized in that earlier discussion, some care must be taken in setting up the hypothesis to be tested and in specifying the implications of the various models. The characterization of the "rational voter hypothesis" offered by Mueller, following from Riker and Ordeshook, revolves around equation (7.1):

$$R = pB + D - C, \tag{7.1}$$

where p is the probability of being decisive, B the benefit that accrues from having one's instrumentally preferred outcome prevail, D the intrinsic benefit from voting, and C the cost of exercising the franchise.

The rational individual will vote if $R > 0$, and not vote otherwise. We have, of course, no argument at all with this formulation. However, in the Riker–Ordeshook discussion and in Ashenfelter–Kelly, the D term is interpreted in terms of civic duty, defined by reference to the citizen's perceived obligation to vote. The implication is that the intrinsic benefits from voting are dependent solely on the fact of voting and not on the direction of the vote. If this is accepted, then the predicted effects of changes in p and B are unambiguous; increase in p and B ceteris paribus will increase turnout. But if, as we have argued, expressive considerations play an important (indeed predominant) role in voter choice *among alternatives,* then the comparative statics of changes in p and B become somewhat less transparent. That was the point of our discussion of these matters in Chapter 4. To recall that argument, consider a choice between two given electoral options, x and y. Voters will divide into two groups:

    (i) those for whom instrumental and expressive preferences are in the same direction, and
    (ii) those for whom instrumental and expressive preferences are in opposite directions.

Now, consider an increase in pB, ceteris paribus. For voters in class (i), the effects are unambiguous: Turnout cannot be reduced. Specifically, some individuals for whom R is initially very small and negative will be induced to vote by the increase in pB. For voters in class (ii), however, the effects are unpredictable – some voters who previously did not vote will not be induced to vote; but some who previously did vote will be induced not to. As we argued in Chapter 4, since expressive considerations dominate in the reason to vote, there is some presumption that the total effect of an increase in expected instrumental benefits on voters in group (ii) is to *reduce* turnout. In short, then, an increase in p and B can be expected to have a rather smaller effect on turnout than a purely instrumental account would imply: Indeed, there may conceivably be no effect at all, or the relationship may prove to be negative.

We should perhaps emphasize at this point that although on our reckoning the pB term is insignificant in explaining voter behavior *on average* across all voters, it is *potentially*[2] significant for those voters who are on the margin of participation – a change in pB need to be no less important at the margin than an equivalent change in net expressive benefits. However, we should note that a change in direct voting costs has the same effect for all marginal voters (i.e., those in groups (i) and (ii)), unlike changes in pB and D for which net effect on turnout within groups (i) and (ii) tend to be mutually offsetting.

On this basis, we would predict:

1. that increases in p, B, and D (as we conceptualize D) would all tend to increase turnout but only by a small amount, and
2. that reductions in C would tend to increase turnout, and do so more than otherwise "equivalent" increases in pB and D.

The differential sensitivity of turnout to changes in $p/B/D$, on the one hand, and to changes in C, on the other, provides an indirect measure of the extent to which instrumental and expressive preferences go in opposite directions (i.e., the relative number of group (ii) voters). In this connection, it is worth noting one finding of Ashenfelter and Kelly – namely the sensitivity of voting turnout to poll taxation and literacy tests (legal in 1960, but abolished by 1972). "A one-dollar (1960 prices) poll tax reduces turnout by an estimated 7 percent" (p. 708). By contrast, perceptions of closeness were not significant in influencing turnout.

Similarly, the wide range of statistical analyses reported by Mueller shows just how inconclusive the evidence on the *sign* (to say nothing of the magnitude) of any connection between turnout and (expected) closeness really is. In one sense this is surprising, because as the discussion in Chapter 4 clearly shows, the probability of being decisive is extremely sensitive to expected closeness. If voting were *solely* instrumental, then one ought to expect enormous changes in turnout with quite small changes in expected closeness. Taking the standard binomial formulation (as outlined in Chapter 4), the probability of being decisive, p, can be approximated by

---

[2] However, as we shall argue, the evidence suggests that such considerations are inframarginal for virtually all voters.

Table 7.1. *Turnout and outcome in U.S. presidential elections, 1940–1972*

Year	Total votes cast (million)	Winner's share in total (percent)	Majority (percent)
1940	49.5	55	10
1944	47.5	54	8
1948	48.4	52	4
1952	61.3	55	10
1956	61.6	58	16
1960	68.3	50	—
1964	70.3	61	22
1968	73.0	50	—
1972	74.1	62	24

$$p = \frac{1}{\sqrt{\Pi n}} (1 - j^2)^n,$$

where j is the expected majority and n is half the number of voters.

Suppose then that the expected majority falls from 6% to 3%. Then expected instrumental returns increase by a factor of

$$k = \left[\frac{1 - j_1^2}{1 - j_2^2} \right]^n = \left| \frac{.9991}{.9964} \right|^n.$$

And in a U.S. presidential election, where expected turnout is perhaps as low as 60 million, the parameter n is 30 million, and k takes a value that is truly astronomical. For example, if n were 30,000, the value of k would be about 2×10^{25}. And that number has to be raised to the one-thousandth power for the U.S. presidential case! Surely, if the instrumental account of voting were true, turnout ought to increase enormously as expected closeness increases. If one were told, in some unidentified case, that a multibillionfold increase in expected benefits made no statistically identifiable change in behavior, one would have doubts that the model was appropriately specified. In our view, the fact that increases in expected closeness do not have a spectacular positive effect on voter turnout comes about as close as one can in this muddy life to a decisive rejection of the instrumental voter hypothesis. Nor does one need elaborate statistical technique to make this point. Consider specifically the data on turnout in U.S. presidential elections for the period 1940–72, taken from Abrams and Settle (1976) and shown here as Table 7.1. Merely by inspection one can see that turnout in 1960 was less than in 1964; and that in the 1968 election was smaller than the 1972 – and this despite the fact that the 1960 and 1968 elections were, ex post, relative cliff-hangers while the 1964 and 1972 elections were relative landslides. If actual closeness can be taken as a rough proxy for expected closeness – indeed, even if the expected vote difference is one-tenth of the actual – the probability of being decisive in the close election would have been many billions of times greater than in the nonclose ones, and the expected instrumental benefit correspondingly so.

The fact that turnout is as insensitive as it is to closeness can be explained either by appeal to the canceling out of category (i) and category (ii) voters, as in the preceding analysis (which accepts a predominant role for expressive considerations anyway), or by the claim (more plausible in our view) that instrumental considerations are inframarginal for virtually all voters. Of course, one could also appeal to conceptual weaknesses in the binomial formulation of decisiveness probabilities[3] or to difficulties in inducing *expectations* about closeness from actual electoral results. But the magnitudes at stake are so huge that any such rescue operations seem bound finally to prove inadequate.

The data in Table 7.1 suggest another puzzle for the instrumental theory – namely, why has voter turnout been increasing? After all, the number of voters who would vote in a pure Nash equilibrium is entirely independent of the number of enfranchised persons. Adding extra *potential* voters to a given group should leave *actual* turnout virtually unaffected in a standard public choice account. If turnout does increase over time, the public choice account must appeal to increases in political stakes, not to increases in voting population. Likewise, in cross-sectional comparisons, the public choice hypothesis should be that other things (including specifically potential political spoils) equal, *absolute* voter turnout should be the same – and independent of the number of enfranchised persons. Any attempt within the instrumental-voter tradition to explain turnout as a *fraction* of the enfranchised population seems to involve a simple mistake. If absolute turnout is positively correlated with enfranchised population – as it manifestly is in both time series and cross-sectional comparisons – this fact is itself a major gesture in the direction of the predominance of noninstrumental considerations.

In summary then, and contrary to what is sometimes claimed in standard public choice circles, the available evidence on voter turnout constitutes pretty decisive rejection of the instrumental theory of voting. Indeed, the evidence suggests that instrumental considerations do not even play a *marginal* role for most voters. The claim that turnout is responsive to expected closeness is itself empirically somewhat dubious, but more particularly, turnout seems nothing like responsive *enough* to changes in expected closeness to support even the mild claim that instrumental considerations play much of a role in voter behavior at all.

It is worth recalling in this connection that even under an expressive theory of voting, expected closeness might be presumed to have some effect. As we argue in Chapter 4, close contests in the sporting arena are more engaging and induce more spectator interest than clear-cut contests. Given the analogy between voter and spectator behavior, it would surely not be implausible if closer contests induced more involvement in the electoral setting as well. In that sense, some small connection between closeness and turnout of the kind that empirical work seems to reveal (or at least does not reject) is quite congenial to the expressive account.

---

[3] We have some doubts on this score ourselves, as we indicate in Chapter 4.

Two puzzles

In the previous chapters and in this chapter so far, we have tried to put the empirical evidence in favor of our theory of voting and against the instrumentalist public choice alternative as impartially as we can. We reckon that the balance of that evidence is pretty clearly in favor of our theory (which is why, perhaps, we can indulge the luxury of impartiality). However, there are two putative facts about political life that at least on the face of things, represent significant problems for the expressive theory of voting. We want in this section to acknowledge these phenomena as problems – as puzzles to be addressed, at least – and to see if those puzzles can be solved with the resources of expressive theory.

The first of these is intellectually interesting but not, as far as we know, enormously significant empirically. The second is highly significant empirically and altogether a cause for taking pause. The first is the phenomenon of so-called strategic voting. The second is the stability in many Western democracies of the two-party system. We explain first why these phenomena are puzzles and then try to wriggle out of them as best we can.

Strategic voting first. A simple example illustrates the possibility. Suppose there is a first-past-the-post election involving three candidates. It is expected that candidates B and C will between them receive most of the votes. Consider now the calculus of some voter who ranks the candidates in the order A:B:C. It is conjectured that such a voter may well vote for B rather than A, because to vote for A is to "waste" his vote. If a voter does this – that is, vote for a "less preferred' candidate (B) over a "more preferred" one (A) – he is said to vote strategically. As elegantly argued by Meehl (1977), this "thrown away" vote argument involves an instrumental calculation: It provides as a reason for voting for B rather than A the consideration that B is more likely to win than A. If the voter takes this reason as compelling, then he ought also, by analogous reasoning, be led to vote "quasi-rationally" as we have earlier defined it.

Of course, no major attack on expressive voting is involved if only a relatively small number of individuals were led to vote strategically. Strategic voting would be a puzzle, but only a small one – perhaps accommodated by an acknowledgment that some voters may be *irrationally* instrumental. But no such escape seems admissible. The existence of a stable two-party system in many Western democracies (and of many parties only where proportional representation allows some chance of "success" by voting nonstrategically) seems to suggest that most voters vote strategically most of the time. It is, after all, somewhat implausible on its face to argue that individuals' expressive preferences will obligingly fall into two well-defined and mutually exclusive sets, each clustered around the positions represented by the rival parties. If individuals do genuinely vote merely as an act of self-expression – and a fortiori as an act of self-definition – one would expect about as many candidates as there are different political expressions in other contexts (letters to the editor in newspapers, perhaps). Surely individuals need a larger repertoire of political positions than two in order to define themselves and/or express their political affections. And, as we know, there are enough single-issue voters to provide some votes for single-issue candidates. How then can a two-party system survive?

A variety of possible answers suggest themselves. One general line involves an appeal to supply-side considerations. There is, one might argue, a "natural" advantage for larger parties attributable to economics of scale in political advertising, rationally habitual voting, and the like that makes entry of new parties and/or unaffiliated candidates unattractive. On this view, entry of new parties/candidates would substantially diffuse the vote but would still leave the major parties dominant and, hence, will not alter political outcomes. Rational candidates recognize this and will not stand as independent candidates; any person with serious political aspirations will seek entry into politics through the established party machinery. Of course, there may be significant institutional barriers as well: Established parties can be expected to expend resources to protect their quasi-monopoly position and typically do so with a variety of policies that penalize small parties or independent candidates.

However, though these supply-side considerations might explain the stability of a two-party system once established, they do not seem to go very far in explaining why the system came about in the first place or why such systems emerged in so many democracies at such different periods in history. Does the expressive theory of voting offer anything that might help here? One possibility is that expressive theory allows not only for expressions of support, but also of antipathy: Booing the opposition is a well-attested spectacle at sporting events, no less than cheering one's own team. At sporting events, booing may be somewhat frowned upon, but in the secrecy of the polling booth, where the scrutiny of fellows is removed and charges of unsportsman-like behavior unspoken, the desire to express antipathy for a *least* preferred candidate may for many voters dominate the desire to express support for the *most* preferred. In our electoral conventions, there is no way of doing this directly. One cannot award a negative vote for C, only a positive one for A or B. If one seeks specifically to make a gesture *against* C, however, it is not clear that a vote for A or B will do equally well: A vote for B may have arguably more of a fist-shaking quality than one for A because B is the more salient opposition. The fact that A is expressively preferred over B is not, in other words, necessarily a decisive reason for voting for A. If A and B are both very strongly preferred expressively to C, the crucial issue becomes rather which vote is the more effective means of expressing one's opposition to C.

This kind of reasoning may well provide an account of why some voters "vote strategically" for what are expressive reasons. But can the reasoning do the work of explaining a two-party equilibrium? To do so, negative expressions would have to dominate positive ones for most voters most of the time. Booing would, as a general rule, have to give greater expressive returns than cheering. Is this proposition plausible? It would seem, perhaps, an unduly cynical view of human nature to hold it, though we have indicated at various points through the book why malice might dominate benevolence in electoral conduct under secret ballot. However, though it strikes us as an interesting possibility and probably of some relevance, it is probably too thin a reed to sustain so apparently robust a phenomenon as the two-party system.

We are, rather, inclined to appeal here to the sorts of considerations we canvass in Chapter 10 dealing directly with Meehl's "thrown-away-vote" argument. There we argue that expressive considerations can give weight to notions like voter responsibility, civil duty, and the like. And a desire to act "responsibly" simply for the sake of doing so will tend to drive voters away from frivolous expressions and toward consequential ones. And lest we seem to paint here too heroic a picture of democratic politics and of human nature, we should also mention a not unfamiliar desire to cheer for the winning team and vote for the winning candidate. Such a desire will clearly tend to generate the two-horse race as an equilibrium.

Perhaps all these considerations taken together amount to an explanation of two-party dominance. We confess that we find our attempts here somewhat ad hoc and only half convincing. We are still inclined therefore to treat the two-party system as something of a puzzle. And it is a troubling puzzle because any satisfactory theory of voting ought to be able to account for the structure of electoral politics to which voting gives rise. And it is a particular puzzle for the expressive theory that seems naturally most congenial to a politics of a thousand voices.

In defense of the expressive theory here, we should note that public choice orthodoxy does not seem to provide a satisfactory theory of two-party dominance either. Most electoral theory in the public choice tradition either assumes a two-party system (as, e.g., Downs, 1957, does) or assumes the party structure *away,* as in the Buchanan–Tullock (1962) model of logrolling. "Party" is a kind of black box in public choice orthodoxy, and it is not clear how a specifically interest-based theory of voting would help much in filling it. If a party is conceived as a more or less permanent coalition of interests, the question has to be raised as to whether a random individual would increase expected returns by joining such a permanent coalition or would do better by selling his vote to the highest bidder on a case by case basis. Since the latter seems likely to be the dominant strategy in most cases, no simple theory of party emerges (or at least does not do so directly) from the standard public choice account.

Conclusion

It is perhaps as well to leave this survey of the "facts," as set out in the preceding two chapters, at this particular point – that is, with a puzzle that neither protagonist seems to be able to handle totally convincingly. The empirical record is not unambiguous; and, as economists have often enough demonstrated, a sufficiently ingenious mind can often explain seeming paradoxes with remarkably spare resources. There are professional rewards for exhibiting such ingenuity, and we do not deny that public choice scholars may be able to explain away many of what we identify as facts uncongenial to the interest-based theory of voting. All the same, we think that there is no shortage of such facts and that the balance of evidence is fairly clearly in favor of the expressive alternative. On the basis of that evidence and its general congruence with the underlying decision-theoretic logic, we must now rest our case.

8 Consensus, efficiency, and contractarian justification

The rule of unanimity is the Wicksellian equivalent of a Pareto move, and the impossibility of securing unanimous consent for any change becomes the Wicksellian criterion for classifying an attained move as Pareto optimal.
James Buchanan, Freedom in Constitutional Contract

Introduction

The argument set out in the foregoing chapters has been developed entirely for the case of simple majority rule. Might the problems posed by the predominance of expressive elements in voters' preferences be overcome, or moderated in a significant way, if the collective decision rule were more inclusive? There is, after all, a strong tradition in public choice theory – most clearly associated with Buchanan and Tullock – that the problems associated with majority rule disappear if unanimous decisions were required.[1] Certainly, majoritarian cycling and the resultant indeterminacy of collective decision-making processes are not present under unanimity, because the requisite redistributions from minority to majority are no longer electorally relevant.

In fact, however, the voter's dilemma problem is also present under conditions of explicit consensus. That is, the revealed preference logic fails not only in large-number majoritarian settings, but also in large-number unanimity ones: The voter's dilemma, the "veil of insignificance," is in this sense a necessary feature of all collective decision making, not just of majority rule.

The reason for this is simply stated. Just as under majority rule, the representative voter is decisive if and only if there is an exact tie among all other voters, so under unanimity, the representative voter is decisive only in the case where no other voter exercises the veto: If any other voter vetoes the proposal, then what the voter under consideration does cannot make any difference to the electoral outcome. Consequently, the representative voter cannot expect, in general, to be decisive; she will therefore be encouraged to behave expressively rather than instrumentally at the polls. In what follows, we shall attempt to render this idea more formally, but the central intuition, at least, should be clear: Under neither majority rule nor unanimity will the individual chooser normally be decisive in the way that she would be in some analogous market setting.

The case of unanimity is, however, of interest beyond its status as a polar limit of possible voting rules. There is a proposition familiar in modern welfare economics, and associated most notably with the constitutional contractarianism of Buchanan and the Virginia school, that unanimous agreement logically implies Pareto

---

This chapter is a development and extension of an earlier paper (Brennan and Lomasky, 1984).
[1] An idea most extensively developed in *The Calculus of Consent* (Buchanan and Tullock, 1962).

desirability. It is this proposition at which the epigraph to this chapter gestures. Yet if our argument here is valid, that proposition is false. Here we follow Buchanan in the contention that the logical connection between unanimity and Pareto optimality is crucial for standard welfare economics (more crucial, certainly, than most welfare economists seem to believe); we part from him in believing that the proposition is *true*. And this is significant not only for welfare economics, but also for the whole array of contractarian arguments that have become current in political theory since the publication of John Rawls's *Theory of Justice*. We do not claim that contractarian justification of, or arguments for, particular kinds of political institutions are necessarily flawed. We do claim that the contractarian line must draw a sharp distinction between arguments based on efficiency (or preference fulfillment) and arguments based on consent. This chapter begins by taking a simple striking example, developing that example for the general case, and then spelling out the implications for welfare economics and for contractarian political theory.

The Kitty Genovese murder

On the evening of March 13, 1964, a young woman was assaulted and stabbed to death in front of her home in the Kew Gardens district of Queens, New York. The victim was twenty-eight years old. Her name was Kitty Genovese.

What made this murder notable was not so much its gruesome character – though the murder was gruesome enough – but rather the fact that the events took place in the full view (and hearing) of most of the residents of the victim's immediate neighborhood. Over thirty persons acknowledged, after the event, that they had observed what was going on. The murder itself took well over half an hour to accomplish, during which time the murderer took himself off for a brief interim and then returned some quarter of an hour later to complete the job. The victim's screams were fully audible for the whole period she was under attack as were her cries for help during the period of the murderer's absence.

But no one went to her aid. No one even bothered to notify the police that the crime was in progress. Had someone done so, it is almost certain that Kitty Genovese would have been saved. And it would have been perfectly possible to notify the police without any danger to oneself – indeed, without even the modest cost of having to make a formal statement, since the tip-off could have been rendered anonymously.

This extraordinary lack of involvement on the part of observers caused widespread press comment at the time. Sociologists, theologians, psychologists, and social commentators of all kinds were wheeled in to give an account of the apparent apathy of New York suburbanites and of the depersonalization of urban communities. How could it be, they were asked, that persons valued the life of one of their neighbors at less than the price of a phone call? After all, since any of the thirty-eight observers could have exercised the veto on the murder of Kitty Genovese, the outcome was tantamount to a unanimous decision on the part of the neighborhood that Kitty Genovese should die. Can we then induce that each observer placed a lower value on murder prevention than the avoidance of involvement?

Table 8.1. *The spectators' dilemma for Kitty Genovese*

	Other spectators	
Typical spectator K	Someone calls police	No one calls police
Calls police	93	93
Does not call police	100	7

The simple answer is no. That is, we cannot infer from the events that all the observers – or indeed any of them – valued Kitty's life at less than the price of a phone call or the inconvenience endured by having to make a police statement. To see this, consider the following construction. Suppose that each valued Kitty's being saved at 100 and believed that phoning the police would indeed save Kitty. Suppose, however, that each placed some small negative value on getting involved, say, a value of minus 7. Then the best outcome for each is that in which *someone else* calls the police. And each recognizes that there are many other potential callers: Each can see other observers at their windows watching the macabre events in the street below. Each may well say to himself, "Surely one of those others will have phoned the police." And none will phone.

The relevant payoff matrix is that given in Table 8.1. For each spectator, the *only* case in which it is rational to notify the police is where no one else does so. Given the assumption that each spectator expects all others to have more or less the same payoff structure, it seems reasonable for each to expect that someone else will notify. To be sure, in the Kitty Genovese case, no one could be certain at any point whether the police had been called or not. What each *could* know is that whatever reasoning he entertains in deciding to notify the police would be replicated many times over in the reasoning of the other spectators. Even if we allow some form of mixed strategy here (the precise nature of which we shall explore later), the probability of achieving the "no one vetoes" outcome can be as high as 7% before it is rational for the typical spectator K to phone the police. Yet the total cost of K not phoning is the net benefit to each of the murder prevented (100) times the number of relevant parties (in this case the thirty-seven other observers), quite apart from the gain to Kitty herself.

In other words, it can be individually rational for no one to call the police, even though all would strongly prefer that someone does. And only one phone call is required. In that sense, the analogy between the Kitty Genovese case and the access to individual veto – in other words, to voting under unanimity – is complete. What is severed is the connection between unanimity and Pareto optimality.

Notice that there would be no analogous problem if there were only one spectator. In that event, we *could* induce the spectator's preferences between Kitty's murder and a troublesome phone call by that spectator's behavior. The problem arises precisely because the number of spectators is multiple: Kitty's problem was not so much that she was the object of indifference, but that she was overobserved.

The generalization

We should at the outset note a couple of features of the foregoing example. First, each observer is led to refrain from vetoing in a case where it would have been optimal for someone to veto. The obverse case is also of interest and no less possible – namely, that persons are led to veto proposals that would leave them better off. Such a prospect has been noted in the literature in the context of strategic behavior designed to secure for vetoers a larger share of aggregate benefit. That is, a project yielding universal benefits may fail to get unanimous support because some voters exploit their veto as a hold-out strategy.[2] But an individual may also veto a proposal that makes her better off even though (indeed in a sense *because*) he has no strategic power – that is, because she believes that her vetoing the proposal is likely to have no influence at all on the outcome and, hence, that she can safely and cheaply indulge her expressive preferences. It is this latter possibility that we will be concerned with here. And this possibility is entirely symmetric. That is, expressive preference considerations can in different circumstances lead a voter either to veto a proposal that makes her better off or to vote for a proposal that makes her worse off. Strategic considerations within a bargaining model of consensual decision making can lead a voter to the former possibility but not the latter. It can never be rational to withhold a veto in order to extract additional rents because all potential bribers have a veto of their own that they can exercise. For this reason, the case we shall focus on in what follows is that in which a voter fails to veto a proposal that makes her worse off. However, we should note that the obverse case is amenable to analogous reasoning.

Another notable point about the Genovese case is that the problem is not merely to be construed as a coordination problem. It is true that each spectator does not know how the others are going to behave, and that if any one of them knew that the others would not notify the police, it would be rational for him to do so. It is also true that the ideal solution is that in which exactly one person notifies the police.[3] What makes that ideal inaccessible, one might argue, is that action is effectively simultaneous and, hence, that each must act in ignorance of how the other will act. If, for example, "play" in the game were sequential, then at least the last player would know how all the others had acted, and the possibility of the Pareto inferior outcome would be avoided. But note that it would be precisely the last player who would veto the murder; nonultimate players all have the incentive, knowing how the last will act, not to veto (i.e., not to call the police). The interaction depicted in Table 8.1 takes the form of the game "chicken." And sequential play can always solve this game, if players have full knowledge of others' payoffs.

---

[2] It is, e.g., this kind of possibility that Buchanan and Tullock (1962) have in mind in emphasizing the increasing "decision-making costs" as more and more inclusive voting rules are used (particularly chaps. 6 and 8). It is also this anxiety that leads Wicksell (1967) to retreat from his pure unanimity ideal to "approximate" unanimity.

[3] Issues of credibility apart. If the likelihood of police intervention is positively related to the number of calls received, then there can be no presumption that the optimal number of calls will be exactly one.

But in the voting case with which we are concerned, neither full knowledge nor sequential play are really feasible options. If the knowledge of citizens' preferences were available independently of their voting behavior, we would not need voting in the first place. And it is an essential feature of standard electoral procedures that voting is effectively simultaneous. Accordingly, in those cases in which expressive preferences and instrumental preferences are in different directions – those cases with the same payoff structure as in Table 8.1 – Pareto-optimal outcomes are not guaranteed.

To formalize the argument a little, consider a community of more or less identical voters – identical at least in respect of the values they place on some electoral option vis-à-vis the status quo. Suppose there are $(s + 1)$ voters, and consider the voting calculus of any one of them. Let the probability that any voter vetoes the proposal be v. Then the probability that the proposal will not be vetoed by someone else is

$$p = (1 - v)^s. \tag{8.1}$$

Now, let the benefits attached to having the proposal not go ahead be b, which we take to be positive. This is the net value placed on the status quo compared with how the world would be if the proposal were to be implemented. And let the intrinsic benefits of voting for, rather than against, the proposal be a – again, assumed to be positive but very much less than b. Then the payoff to each of voting for the proposal is

> a if no one else vetoes and
> $a + b$ if someone else vetoes,

while the payoff to each of voting against the proposal is b.

So the expected net benefit of voting for the proposal is

$$E(B) = [ap + (1 - p)(a + b)] - b, \tag{8.2}$$

where p is the probability of no one else vetoing. Simplifying,

$$E(B) = a - bp \text{ and is positive iff } p < a/b. \tag{8.3}$$

There is, of course, a value of p at which each individual voter is indifferent between voting for and against the proposal – namely, where $p = a/b$. The individual behavior, therefore, that is consistent with each agent behaving identically is where each vetoes with probability v^*, where

$$(1 - v^*)^s = \frac{a}{b}. \tag{8.4}$$

$$v^* = 1 - \sqrt[s]{\frac{a}{b}}. \tag{8.5}$$

The outcome in which each voter vetoes with probability v^* is a Nash equilibrium in the sense that no one will have an incentive to change from that behavior if he takes others' behavior as fixed and independent of his own. Such an equilibrium seems unlikely to be stable: As in more familiar versions of the game of chicken, players have incentives to declare their intentions to vote expressively in order to induce others to vote instrumentally. However, it is useful to focus briefly on the Nash independent adjustment equilibrium and compare it with the Pareto-optimal case.

As we noted, the ideal outcome is where exactly one person vetoes the proposal. This ensures a total gain of

$$B^* = (s + 1)b + sa. \tag{8.6}$$

But this outcome is inaccessible under simultaneous voting. It is also inaccessible under an appropriately decentralized market equivalent, because in that case each individual would choose her separate b rather than a, and the total payoff would be

$$B^M = (s + 1)b. \tag{8.7}$$

We emphasize an important implication of (8.6) – namely, that voters' expressive benefits derived from voting for the proposal are not irrelevant to optimality calculations. It will be Pareto desirable to have an occasional project that no one would choose if decisive: The important thing is not to have too many such projects. Unfortunately, as we shall show, the actual outcome under unanimity does give too many. We shall, in fact, prove two propositions: first, that the Pareto-optimal solution under feasible unanimity is unstable; second, that the Nash solution is dominated by the universal veto solution (or market solution) B^M. We proceed to these propositions immediately.

It should be clear that there is a mixed strategy that yields a higher total payoff than B^M. Suppose voters vote probabilistically, in such a way that the probability of no one vetoing is p, and the average number of vetoers on any trial is m. Then the total payoff is

$$B_U = (1 - p)[(s + 1)b + (s + 1 - m)a] + p(s + 1)a \tag{8.8}$$

$$= (s + 1)b - (s + 1)bp + (s + 1)a - ma + map$$

$$> (s + 1)b \text{ iff } p < \frac{(s + 1)a - ma}{(s + 1)b - ma} = \frac{a - a[m/(s + 1)]}{b - b[m/s + 1]}. \tag{8.9}$$

Denote the p that maximizes B_U by $\hat{p}$, and the associated value of B_U by $\hat{B}_U$. We know that $0 < \hat{p} < [(s + 1)b - ma]/[(s + 1)a - ma]$. And we also observe that

$$\frac{(s + 1)b - ma}{(s + 1)a - ma} < \frac{b}{a}. \tag{8.10}$$

As pointed out in (8.3), when $p < a/b$, it is individually rational to vote for the (undesired) proposal. Accordingly, if it happened that everyone were following a mixed strategy that would generate the optimal probability of the proposal passing,

$\hat{p}$, rational voters would find it beneficial to depart from that strategy. In short, the outcome $\hat{B}_U$ is unstable.

The Nash solution outcome can be derived, at this point, by substituting the value $p = a/b$ in (8.8) to obtain

$$B_N = (s + 1)b + (s + 1)a - ma - \left(\frac{a}{b}\right)(s + 1)b + ma\left(\frac{a}{b}\right)$$

$$= (s + 1)b - \frac{ma}{b}(b - a) \tag{8.11}$$

$$< (s + 1)b, \quad \text{since } b > a > 0.$$

Thus, the Nash solution under unanimity is less efficient (generates a smaller aggregate payoff on average) than the universal veto solution, B^M, and a fortiori than the best unanimity solution, $\hat{B}_U$. Moreover, the differences at stake need not be negligible. It seems quite conceivable, for example, that $\hat{p}$ may be, say, a half of a/b; and in that case, "undesirable" proposals would be unanimously approved twice as often as would be optimal.

We do not, of course, claim on the basis of anything argued so far that the problems posed by expressive elements in voting are more significant under unanimity than under less inclusive decision rules or, for that matter, that they are less significant. The comparison of unanimity with Wicksellian "proximate unanimity" and with simple majority is an exercise we shall not here pursue. Our object has instead been to disprove the proposition that unanimous support under a rule of explicit unanimity implies Pareto desirability. That object we believe we have met.

There is, however, one feature of the argument that we ought to note. This is the significance of the assumption of roughly identical voters. Consider by contrast the case of a redistribution away from one voter-citizen to all the others, where the others are assumed to be nonaltruistic. The voter-citizen to be harmed will clearly have reason to veto the proposal: He cannot rely on others to defend his interests for him. But where there is a redistribution from many to many and there are expressive reasons to vote for the redistribution, each of the losers will rationally tend to free ride on the others (in the relevant probabilistic sense). We can then confidently rely on the unanimity rule to protect small minorities against exploitation (one traditional source of anxiety about majority rule); we cannot, however, rely on unanimity to promote all or only Pareto-desirable policies.

Unanimity in welfare economics

The idea that unanimity is a decisive test of Pareto optimality – in the sense that any policy proposal that survives the consensus test can be identified as Pareto optimal – occupies an important place in welfare economics. This is so because the explicit grounds on which welfare economics rejected the older utilitarian schema in favor of the Paretian alternative relied primarily on the "unscientific nature" of interpersonal comparisons of utility. What epistemological warrant is there, the critics of utilitarianism asked, for the claim that transferring income from A to B will increase B's utility by an amount more than A's is reduced? Where is the common numeraire of human satisfaction to which such judgments make appeal? By what faculty of mind reading can the observer ascertain the relevant psychological balance? These questions were taken by the economics profession to be unanswerable and their unanswerability to be decisive grounds for the rejection of the utilitarian program.[4]

Other kinds of attacks on utilitarianism of a more philosophical kind are of course possible and have been vigorously pursued over the doctrine's history. The allegations include the violence done to elemental notions of fairness, the failure to make proper allowance for the distinctiveness of persons, the failure to provide an adequate account of personal integrity, and so on. We shall not pursue such lines here. Our interest is in a different kind of question, one more central to the traditional welfare economics literature – namely, does the Paretian welfare framework deliver the kind of epistemological solidity that utilitarianism is seen crucially to lack?

What, in other words, is the epistemological status of claims that a particular change makes someone better off and no one else worse off? Are such claims supportable without the "reading of minds" that was seen to tarnish the utilitarian's program? What are the empirically well-grounded observations of individuals' behavior that will count as decisive evidence that a particular change in the prevailing state of affairs does indeed satisfy the strict Pareto test? Or, under other variants of the "new welfare theory," such as the hypothetical compensation schemes of Hicks (1940) and Kaldor (1939), how can one *know*, without independent knowledge of the utility functions, that gainers *can* compensate losers?

Strangely enough, such questions have not much disturbed welfare economists (Buchanan apart). And this is strange because much of the past fifty years of welfare economics scholarship can be interpreted as demonstrating just how troublesome these questions are. Consider, for example, the paradigmatic case of voluntary bilateral exchange, and assume, as in the standard account, that individuals are the best judges of their own interests.[5] We can certainly conclude from the fact of such exchange that both parties are, or expect to be, made no worse off. What we cannot conclude is that the two parties are the only ones affected by the exchange. We may of course hypothesize that only those who are party to the exchange are affected – that the market in question is ideal – and then use the model of exchange in ideal markets as a conceptual benchmark to exemplify the notion of Pareto desirability. But from an epistemological perspective this surely begs all the crucial questions. What is the observational content of a determination that a market is "ideal"? Even if the goods exchanged have all the *technical* properties of privateness, how can we know that some third party or parties are not affected via "psychic externalities" in Pareto-relevant fashion? Equally, how can we know that

---

[4] The decisive attack along such lines is Robbins (1932). For an evaluation of Robbins's position more favorable to the feasibility of interpersonal comparisons, see Little (1950).

[5] Questions about the authority of such individual judgments might at this point be raised, but their bearing on the argument of this book will be postponed to Chapter 9.

the trade in question does not lead, via cross-substitution effects, to greater distortions in other markets where distortions already prevail? After all, we have no grounds for thinking that governments will provide all public goods in exactly the correct amounts – and no independent test of what those correct amounts are. And we have good grounds for believing that monopoly elements will abound in some markets, that some policy interventions (such as tariffs) will create rather than remove distortions. In short, the reality of abundant preexisting distortions and the fact of interdependent markets as well as the logical possibility of Pareto-relevant psychic externalities imply that even the simplest cases of bilateral exchange have welfare implications that are utterly opaque. The same conclusion applies a fortiori when dealing with public policy questions of the standard kind: Should higher education be subsidized and by how much? What is the optimal expenditure on AIDS research? What level of pollution is efficient? And so on. We can accept that what welfare economics requires of us is to apply the *cherchez les externalités* rule, but where do we begin the *cherche?*

If, as Robbins argues, only preferences as revealed through actual choices can have full epistemological authority, then we are indeed totally at sea – or so, at least, it would seem. Of course, it could be claimed that, somehow, reading individuals' minds to obtain information about the various elements that enter their utility functions and the relative values placed on each is somehow less exacting than reading minds to obtain comparative information or interpersonal variations in the marginal utility of income. Such a line may be buttressed by the observation that various mechanisms of the kind suggested by Clarke, Groves and Ledyard, Tullock and Tideman, and others, can be used to elicit asymptotically accurate estimates of demands for public goods – while no such techniques yet exist to gauge the marginal utility of income, and arguably cannot be invented. Perhaps all this is true, but it seems to us highly dubious. It seems that Paretian welfare economics founders on exactly the same epistemological shoals as utilitarianism was taken to.

Or at least, Paretian welfare economics would so founder, were it not for unanimity. As standardly interpreted, unanimous decision making provides a decisive test of Pareto desirability. And as Buchanan has vigorously argued, if a proposal cannot ultimately secure unanimous support, we have no warrant for regarding it as Pareto desirable. In the Buchanan scheme, unanimous consent becomes a kind of epistemological Archimedean point from which (and uniquely from which) the Paretian welfare framework can properly be launched.

Our argument in the preceding section is that Buchanan's attempted rescue operation fails – that, as a matter of pure logic, unanimous consent is neither necessary nor sufficient for Pareto desirability. In other words, the "new" welfare economics cannot meet its own stringent epistemological standards, and Robbins is well and truly hoisted with his own petard.

Consent and justification

Although the characterization of the Pareto criterion as a kind of informationally feasible variant of utilitarianism is naturally invited by the Robbins-inspired rejection of interpersonal utility comparisons, that characterization is unduly narrow – even within economics. Certainly many of the exponents of the Paretian framework, and most notably Buchanan himself, have seen the virtues of the Paretian framework in terms much closer to those of contractarian political theory.

The object of contractarian political theory is to provide a compelling justification for political arrangements in the face of essential moral pluralism – or rather, to seek out those political arrangements that can be so justified. Consensus plays a critical role in this exercise. That to which everyone has agreed has successfully run the gauntlet of justification, even though the grounds on which each consents may be very different. Indeed, A may be appalled that anyone could have agreed on the basis of grounds that are determinative for B. No matter, so long as each, acting as a free and rational being, concurs. Let a thousand conceptions of the good bloom. The liberal gardener tolerates, may even relish, certainly adjusts himself to, their variety. His concern is to find bloom-watering arrangements that are, for whatever reason, accepted by all.

The analogy to Pareto desirability is clear. Just as the Pareto criterion accepts as authoritative the preferences of all affected parties in some policy action and requires that the policy be preferred by all those parties, so contractarian justification of political arrangements accepts rival conceptions of the good. Indeed, for some contractarians (and for most economists, we suspect), conceptions of the good are simply preferences – though preferences defined specifically over political institutions rather than particular policies. And contractarian theory, like Paretian welfare economics, seeks a kind of unassailably high moral ground. One may cede a lot of territory, in the sense that one is reduced to silence on many issues but when one speaks, one deals in what ought to be knock-down arguments. Who, after all, can plausibly reject a policy that makes her better off and who can complain about institutions to which she has already knowledgeably consented?

Moreover, as Buchanan and Tullock (1962) have plausibly argued, unanimous consent may be impossible to solicit (or excessively costly) at the level of day-to-day decision making. Accordingly, the natural domain of the Pareto criterion is at the level of decisions about the day-to-day decision-making *procedures.* At this more abstract ''constitutional'' level of decision making, individuals can be presumed to be more ignorant about what their particular interests will be and are therefore more likely to take a public-interested line. At this constitutional level, decision-making costs are lower and consensus can be agreed to be the appropriate decision-making rule. The connection with Rawls's ''veil of ignorance'' in the ''original position'' is clear. Of course, Rawls's project is not that of applying Paretian efficiency concepts at the relevantly feasible level. But if Buchanan's general argument is accepted – if, that is, Paretian concepts can plausibly only be applied at the level of choice among alternative political-economic institutions – then contractarian political theory and Paretian welfare economics share not only a common appeal to consensus, but also a common domain.

The question naturally arises, then, as to whether contractarian political theory is susceptible to the problems that we have argued plague consensus as a definitive test of Pareto optimality. The answer to this question depends on whether social contract is seen as a method of determining arrangements that are conducive to maximal furthering of the various conceptions of the good that persons hold, or as authoritative for some other reason; for if the former, then our critique applies.

A distinction could, of course, be drawn between Pareto efficiency and social contract theory on the grounds that the former deals simply with preference satisfaction, while the latter deals with competitive conceptions of the good that different persons seek to promote. For the purposes of the argument here, we can accept that distinction without in any way losing the force of the proposition. An individual may, for example, be "excessively" influenced by the opinions of others in delivering his consent in an environment where his consent is unlikely to be influential on the prevailing outcome. Or he may be excessively distracted by other non-outcome-relevant considerations. The point is that the *grounds* on which he values options and outcomes is irrelevant to the fact that option-related and outcome-related considerations are inappropriately weighted unless the agent is decisive.

This observation does not, however, necessarily exhaust the normative resources of consent. We may deny that consent matters solely – even primarily – as a means for arriving at efficiency. We may want to insist that voluntary consent puts one under an obligation to comply whether or not one prefers that to which one consents. This is to take the normative thrust of consent as *deontological* rather than *teleological*. The deontological reading of consent's significance indeed seems to be more in keeping with the spirit underlying contract theory than is the teleological alternative: It is not, by and large, behavioristic scruples that keep contract theorists from appealing directly to the preferences of individuals and thus to induce straightaway a political constitution that optimally fits these preferences. Consent figures importantly not so much because it leads to good outcomes, but because of the way in which these outcomes arise. Rather than falling from the heavens, or from the axioms of an impersonal deontic calculus, a society's basic institutions are *chosen* by persons acting in their capacity as rational and autonomous agents. That to which one gives one's consent is to be seen not merely as something good for one, but as something that one has actively participated in bringing about. It can then plausibly be maintained that one who is (co)responsible for the framework of a polity is bound to respect its determinations because she has bound herself.

The analogy that comes immediately to mind is a *promise*.[6] One who promises to do *x* thereby places himself under an obligation to do *x* even if he subsequently finds out that keeping the promise is more costly than had been anticipated. Even more importantly, the normative force of a promise to do *x* is not that the promiser has reliably indicated that doing *x* will advance his welfare; promises are not binding because – and to the extent that – they are efficient. The normal way to construe the normative force of promises is as *intrinsic* to the act of promise giving, rather than as instrumental. By parity of reasoning, one who through his vote consents to some policy that he had the power to veto unilaterally can be understood as

---

[6] Promising *invariably* seems to come to mind when philosophers set themselves to analyzing moral obligation. We feel some discomfort in trotting out a warhorse that has so often been put through its paces but suppose that it would not have been taken out of the stable so frequently if it did not give good mileage.

doing more than indicating (perhaps reliably, perhaps unreliably) the direction of his preferences; he is *agreeing* to be bound by the policy should it be accepted by all.

It may seem that while the phenomenon of expressive voting is of *every* significance to contract theories for which the authority of consent is teleological, expressive voting matters *not at all* to theories that understand consent's authority to be deontologically grounded. That, though, is too quick. There are at least two respects in which expressively motivated action remains troublesome for deontologically based contract theories. First, what may have appeared to be adequate grounds for inferring the existence of consent under the assumption that consent reliably reveals preferences over outcomes might prove insufficient once it is allowed that individuals can rationally assent to proposals that do not reflect those preferences. If so, the results of contract become indeterminate or a mere proxy for preference. Second, the presence of significant prospects for the achievement of expressive gains can be argued to vitiate the authority of consent by rendering it less than fully voluntary. We consider these two arguments in turn.

Inferred consent

Precisely because consent renders benign many undertakings that would, in its absence, be morally dubious (e.g., the difference between rape and romance), the temptation to extend the range over which consent can be deemed to operate is well-nigh irresistible. Thus, social contract theorists have been led to augment the original explicit consensual performance that undergirds the constitutional structure of a regime with an *implicit* consent that can be presumed of anyone who chooses to remain within the domain of a governing authority.[7] It will obviously make the task of justifying political institutions a far more manageable task if the theorist can get away with positing just one founding convention in which consent is explicitly given and which retains continuing legitimacy in the face of new entrants to the polity, through immigration or birth.

Although implicit consent is not the product of any specific performance that can be cited as the *act of consent* to social rules, it is presented as no less bona fide a representative of actual consent than is explicit consent. What agents in fact do or refrain from doing is appealed to in order to justify the claim that their consent has been elicited. By way of contrast, *hypothetical consent* theories build construction of moral rights and duties on counterfactual considerations of that to which agents *would* agree under stipulated circumstances. The resultant genesis of moral

---

[7] "Nobody doubts but an *express Consent,* of any Man, entering into any Society, makes him a perfect Member of that Society, a Subject of that government. The difficulty is, what ought to be look'd upon as a *tacit Consent,* and how it binds, i.e., how far any one shall be looked on to have consented, and thereby submitted to any government, where he has made no Expressions of it at all. And to this I say, that every Man, that hath any Possession, or Enjoyment, of any part of the Dominions of any government, doth thereby give his *tacit Consent,* and is as far forth obliged to Obedience to the Laws of that government, during such Enjoyment, as any one under it; whether this his Possession or be of Land, to him and his Heirs for ever, or a Lodging only for a Week; or whether it be varely travelling freely on the Highway; and in Effect, it reaches as far as the very being of any one within the Territories of that government" Locke (1960), sec. 119, p. 392.

imperatives is a function both of the features attributed to the arena within which contract is envisioned to occur and to the (hypothetical) contractual undertaking itself. Although it is not entirely clear which versions of classical social contract were taken by their expounders to be loosely historical and which purely hypothetical, the most distinguished contemporary invocation of social contract theory, that of Rawls (1971), is firmly located within the province of hypothetical consent:

> In justice as fairness the original position of equality corresponds to the state of nature in the traditional theory of the social contract. This original position is not, of course, thought of as an actual historical state of affairs, much less as a primitive condition of culture. It is understood as a purely hypothetical situation characterized so as to lead to a certain conception of justice. . . . No society can, of course, be a scheme of cooperation which men enter voluntarily in a literal sense; each person finds himself placed at birth in some particular position in some particular society, and the nature of this position materially affects his life prospects. Yet a society satisfying the principles of justice as fairness comes as close as a society can to being a voluntary scheme, for it meets the principles which free and equal persons would assent to under circumstances that are fair. In this sense its members are autonomous and the obligations they recognize self-imposed. (pp. 12–13)

Critics of the method of hypothetical consent will reject the assertion that a society consonant with principles to which individuals would have assented in some imaginary setting provides any basis for categorizing the society as even remotely approaching a "voluntary scheme." That Jones would have traded his bicycle to Smith for $100 and that Smith would have given up $100 for the bicycle does not vest Smith with title to the bicycle and Jones title to the $100. And a social mechanism that removed the bicycle from the one and the cash from the other in order to effect a redistribution may be claimed justifiable on grounds of enhancing efficiency but not because it can be said to have played midwife to the implementation of a voluntary transaction. On such grounds it is certainly possible to criticize hypothetical contract as falling short of demonstrating a social order to be voluntary in any morally compelling sense.

We wish to suggest a different though related criticism of the underpinnings of social contract theory. Let it be granted that what individuals would agree to can, in an appropriate setting, settle what ought to be the case in the world.[8] Let it be granted in particular that what persons in the Rawlsian original position would agree to (as foundational principles of justice) determines which arrangements satisfy criteria of fairness for actual societies in which citizens have never bargained with each other behind a veil of ignorance. There still remains the question as to the basis on which we can determine what it is that would command the assent of individuals so described.

The Rawlsian account assumes, as does every other version of hypothetical contract of which we are aware, that individuals will endorse that set of rules that they judge to be most conducive to the success of their own interests: Individuals would

---

[8] E.g., questions about what course of medical treatment ought to be given to comatose individuals might plausibly be supposed to hinge at least in part on what that individual, were he in a position to be able to rule on his own medical destiny, would elect as a course of treatment for himself.

consent to that which they prefer. It is this inference, however, that has been shown to be erroneous. If expressive factors are present, then rational individuals may well *withhold* their assent from a proposal that maximizes their well-being in the expected sense and give it instead to a proposal under whose auspices they would be worse off. Moreover, *everyone* can be rationally led to do so under a rule of unanimity just as much as under majority rule. It follows then that the Rawlsian argument is very much at risk. Many critics have contended that contractors in the original position would not be led to see their interests best served by Rawls's two principles of justice and, most especially, not by the difference principle. What we maintain, though, is that even if Rawls were entirely correct in his argument that the two principles of justice would be *preferred* by contractors under the extreme uncertainty of the original position, it does not follow that those principles would be *chosen*. Preference is one thing, choice another. Full knowledge of individuals' preferences over outcomes simply does not translate into knowledge of that to which they will assent.

It could be responded that the gap in the Rawlsian argument is easily repaired. The original position is not meant to replicate a setting in which any actual deliberations have taken place. Rather, it is highly stylized, building into the beliefs and attitudes of the participants precisely what will generate the agreement that constitutes justice as fairness. So, for example, contractors are allowed to know general truths of economics, political organization, and psychology but not their own level of material endowments, the circumstances of their own society, or the generation to which they belong (Rawls, p. 137). And precisely in order to derive a principle of just savings, Rawls construes the participants as representing family lines, with ties of sentiment binding the generations (p. 292). Why then not decree as a matter of faith that individuals have no expressive interests, or that they do not know what those expressive interests are and thus cannot act on them, or that their expressive interests are entirely congruent with their preferences over outcomes? By availing himself of one of these expedients, Rawls (and hypothetical contract theorists in general) can sidestep the roadblock thrown up by expressive considerations and move directly from an assessment of the preferences of contractors to their hypothesized consent.

While logical validity can be preserved by such a stipulative strategy, it comes at a cost, one that must be high for a theory that bills itself as contractarian; for if preference over outcomes is necessary and sufficient to constitute the grounds for inferring an agent's assent, then the act of consent is rendered morally otiose. It is underlying preference that is uniquely decisive. Nothing else can matter because nothing else is allowed to count for a person as a reason for coming down one way rather than another. Therefore, the proposed emendation is one that takes the significance of consent to be merely instrumental, as no more than a check mark indicating the direction of preference, and simultaneously it takes the normative authority of contract to be thoroughly teleological. It is not the *act of consent*, hypothetical or actual, that binds agents, but rather the shape of utility functions imputed to them.

It may, of course, be reasonable to ground the proper structure for political principles and institutions in agents' interests – rather than in facts about how persons choose to act on or refrain from acting on these interests, or in any deontological principle that ties the existence of obligations tightly to voluntary acts of pledge. This may be reasonable, but not in any obvious way contractarian. The ploy to validate by stipulation the inference to the targeted principle of justice simply transforms consent into a quasi-mechanical procedure by means of which preference is recorded. An agent's autonomy no longer will be allowed to include decision on his part between expressing support because value is assigned to that which is supported and expressing support because the expressive act is itself valued. As was previously noted, critics of hypothetical consent theory have challenged the claim that any significant measure of voluntariness attaches to the determination of what someone *would have* agreed to and that, therefore, hypothetical consent does not inherit the moral cachet of actual consent. To this we add that consent which is not, even in theory, separable from the holding of preference is yet a further step removed from the paradigmatic consent to which we naturally tend to ascribe moral significance. Its force cannot be deontological but rather teleological. Contra Rawls, there is not even the simulacrum of self-imposed obligation if it is preferences rather than agents that yield political determination. If contract is an appealing device to employ in political theory in virtue of deontological considerations such as the bindingness of promises on which it leans, hypothetical contract confronts a dilemma. Either the argument from preference to that which would receive consent must be rejected, or else the normative significance of the hypothesized contractual setting must be taken as based on preference itself and not at all on the giving of consent. Whether this dilemma can be surmounted and, if not, whether it is merely inconvenient for hypothetical contract theory or whether it is fatal to it we leave as questions for another occasion.

Procedural criteria for the normative authority of consent

Even a strictly deontological construal of the authority of consent can discount its bindingness when the conditions under which consent is achieved involve unfairness, coercion, or some other feature that renders consent less than the fully voluntary act of an autonomous agent. If the institutional context within which agreement occurs is such that agents are systematically prompted to agree to outcomes detrimental to their interests, we might judge that the formal conditions for morally binding consent fail to obtain. Note that this is not equivalent to the teleological reading in which the fact that assent diverges from preferences is itself held to undermine the authority of consent. Rather, the deontological conception is one in which procedural standards are criterial for the moral adequacy of consent but such that a systematic tendency to produce outcomes that diverge from interests is held to be symptomatic of a procedural defect. Without any pretension of their being exhaustive, the following illustrate familiar grounds on which it can plausibly be maintained that procedural criteria for voluntary agreement have not been satisfied:

Coercion. A holds a gun to the head of B and proposes the transaction "Your money or your life!" B hands over his money to A and A does not shoot.

Threat. A, who holds compromising photographs of B, threatens to release them to public view unless B agrees to pay a sum of money to A on a regular basis. B considers the offer and agrees to pay.

Duress. A's spouse has just died and B comes around to sell A a top-of-the-line gold-inlaid casket. A at first turns down the purchase, but B does not take no for an answer, and after hours of being badgered, A agrees to buy.

Fraud. A offers to sell B Leonardo's *Mona Lisa* for $10,000. B pays the money and A delivers a painting completed a week earlier by one Leonardo Schultz. It has the title "Mona Lisa."

Incompetence. A is 98 years old and conspicuously senile. B comes by to sell life insurance policies. A has no dependents and only a hazy understanding of what an insurance policy is but purchases a policy. The sale is repeated another dozen times.

Grossly unequal bargaining power. A comes across B, who is suffering from extreme hunger. A offers B a mess of pottage in exchange for B's birthright. B considers briefly and then accepts.

We need not claim that, in each of these cases, the transaction is to be accounted null and void due to procedural defect, only that, for each, there is at least some prima facie indication of impropriety that calls the transaction's bona fides into question. Elucidation of a full theory of procedural fittingness for agreement is beyond our present aspirations. However, we take it to be uncontroversial that *some* procedural failings can undercut the bindingness of agreement.

With this in mind, might it not be reasonably argued that the institutional setting of a rule of unanimity in large-number electorates contravenes conditions of procedural fairness? Individuals who recognize that their own likelihood of being decisive is very small, and who stand to accrue large expressive gains by voting against their interests, are strongly induced to vote for the outcome the emergence of which they do not prefer. Yet that outcome does in fact emerge, because each confronts the same choice calculus. In this case is the result morally acceptable, on a strict deontological construction, because it did in fact achieve consensus? Or is the procedure under which unanimous approval was forthcoming sufficiently tarnished that the agreement should be null and void?

We confess ourselves uncertain about the correct answer. On the one hand, each individual was perfectly free to veto the proposal and thus avert the unwanted result. No vote was coerced. Each voter, looking back on the process, is barred from declaring "There was nothing I could have done about it." In effect, each gambled on the willingness of someone else to cast the veto, and the gamble was lost. We do not wish to put forward a general principle that one's act of voluntarily assuming a risk is automatically annulled should the result turn out to be adverse – not even if it could be known ex ante that one's expected return was negative. That would be to strip away nearly all the normative flesh from the frame of consent.

On the other hand, there seem to exist close parallels to standard cases of duress. B, the casket salesman, does not employ coercive force against A. A is free to reject B's offer of the casket. A cannot retrospectively conclude, "There was nothing I could have done about it." A recognized a long-term interest in not purchasing the casket but also a gain to be accrued through inducing the importunate salesman to depart. The latter motivated A's decision, and as a result, an outcome emerged that contravened A's preferences. If there exist procedural grounds for annulling the sale, what relevant features distinguish this case from that of the proposal that secures unanimous approval?

Consider a standard prisoners' dilemma in which a strategy dominant for each player gives rise to an outcome in which both are worse off than they would have been with another strategy. Of course, prisoners' dilemmas can yield results that the observer will judge to be "good," based on her own independent standard of appraisal. Indeed, to the extent we believe that malefactors ought to get their just deserts, the original prisoners' dilemma might present itself to us as a salutory basis for law enforcement. But the outcome does not present itself as desirable to those bound up in the prisoners' dilemma, and at least in some cases, observers will concur with their judgment. What is it that leads the observer in some cases and the players in all cases to decry the suboptimal outcome?

One possible response is that it is suboptimality itself that offends. An outcome in which each would be better off is available, and by application of the Pareto test, the one in fact achieved is judged to be inferior. This is a straightforwardly teleological appraisal and, as such, is subject to deontological critique. So long as each party has acted voluntarily in choosing as he did, it can be claimed, formal criteria of normative acceptability have been satisfied. To be sure, no one of the players himself determined the outcome, but their acts of rational free choice jointly brought it about. As in the case of having bet and lost, one is bound to accept the results of one's voluntary actions. Consequential considerations simply do not come into play.

We say that a deontological critique *could* be constructed along those lines. It has, however, the appearance of oddness because it professes to find nothing to gainsay about a prisoners' dilemma outcome. Because most of us feel a strong disinclination to be thrust into a prisoners' dilemma environment ourselves and perhaps feel sympathy for others unfortunate enough to find themselves there, most persons will be disinclined to accept the appraisal of the prisoners' dilemma as morally benign. It does not follow, however, that this intuition must land one back in the teleological camp, for one can situate the objectionableness of prisoners' dilemma situations not in the suboptimality of their outcomes but in the structure of the choice situation itself. Individuals are induced within a prisoners' dilemma to generate outcomes that no one of them wants, and it is the fact of *inducement* rather than the undesirability of the outcomes that render the proceedings normatively suspect. Reverting to the analogy of a losing bet, a person who wagers in circumstances where he is impelled neither to wager nor to refrain from wagering but just decides for himself to bet has no ground for complaint about the propriety of his being required to pay up. In particular, though he dislikes the outcome, the process that led up to it must be admitted to be unexceptionable. Not so with the prisoners' dilemma. Its badness is not simply a function of its failing the Paretian test but because of the fact that individuals are put into a position where they are induced to bring about that failure.[9]

These reflections are neither systematic nor conclusive. We repeat that we find ourselves puzzled about which conclusion to draw. This seems to be a matter about which reasonable deontologists can disagree, but there is at least a plausible case to be made for the claim that something like duress renders unanimous agreement in the presence of countervailing expressive returns less than fully voluntary and thus, on deontological grounds, normatively inconclusive. And for one who adopts a consistently teleological line, the conclusion seems to be not merely plausible but inescapable: Unanimous consent is not a reliable indicator of common preference.

Summary

The object of this chapter has been to extend the earlier discussion of nondecisiveness in collective decision making from the case of majority rule to that of unanimity. We have argued that qualitatively the same problems apply – that just as under majority rule, individuals may vote for policies that make them worse off, so under unanimity, no one may veto a policy that makes many (and, in the limit, all) worse off.

This fact has implications for Paretian welfare economics, in that the institutional setting traditionally identified as isolating Pareto-efficient moves is collective decision making under consensus. To have some such institutional setting is important because it provides a behaviorist foundation for the identification of Pareto-optimal moves and a feasible institutional setting in which such moves can be realized. The Pareto framework's possession of an institutional equivalent is exactly the source of its alleged superiority over utilitarianism: Claims about Pareto-desirable moves can be decisively tested by observation (at least in principle) in a way in which utilitarian proposals with their problematic interpersonal comparisons cannot. Accordingly, if the connection between Pareto optimality and consensus is at risk, so is the alleged epistemological superiority of the Paretian framework.

The argument also has implications for social contract theory in political justification. To the extent that the normative force of consent is seen to derive from consent's authority as an indicator of preference satisfaction, then the argument applies directly. But if consent is seen to be intrinsically binding, as in a promise

[9] That is not to claim (or deny) that the structure of the choice situation *caused* them to fail. For obvious reasons we do not wish to fall into a discussion of causal determinism and freedom of the will at this juncture. We note only that to describe the prisoners' dilemma as a "choice situation" is to imply that the players could have chosen otherwise and thus that they could have secured an outcome other than the Pareto-dominated one. Being strongly induced to adopt a strategy is not equivalent to literally having no choice about which strategy to adopt.

given, the argument has little direct force – though it may not have no force at all. One might construe the multiperson nature of the consent given, and the resultant ex ante expectation of nondecisiveness, as modifying the bindingness of the consent – as if the context were a mild form of duress. Such a construal seems unpersuasive to us, but we are not entirely confident of our intuition here. What does seem clear is that a sharp distinction should be drawn between actual consent and hypothetical consent, the latter having virtually no binding force beyond its preference satisfaction properties (such as they are). Tacit consent and implicit consent are closer to actual consent than to hypothetical for the purposes here. Hypothetical consent seems to us to differ in only a minor way from pure preference satisfaction and, accordingly, to be extremely susceptible to the problems that this chapter has addressed.

9 Paternalism, self-paternalism, and the state

> *We cannot accept want-satisfaction as a final criterion of value because we do not in fact ourselves regard our wants as final; instead of resting in the view that there is no disputing about tastes, we dispute about them more than anything else; our most difficult problem in valuation is the evaluation of our wants themselves and our most troublesome want is the desire for wants of the "right" kind.*
>
> Frank Knight, *"The Ethics of Competition"*

Merit goods

Some goods are underproduced and underconsumed. Least controversially, the class of such goods will include Samuelsonian public goods of varying degrees of purity (i.e., goods that exhibit significant nonappropriability and/or joint consumption characteristics). Unless market provision of such goods is supplemented by nonmarket provision of an appropriate kind, a Pareto-inferior output will result. More controversial is the existence of *merit goods*, items underconsumed even in ideal markets.[1] Among the goods for which such status has been claimed are the fine arts, attendance at economics lectures, and nutritious cholesterol-free diets. And as well, there can be *demerit* goods – those that are *overconsumed* at market prices. A representative listing of contenders for this status would include heroin, cigarettes, gambling, whiskey, and perhaps rock music. While the concept of a public good can be presented in terms that may appear to be value free,[2] it is apparent that the concept of a merit good is fundamentally and ineliminably normative. Better put, the merit goods notion seems to require a rather stronger normative apparatus to sustain it. Accordingly, a sharp debate has ensued over the proper place, if any, of merit goods considerations in the economic theory of government action. The controversy has two strands. First, if there are merit goods, then their underconsumption cannot necessarily or primarily be attributed to market imperfections as such: The central feature seems to be irrational or otherwise mistaken individual preferences. The question naturally arises as to whether it is meaningful to characterize preferences as defective, and if meaningful, what could be the epistemic basis of judgments to the effect that individuals fail to prefer, or fail to prefer sufficiently, that which they ought to prefer. Second, if the conceptual problems surrounding merit goods can somehow be resolved, can a case be made for the *political* provision of merit goods? This second question is relevant because it is one thing to argue that individuals are not perfect judges of their own interests or

---

[1] The term was first introduced by Musgrave (1959), pp. 13–14.
[2] We quite deliberately say "appear"; claims of the insufficiency of public good production on the market are hardly intelligible without some underlying normative presuppositions concerning the relative authority of preferences revealed in the presence of externalities and those that would be revealed if all relevant externalities were internalized.

143

even that they are not the best judges, and quite another to argue that superior choices will emerge from political processes. Without that additional step, merit goods remain institutionally empty, whatever their conceptual and epistemic status, and the whole enterprise of developing a case for public intervention based on the merit goods concept fails utterly. If individuals left to their own devices will satisfy erroneous or otherwise deficient preferences, then there is scope for the state to *attempt* to exercise paternalistic intervention through which "better" preferences will be imported. Whether we have grounds for believing that it will succeed in such enterprises is an independent question.[3]

Strangely, much of the discussion of merit goods in the economics literature[4] has been restricted to the purely conceptual level of discourse. Musgrave's original treatment is, like his discussion of "social wants" (public goods), essentially an exercise in supplying the normative foundations for his theory and is completely institution free. This is not meant as criticism. It is important that questions about the normative authority of individuals' revealed preference be pursued, both by and for economists. Recent history in welfare economics with its strongly behaviorist orientation has rather tended to sweep away these questions: Individuals' "interests" have been taken to have no meaning apart from their observed choices. The claim that there may be a meaningful and useful distinction between *choice* and *preference* (or, variously expressed, between *utility* and *true welfare,* or between tastes, preferences, and values) even in markets for purely private goods may therefore strike the modern welfare economist as strange and perhaps even objectionable, as it apparently does for McLure (1968). That behavioristic inclination does not, however, provide a secure methodological stronghold from which unwelcome normative intrusions can easily be repulsed.[5]

But it is at least as important that the implications of such claims for the choice between decentralized (market) and centralized (political) processes be thoroughly developed, since it is this latter aspect that is crucial for purposes of policy. Just as in public goods theory, the mere demonstration of market imperfections does not constitute a case for government intervention: We need additionally to demonstrate that the political process can reasonably be expected to improve on the market. Any

[3] J. S. Mill was actually aware of the independence of these issues. In *Utilitarianism* he acknowledges the existence of merit goods, there referred to as "higher pleasures" and presents, as an epistemic criterion for their identification, judgments by the "man of experience." Yet he also argues eloquently in *On Liberty* for governance that is nonpaternalistic, subject to a few minimal qualifications (dealing primarily with children and uncivilized peoples). Gertrude Himmelfarb (1974), among others, has argued that the Mill of *On Liberty* has experienced a drastic sea change from the Mill of the earlier work, from whom he now dissociates himself – though this allegation of inconsistency is disputed by Ten (1981).
[4] See the discussion in Head (1966, 1969) and for a more recent appraisal Brennan and Walsh (1990). There is a complementary literature that occurs at a more methodological level, dealing with rationality (in particular Elster, 1979, 1983), the economics of self-control, and related issues. The extensive bibliography in Brennan and Walsh (1990) indicates much of the relevant material.
[5] In the preceding chapter we attempted to show that the behavioristic postulates of the new welfare economics are inadequate for much of the task that welfare economics sets for itself. If the welfare economist restricts himself to the Spartan diet of (behaviorally) revealed preferences, then he will perish from epistemological malnutrition; market failure, even in extreme cases, must be considered entirely a matter for metaphysical speculation. The merit goods discussion, in its purely normative variant, is complementary to that critique: Both involve a denial of the behaviorist's reductionism.

such demonstration invariably involves a comparison of two imperfect institutions and a careful weighing of the particular virtues and inadequacies of each in the case in hand.

The only contributor to the merit good literature to deal explicitly with this institutional aspect of merit goods analysis is Head (1966, 1969), and in this sense his early contributions are conceptually complete in a way that much of the subsequent literature is not. Head's conclusions in this connection are worth quoting at some length. His basic claim is that

> there are very good reasons for supposing that the irrationality and uncertainty characteristics of merit goods pose far more difficult problems for the political mechanism than those associated with pure nonappropriability. . . . Since it would obviously be naive to rely upon the emergence of an absolutist government inspired by an altruistic desire to rectify irrational preferences, and since the democratic process (as envisaged by Downs) is evidently incapable of performing this function, it would appear that this aspect of merit want theory is *completely nonoperational* in a fundamental sense. (p. 225, emphasis added)

Head considers but rejects the notion that the preferences revealed in political and market contexts may be systematically different in any way relevant to the merit goods issue. Such differences would, he claims, require "genuine schizophrenia" – and in the spirit of modern public choice theory, he rejects such institutional schizophrenia as implausible. "Even if government experts or party elites could somehow determine the true preferences of individuals, the inclusion of merit goods policies would result in electoral disaster" (p. 224). The bottom line, therefore, is that "the political problem of improving on market performance is likely to be even more difficult in the case of merit goods than in the case of pure public goods." Indeed, the logic of Head's argument is that there can be virtually no presumption that the political process can ever improve on market performance in provision of merit goods, except perhaps by luck. In this sense, the merit goods case is quite unlike the public goods counterpart. Any possibility of creating a normative justification for government activity based on merit goods is illusory. It is the dynamics of political processes rather than any complaint with the concept of a merit good or unquestioned reliance on the authority of "consumer sovereignty" that leads Head to this strongly antipaternalistic result.

In developing his argument, Head explicitly invokes a Downsian model of rationally self-interested voting behavior. It is apparent that once this model is replaced with the one developed in this book, the possibility of successful state paternalism becomes once again an open issue. In particular, if the state that manipulates relative prices in order to bring about increased consumption of merit goods is not an absolutist order but rather one responding to the preferences expressed by an electorate, then we will have to consider quite seriously whether voters will not utilize the instrumentality of the state for "self-paternalism." Three implications relevant to the merit goods discussion suggest themselves. First and most obvious, Head's claim that provision of merit goods necessarily leads to "electoral disaster" must be rejected. It seems clear that, at the very least, some merit goods may emerge in political equilibrium. But this weak proposition can be strengthened. We shall aim to show that majoritarian policies are such as to *encourage* political provision of merit goods; electorates are likely to vote for the provision of merit goods that they would not choose to consume in comparable quantities in an analogous market setting. Stronger still, they will be motivated to vote for the provision of these goods precisely because they take them to be merit goods.

This fact leads to a second implication. Because preferences revealed in political and market contexts differ, it is not possible to make valid institutional comparisons without some prior decision as to whether political preferences or market preferences should be decisive. The rejection of any ascription of genuine schizophrenia to individuals in their capacities as consumer and voter (a rejection we emphatically second if "genuine" is properly interpreted) does not allow one to appeal to "individual sovereignty" as if that notion were well defined. "Individual sovereignty," we shall argue, may refer to *consumer* sovereignty as familiarly understood in market context; to *voter* sovereignty as revealed in electoral contexts; or yet more inclusively, to *reflective* sovereignty, which concerns preferences over alternative possible sets of preferences (i.e., the individual's own metapreference norms). If the individual is to be reflectively sovereign in this sense, he must be assigned the capacity to choose between institutional forms in the light of the preferences to which those forms predictably give effect. Once it is recognized that the subjective determinations of individuals are themselves institution dependent, it is no longer coherent to suppose, as normative economics characteristically does, that all questions of value can be left to subjective determination as such; for the question now becomes: left to *which* subjective determinations? An *argument* is required from those attempting to design and evaluate alternative institutional structures concerning which species of preferences is to be preferred. Since comparative institutional analysis is a central part of our own concerns, that onus fairly rests specifically on ourselves (among others). We have alluded to this problem in previous chapters: It must now be faced head-on.

Third, arguments of a more conventional public goods sort for assigning decisions to political processes have to be reevaluated. The replacement of market choice by political choice may effect not so much the internalization of externalities as the subsidization of merit goods. Such an outcome will, definitionally, be "inefficient" within the standard conception of that term: But whether the outcome is nonetheless normatively justifiable is not a consequence of the definition but must be considered in its own right.

In this chapter, we aim to explore all these matters. In the next section we contest several interrelated assumptions that characterize much of the standard welfare economics literature. These assumptions are (1) that while interpersonal preferences may be incommensurable, intrapersonal preferences are readily commensurable by virtue of trade-offs individuals will reveal themselves prepared to make; (2) that the epistemically authoritative revelation of preferences is through market transactions in which individuals voluntarily assume costs in order to achieve what they take to be benefits; (3) that it is insofar as individuals are able to give effect through their market transactions to their preferences that they enjoy "sovereignty," and (4) that if consumers are, in this sense, sovereign, then from their perspective there can be no reason to believe that market processes are inferior to any alternative institutional arrangements.

Against this array of assumptions we argue that the structure of individuals' preferences is *complex,* and introduce a taxonomy, itself abbreviated, in which preferences revealed in the market are but one among the kinds of preference that individuals entertain and to which they have reason to give effect. As a result, the notion of "consumer sovereignty" is exhibited to be but one component of individual sovereignty. For this reason, the political provision of merit goods can in principle be argued for in terms of individuals' own preferences – although these are not the preferences revealed in their market behavior. The state that provides such merit goods will be acting paternalistically, but its normative authority is sought not from some external standard of value known to a special coterie of sages or technocrats but from the value judgments of the individuals over whom paternalistic control is to be exercised. It is thus a kind of self-paternalism that presents itself for evaluation; and such self-paternalism cannot easily be dismissed through invoking standard liberal or methodological subjectivist caveats. The chapter's penultimate section addresses this argument by considering the institutionally relevant question as to which preferences should be preferred, and a concluding section follows with a brief discussion of the relevance of merit goods considerations to the actual workings of democratic political processes.

m-Preferences, p-preferences, and reflective preferences

That an individual's preferences are not all of a kind and thus readily commensurable one with another is suggested by the existence of the voter's dilemma. Recall that we have characterized the voter's dilemma as an interaction in which individuals vote as they prefer but collectively generate an outcome that no one of them prefers. The term "prefer" does double duty in the preceding sentence: In its first appearance it refers to the expressive factors motivating a vote; its second appearance refers to what an individual would have been motivated to select had she been in a position where she was decisive. Preferences revealed in contexts where agents act decisively will tend to be outcome oriented, while preferences revealed by voting will tend to be non-outcome-oriented. Let us call the preferences that motivate a vote "p-preferences," and since outcome-oriented preferences are preeminent in market contexts, we shall call these "m-preferences." What makes the voter's dilemma deserving of its name is that individuals' p-preferences are observed to diverge from their m-preferences. What a person has reason to p-prefer, she m-disprefers and vice versa. Were p-preferences extensionally equivalent to m-preferences, there would be no dilemma.

Has it been shown, though, that p-preferences are different in kind or stand on a different level from m-preferences or merely that they (sometimes) stand opposed to m-preferences? By the latter is meant the familiar sort of circumstance in which an agent wants to do *x* and wants to do *y* but cannot do both. The preferences standing behind *x* and *y* are in opposition but are on the same level. They are weighed against each other when the agent decides to do *x* rather than *y* in virtue of his stronger preferences running in that direction. To call an outcome "efficient" is to indicate that the strongest of opposed preferences is determinative. However, when Jones prefers that x be done and Smith that y be done, their preferences are not merely opposed but, in the relevant sense, different in kind. There does not exist an overall standard of appraisal common to Jones and Smith in terms of which the conflicting preference can be weighed, and thus neither outcome can be said to be more efficient than the other (unless some mutually beneficial exchange emerges in which Jones gets his way on x in return for Smith getting her way on some other issue).

If the outcome yielded by a voter's dilemma is taken to be the "wrong" one, that judgment presupposes an implicit prior judgment that the conflicting p-preference and m-preference are opposed but not different in kind. The outcome is labeled "inefficient" because it does not maximize the payoff to citizen-voters. But that is to presuppose that the "right" point of view is from the perspective of m-preferences; had the individuals been "buying" outcomes as they do in the market, they would have given effect to their m-preferences and thus procured a different result. If "efficiency" is simply defined in terms of m-preferences, then it is tautologous to assert that outcomes which do not fully reflect individuals' m-preferences are inefficient. However, to then assert the wrongness of the political outcome on grounds of its (m) inefficiency is entirely to beg the question of the relative normative authority of p-preferences and m-preferences. We could define a criterion of "p-efficiency" such that x is p-efficient relative to y if and only if x more fully reflects agents' p-preferences than does y. It will then be the case that political determinations that faithfully reflect electoral preferences are p-efficient and efficient market determinations p-inefficient. Before the market result can be judged to be "better" than the political determination, it has to be established that it is m-efficiency that is the normatively crucial notion and not p-efficiency.

It may appear quite bizarre to insist that the normative authority of m-preferences, and thus of efficiency, needs to be argued rather than simply taken as self-evident. But that is precisely what is implied by the recognition of merit goods. If it makes sense to say that an item may be underconsumed at Pareto-optimal prices, there must then be a meaningful sense in which individuals' m-preferences can be "wrong," some sense in which the m-efficient outcome is undesirable. Methodological subjectivists who assert that ascriptions of value are to be explained in terms of the subjective preferences of individuals accordingly tend to give short shrift to the concept of a merit good. They will maintain that it is epistemologically unsound to posit some external vantage point from which one can ascertain that individuals "undervalue" some good. m-Efficiency, they maintain, is authoritative because it issues from the uniquely legitimate fount of values, subjective determinations of individuals.

Although we see problems in the subjectivist's epistemological stance, we shall not seek to criticize that stance here. Certainly, we concur with the subjectivist's rejection of political authoritarianism. However, doing so does not imply that the conception of merit goods is vacuous. It is not required that there be an external, omniscient evaluator who weighs consumer preferences and finds them wanting:

Rather, individuals can – and do – evaluate their own preferences. One who gets everything that one m-prefers may nevertheless wish to have quite different m-preferences. For example, a smoker may desire cigarettes, may get them in the quantity she prefers, yet urgently desire to be rid of the m-preference that gives rise to her smoking. It is genuinely open to question whether the "efficient" result, that in which the smoker's m-preferences are fully effectual, is the normatively superior result – and this not from the point of view of the surgeon general or some self-appointed "moral expert," but more importantly and more immediately, from the standpoint of the smoker herself. It requires no denial of subjectivism to conclude that the smoker may have good reason to desire that her m-preferences not be satisfied, and that such nonsatisfaction may be the normatively optimal outcome for her. In particular, she may have reason to vote for policies that will tend to frustrate and/or eliminate her desire to smoke. Should she do so, she will be revealing p-preferences that conflict with her m-preferences, but she could not be criticized for voting irrationally. And should an electorate vote along these lines, then they would generate a collective outcome through which their m-preferences would be dissatisfied. It is not obvious to us that such a result deserves to be called "perverse" or "suboptimal" even though it is, definitionally, m-inefficient.

There is an old and distinguished tradition in philosophical ethics that maintains that m-preferences are not definitive, that individuals can be mistaken in their m-preferences, know they are mistaken, and thereby express preferences that contravene their own m-preferences. Aristotle's analysis of *akrasia* stands at the heart of this tradition.[6] The morally weak man is one who discerns what the right course of action is and who prefers, at some volitional level, that this knowledge be effectual in action. Nonetheless, his m-preferences run against his beliefs concerning what is best for him, and when he comes to the point of acting he does what he believes he ought not do. St. Paul's understanding of akratic sin is similar: The sinner perceives what is good but fails to behave accordingly because of his fallen nature. "That which I would, I do not," observes Paul, in some anguish, "while that which I would not, that I do" (Romans 7:19).

Kant (1913) raises the conflict to the level of metaphysics, distinguishing in the *Groundwork* "inclination" and "reason" as two totally disjoint sources of motivation. Kant argues that any action that can appropriately be described as "moral" necessarily must be motivated by purely rational considerations (whose synthetic a priori form is that of the categorical imperative) irrespective of all tugs and pulls from inclination, those obstreperous m-preferences that constantly threaten to deflect us from our duty. Although within the Kantian theory it need not be the case that reason and inclination conflict, they typically do: And it is the task of practical reason to dissociate itself from whatever m-preferences might be impinging on the agent and through this dissociation to propel her to act for the sake of duty.

A theorist professionally closer to home for economists is Adam Smith. While in the *Wealth of Nations* Smith almost entirely confines himself to an analysis of how m-preferences work themselves out in the market, he clearly believes that

---

[6] In particular in the *Nicomachean Ethics*, bk. 7.

m-preferences are themselves subject to moral evaluation. In his *Theory of Moral Sentiments* Smith presents an account of those psychological impulses that give rise to individuals' moral judgments by reference to *sympathy* felt for motives or action by an "impartial spectator." The spectator is not some hypothesized "ideal observer" but rather the agent himself, insofar as he reflectively dissociates himself from the immediacy of his m-preferences and holds them up to scrutiny. The "man within the breast" will rule in contravention to those m-preferences that fail to prompt a sufficient degree of sympathetic harmony.

The point of this quick tour through twenty centuries of philosophical thought is to illustrate the persistence and varied exposition of the idea that preferences themselves are properly subject to evaluation, and to evaluation by the agent himself. Although the thinkers cited hardly constitute any one school, there is a common thread running through their various expositions. All agree that individuals at least sometimes do what they know or at least believe to be wrong.[7] When a man knowingly does what is wrong, he acts on the basis of a preference that he would prefer not motivate his actions. He nonetheless acts akratically because the *costs* of right action are too great. If he were a better man he would be willing to bear those costs, and were he a worse man there would be no preference counterpoised against the m-preference from which he acts. But he is morally weak, and so the costs that confront him directly at the point of action dissuade him from restraining the m-preferences that he himself judges to be disreputable. Were costs reduced or altogether eliminated, the morally weak man would act differently. The m-preferences that he would then find least costly to fulfill would be consonant with his beliefs concerning what it is best that he prefer. He would, of course, remain morally weak in the sense of not being disposed to assume moderate costs in order to act on what he believes to be best, but it will be his good fortune not to be called upon in practice to act on the disposition he lacks. He will not be "led into temptation."

Such costs are typically negligible when one is engaged in quiet reflection that will not immediately issue in action. The glutton contemplating his conduct at last night's dinner party may sincerely bemoan the fact of his taking a third serving of chocolate mousse; he retrospectively prefers that he had not done so. But to indulge such preferences the following morning is merely to give oneself over to remorse and not to give up anything sweet and delicious. Had he indulged that preference the previous evening, the opportunity cost would have been chocolate mousse forgone, a cost he evidently was unwilling to bear at the time. Now, however, he may reflectively judge that he would have been better off had that cost been paid. He will regret not only that he did not forbear from the third serving of mousse, hard as that would have been to do, but also perhaps that the forbearing was so hard. If, for example, the hostess had not offered another helping after the second, there would have been no challenge at all.

It may seem that the man who lustfully and eagerly does what he says he should not bemoans his transgression and then once again lets his passions "get the better

---

[7] The best-known denial of the proposition that individuals sometimes knowingly do what is wrong constitutes half of the so-called Socratic paradoxes.

of him'' is nothing but a hypocrite. There is, however, a crucial difference between the hypocrite and the morally weak man. The hypocrite professes allegiance to a principle to which he assigns zero (or even negative) value. He would voluntarily assume *no* cost to act on the principle and might even be willing to undergo expense in order not to act on it. The morally weak man is different. The assent he gives to the principle is sincere in that he is willing to assume *some* cost to act on it – only not as large a cost as is often required at the moment of choice. Furthermore, the cost he believes he ought to be willing to pay is not the cost that he is in fact disposed to pay. So the hypocrite is merely false, while the akratic is divided against himself. The preferences to which the weak man tries to bind himself in a cool, quiet moment are not those that motivate him when action is immediately at hand.

We shall call preferences that range over other preferences and that do not directly issue in action "reflective preferences." A distinctive feature of reflective preferences is that their expression is not costly in the way that expression of m-preferences is. Because reflective preferences do not motivate an individual to procure an outcome (and thus to forgo other outcomes), the opportunity cost of a reflectively preferred *outcome* is negligible. Reflective preferences then are not informed – or misinformed – by a lively apprehension that one will reap the benefits and costs associated with the outcome those preferences commend.

It should be immediately apparent that p-preferences share some important features with reflective preferences as here defined. In the usual case where one's vote is unlikely to be decisive, one is free to vote for the candidate, policy, or option one reflectively prefers without thereby accruing the benefits or burdens associated with the imposition of the reflectively preferred outcome. That is to say, the constraints of majoritarian voting (as contrasted with the constraints imposed by the market) seem differentially to favor the expression of reflective preferences (relative to m-preferences). Institutional structures that elicit p-preferences will thus give more play to reflective preferences than will institutions designed to elicit m-preferences.

p-Preferences are not the only avenue through which reflective preferences are revealed. The rueful lament that one did not act better, the New Year's resolution that one *will* act better – these too express reflective preferences. They differ crucially from p-preferences in that p-preferences when aggregated do produce outcomes. To the extent that political outcomes faithfully reflect p-preferences,[8] the political process will tend to provide those goods that in aggregate are highly p-preferred in larger quantities than would prevail in the market. Equally, goods that are, in aggregate, highly m-preferred and less highly p-preferred will tend to be "undersupplied" in political processes – undersupplied, that is, relative to a reference class of market allocation. It is precisely this relativity that renders it illegitimate to assume without further ado that the workings of ideal markets generate an efficient *and thus optimal* allocation. Normative economics cannot evade the necessity of evaluating the relative weight of p-preferences and m-preferences.

---

[8] Which they may not do – as when, e.g., imperfections in the rules by which votes are aggregated generate *p*-inefficiency.

Whatever institutional arrangement is advocated will differentially favor one sort of preference over the other.

It is useful at this point to define yet another set of preferences – those that the agent reflectively prefers herself to bring to bear in the arena of action. Call these "r-preferences." These are unlike reflective preferences in that they are defined over actions, not over preference orderings. And they are unlike m-preferences and p-preferences in the sense that they are not defined by reference to some institutional structure in which they are revealed. However, like m-preferences and p-preferences, they are defined over the set of actions and/or outcomes to which those actions give rise.

Economists have overwhelmingly supposed that, in the name of individual sovereignty, m-preferences ought to be decisive in the choice of alternative institutional designs. They have failed to realize that m-preferences, p-preferences, and r-preferences are conceptually distinguishable and, more to the point, will often enough fail to coincide. It follows that the concept of individual sovereignty is ambiguous. "Individual sovereignty" can mean *consumer sovereignty,* getting what one m-prefers; *political sovereignty,* getting what one p-prefers; or *reflective sovereignty,* getting what one r-prefers. When the methodological individualist bases his normative theory on the premise that institutional arrangements are to be evaluated in terms of their fit with what individuals really want, he is, we believe, on the side of the angels. But what it is that individuals want, or even what it is that individuals most want all things considered, is not, for better or worse, a simple question. What will register as a want is itself institutionally dependent; want fulfillment cannot therefore be used directly to assess the adequacy of alternative institutional arrangements. Because preferences are not identical across institutions, the task of social appraisal is hard. So too, and for much the same reason, is it hard to decline the third serving of chocolate mousse that one *knows* it would be better not to have.

Political processes and the effective provision of merit goods

Exploiting the terminology of the preceding section, merit and demerit goods are those where m-preferences and r-preferences diverge – where the agent finds himself acting in market choice in a way that he reflectively prefers that he did not act. Is there any reason to believe that in those cases where such divergence occurs, that p-preferences might be closer to r-preferences than m-preferences are? We believe so, because the cases where m- and r-preferences diverge are generally cases of weakness of the will, where the distractions of a narrow self-interest or of the immediacy of consumption options lure the actor away from the course of action she thinks she ought to take. The polling booth is a quieter venue than the market – quieter in the sense that action is divorced from outcome in a radical way. If one has reflectively judged that x is to be preferred over y, it seems reasonable to suppose that this judgment will not be abandoned when one pulls the x lever in the ballot box, while it may be overtaken when the benefits of y are immediately to hand as they are in the market. What one is likely to focus on in electoral choice is the virtue of x over y tout court – one expresses one's assessment of the value of x qua x, with little hanging on that assessment apart from the assessment itself. Whatever grounds one might have for believing that x is to be preferred *in principle* are grounds that seem likely to secure one's support in the electoral context.

We have previously characterized voters as acting *inconsequentially*. This has a derogatory ring, connoting a circumstance in which agents are free to indulge their fancies because their actions are not tempered by a lively apprehension of costs to be borne. One may, however, view voting instead as exhibiting *detachment*. The individual is able to consider his electoral decision from an overall, impersonal standpoint rather than, as is the case in the market, in terms of narrow costs and benefits redounding immediately to himself. As no consequences directly issue from the particular voting act, a long-term appraisal of the merits of contested policies will not be overwhelmed by short-run factors that the individual reflectively judges should not be determinative but that, in the market, might well be. If the hurly-burly of the market leads morally weak individuals[9] to do what they believe they ought not, then the quiet of the polling booth might well commend itself as the indicated corrective. To say this is not to make the absurd claim that voters will survey electoral possibilities with Olympian detachment and invariably vote wisely as their reflective preferences commend. Nor is it to advance the equally absurd claim that individuals in the market are routinely overcome by a myopia blinding them to an adequately comprehensive apprehension of where their best interest lies. Rather, a modest comparative proposition is being advanced concerning how imperfectly rational beings might on balance be expected to act under the constraints of different institutional settings that are themselves imperfect. The proposition is that the detachment which political procedures afford provides some reason to believe that political determinations will be more in accord with reflective preferences than will corresponding market determinations.

If individuals were, at a reflective level, fully in control of their own lower-level preferences, then there would be nothing to choose between m-preferences and r-preferences; m- and r-preferences would be identical. What one reflectively believed ought to motivate one *would* motivate one, and would do so in all circumstances calling for choice. Full harmony as a volitional being would have been achieved: One would have preferences over outcomes, prefer to have just those preferences, prefer to prefer those preferences, and so on as far up the ladder as reflective preference ascends. Such complete harmony is admirable, but unfortunately it is not a condition most of us can recognize in ourselves. A perfectly rational being will never be tempted to act other than for the best; she is what Kant calls a being with a "holy will." Because we do not partake of a holy will, success for us will often entail avoiding temptation rather than triumphing energetically over it. One acts rationally then – albeit not as a perfect (rational) being would act – in attempting to bring about circumstances such that preferences in conflict with one's reflective preferences will not be satisfied.

---

[9] A categorization that includes almost all of us to some degree.

There are two paths by way of which one can build a fence around one's reflective preferences in order that they not be contravened in practice. The first consists of internal housekeeping, building up one's strength of will so that, when temptation does arise, one will be disposed to grit one's teeth and overcome it. This is the path of character building. The ninety-nine-pound moral weakling becomes, if not a tower of strength, then perhaps a middleweight counterpuncher, capable of offering reasonable resistance to inclinations that ought to be resisted. Character building is, when achievable, perhaps the better path in that it renders one more independent of external contingencies; should external factors prove more adverse than one had hoped, there is still a good prospect of saying no to their deleterious suasion.

The second path is that of managing one's environment. One attempts to arrange circumstances so that a given supply of motivational energy will go further. That can be accomplished either through ensuring that one will not be put to the choice that one would likely get wrong, or through manipulating the cost structure of the choice situation so that one's likelihood of getting it right is increased. An example of the first kind, indeed the classic example, is that of Ulysses lashing himself to the mast in order not to become the Sirens' victim. The choice of whether or not to remain on board once the Sirens commence their haunting melody, a choice Ulysses has reason to believe he will fumble, is thereby closed off to him. This second sort of strategy is followed by the reformed alcoholic who declines to enter bars or attend cocktail parties. He reflectively prefers that he not drink, and that preference supplies him with sufficient reserves of motivational energy not to rush into liquor stores. Actually to find himself face to face with an icy martini may well raise the psychic cost of refraining from drink above the threshold at which his reflective preference is reliably effective. Alternatively, the alcoholic may endorse as truly optimal the m-preference of desiring to have one drink but not a second, while realizing that the subjective cost of declining the second drink will be much greater than that of declining the first. Therefore, given a realistic appraisal of his demand schedule after having had one drink, he adopts the total abstinence policy as most indicated for the imperfectly rational being he recognizes himself to be.

A slight variation on this theme is for an individual to raise the costs inherent in an activity in which she prefers that she not indulge. So a smoker might widely proclaim to others that she will not, after a certain date, smoke another cigarette, thereby bringing upon herself the derision of others should she backslide. This is to make a gamble with oneself. By having upped the ante, the individual will subsequently find herself worse off than the benchmark situation should her m-preferences lead her after all to lapse back into smoking, but she will be better off if her apprehension of the cost of social disapproval should prove sufficient to override the desire to smoke. Wagering with someone else concerning which of them will smoke first represents an external management strategy incorporating two distinct bets, one with the other person and one with oneself. Such examples are neither far-fetched nor uncommon; they represent a rational response on the individual's part to the fact of her imperfect rationality.[10]

---

[10] See Elster (1979, 1983) for illuminating discussion of these and related issues.

It is, therefore, not surprising that individuals may equally be rationally motivated to utilize political mechanisms toward the same end. Hobbesian social contract can be so conceived. Persons living in the state of nature prefer a life less nasty, poor, brutish, and short, so they contract with each other to forbear from aggressive incursions, subject to reciprocal forbearance from others. Such a contract is unstable because each will be tempted to violate it for temporary advantage, even though the ultimate consequence of violation will be a return to the abhorred condition whence they emerged. Selection of a sovereign is the solution to the stability problem. The standard motivational explanation given of the introduction of the Hobbesian sovereign is in terms of the desire of each person to ensure the compliance of *others;* severe penalties for noncompliance is the means to deter them from defecting. While that does indeed supply part of the motivation for establishing a sovereign, it is also the case that each individual reflectively has reason to judge that he himself ought to prefer to refrain from aggression. If he knows himself to be at all morally weak, vesting enforcement powers in the sovereign will make it more likely that he acts as he reflectively prefers to act. Note that the individual finds it relatively cost free to bind himself in solemn assembly to forbear from aggression and to cede enforcement to the sovereign. No pretty bauble beckons, inviting expropriation, while the cost of not consenting – to be thrown back into the war of all against all – vividly impresses itself on him. It is accurate then, though perhaps unconventional, to classify sovereignty, or law and order in general, as a merit good – a merit good that even the flintiest methodological subjectivist might find difficult to dismiss.

The connection to the earlier discussion of voter inconsequentiality, the other side of which is voter detachment, ought to be clear. Individuals have reason to utilize collective mechanisms to subsidize the provision of merit goods and to prohibit or raise the cost of demerit goods. It is not schizophrenic for someone both to consume some commodity (say, alcohol or pornography) when it is provided in the market and yet to vote for prohibition of that commodity, or to vote to be taxed to subsidize a product that he and others decline to purchase at Pareto-optimal prices. This rather is rational activity by someone who does not quite have his volitional house in order and who sees that appropriate political determinations might help to do the job for him. What justifies political provision to the actor is as much the reflective disapproval of his own m-preferences as it is worries about externalities in consumption of these things or solicitous concern about the "weaker brethren."

Let us consider a standard merit goods case – that of prohibition of some addictive substance (alcohol, perhaps) – in terms of our standard matrix construction. The structure of payoffs is that indicated in Table 9.1 and indicates a vote for prohibition even though the individual would, were he to believe himself to be decisive, opt against.

The representation looks familiar; it is indeed *formally* equivalent to the prisoners' dilemma interaction originally introduced in Chapter 3. There is, however, a crucial difference in interpretation. Emergence of a voter's dilemma gives rise to regret on the part of citizen-voters that the less desired outcome was victorious (though not regret from any individual concerning the direction in which he cast his own ballot). Each has reason after the fact to regard the voter's dilemma as an in-

Table 9.1. *The prohibitionist's calculus*

	All others		
Each	Majority for prohibition	Majority against prohibition	Tie probability $(p \to 0)$
Vote for prohibition	5	105	5
Vote against prohibition	0	100	100

stance of political failure and reason before the fact to resist the introduction of collective determinations that issue in such an outcome. But he who reflectively prefers that he not drink but who finds his m-preferences pressing Demon Rum upon him will have reason to regard the outcome whose payoff determinants are sketched in Table 9.1 as a substantive *success*. What weakness of character imperils, collective decision procedures have made secure. Voters have succeeded in disowning their recalcitrant m-preferences and in doing so have achieved what they reflectively prefer.

The formal indistinguishability of political provision of merit goods from the voter's dilemma reveals that the badness of the latter is not something that can just be read off the numbers, that it is not a consequence of the behavioral logic of the matrix. Those numbers reflect the voter's m-preferences; and those in the final column predict how the agent would behave *were he decisive*. But they do not show how the agent would prefer that he behaved. The normative force of the voter's dilemma presupposes the premise: m-preferences are normatively authoritative. Should that premise be withheld in a particular case, should its contrary instead be affirmed, then what has the form of a voter's dilemma becomes benign from the point of view of the voters themselves. They are coerced by the agency of the state to refrain from that which they m-prefer, but they desire at the level of reflective preference to be coerced. Although the prohibition ordinance is paternalistic, it is a paternalism exercised by and on the same set of individuals. It is, in a word, self-paternalistic.

We do not mean to imply that when an individual votes for the provision of a merit good or the prohibition of a demerit good she is to be conceptualized as deliberately acting to bring about the policy for which she votes. In this case, no more than in any other, should voting be conceived of as an outcome-instrumental performance. When the individual votes for the provision of a merit good, she is to be deemed as expressing support for it rather than as acting with the intention to bring about its political provision. The p-preference expressively revealed is opposed to the agent's m-preference, but because voting affords inconsequentiality/detachment, the p-preference is more congruent with the individual's r-preference. Should a majority of voters exhibit a similar preference structure, the merit good will be provided though no one acts with the intention of procuring it. The invisible hand can be seen at work here, not angling to achieve efficiency – the merit goods outcome is definitionally "m-inefficient" – but to give effect to those sentiments of which the impartial spectator approves.

Politics as the midwife of reflective preferability: a critique

In the preceding section it was shown that merit goods considerations afford a prima facie argument for the utilization of political mechanisms in place of market determinations. Individuals may reflectively disprefer their own m-preferences and believe that the p-preferences they and others express in the voting booth give a better fit with reflective preference, so there will be a self-paternalistic justification for removing certain choices from the market and placing them in an institutional setting in which p-preferences are determinative. That is not, however, to be taken as an unreserved endorsement of collectivized choice. There is a case to be made *against* the political provision of merit goods, and that case is what we undertake to explore in this section.

Even were it the case that p-preferences mirrored reflective preference with the utmost faithfulness, there would be no guarantee that political processes would generate p-preferred outcomes. There may be a slip between cup and lip lying in the imperfections inherent in the majoritarian aggregation rule. But, in addition, the antecedent clause of the conditional is false; p-preferences do not necessarily mirror reflective preferences and may radically diverge from them. As has been noted in previous chapters, separation of costs from choice in the polling booth can lead one to vote more *immorally* than one would act in an analogous market setting. We can now extend that proposition: Individuals may be induced to vote in a direction that *they themselves believe to be immoral* and of which they *reflectively disapprove*. Consider the case of someone prejudiced against blacks, aware of his own prejudice, and disturbed by it. At a reflective level he judges racism to be evil and disowns the racist impulses he finds within himself, but he lacks the power entirely to rid himself of his prejudice. In his market behavior, the individual will generally avoid acting from his racist inclination because such action tends to be costly: To forgo working with, selling to, or employing blacks is to forgo the economic benefit that these transactions would afford. To publicly express disdain for blacks is to incur costly social disapproval from those who find the sentiments offensive. But once inside the voting booth, anonymity reigns, expression is virtually costless in terms of economic opportunity forgone; and so the expression of a bigoted p-preference is unconstrained by external factors and restricted only by the individual's own reflective judgment, which may prove insufficient for the task. In this case the costs inherent in market behavior *reinforce* adherence to what one reflectively prefers, while it is the shedding of costs that conduces to weakness of will.

That politicizing the decision presents this other aspect is exactly what one would be led to expect from earlier arguments; if voting behavior tends to give effect to expressive *extremes*, both moral and immoral, then it can either reinforce or undermine reflective preference. This is to assume – perhaps too charitably – that reflective preferences by and large deserve the designation "moral." The assumption is not crucial to the argument; whatever the nature of an individual's reflective preferences, voting will tend to generate extremes relative to those preferences. Merit goods will win electoral approval but so too will demerit goods, and both in greater quantities than would be provided on the market. Given this double-edged result, those who are risk averse may have reason to prefer (reflectively) the decentralization of decision making.

There is then a prima facie case against employing the political mechanism on the grounds that it will provide merit goods, and it is symmetrical to the prima facie case for employing political mechanisms. The two need not balance out. Suppose that we were able to determine that certain sorts of voting determinations were much more likely to generate merit goods than demerit goods, while others were much more likely to generate demerit goods than merit goods. What would be called for then would not be to depoliticize all determinations to the greatest extent possible, but rather to use political mechanisms for the former sort and to avoid them for the latter. This may be part of what is accomplished by recognizing in individuals certain *rights* that act as side constraints on what politics may undertake through majoritarian decisions. The suggestion appeals, but absent any well-worked-out theory combining merit goods considerations with rights considerations, it remains highly speculative. We are not aware of any such well-worked theory, and we believe that the onus properly rests on the proponent of publc provision in merit goods cases to exhibit the connection if indeed it does exist. More generally, the onus is on the proponent to develop a taxonomy of voting determinations in which principles are specified for separating merit goods–conducive issues from demerit goods–conducive issues.

For the sake of argument let us grant that weakness of will more frequently arises in the market than in the polling booth (either because the market just is more conducive to *akrasia* or because a filtering mechanism has been devised to keep determinations that are threatening to reflective preference out of the political arena). There would still be a strong case for leaving decisions to the market, even though we know that individuals would thereby go wrong more often. Weakness of will need not be entirely a negative phenomenon; its brighter side is that individuals can *learn* from their akratic lapses so as to do better next time. The market is conducive to learning. She who goes against her own reflective preference subsequently incurs the cost of that preference unsatisfied and will be in a position to realize that the cost was self-inflicted. When she is subsequently faced with a similar choice, she may, in virtue of the previous costly experience, stand a better chance of resisting deflection by peripheral considerations so as to get things right this time. We do not, here, make the incredible claim that market transactions always penalize the foolish and reward the wise, or that the operative conditioning imposed by the market invariably succeeds in transforming dull consumers into clever ones; in both of these respects there doubtlessly are numerous "market failures" to be noted. What we observe is not a surefire palliative for error, but simply a *tendency* inherent in choice settings in which agents have to live with the consequences of their actions to bring about the correction of mistakes.

While the market conduces to learning by concentrating the costs of mistakes on those who make them, politics diffuses costs and thereby encourages the perpetuation of ignorance. If I hire a plumber because his wavy hair and broad grin are attractive, or because he speaks in pleasing generalities about the attractions of unobstructed pipes, I shall subsequently be led to reflect seriously on whether these are the prime requisites for choiceworthy plumbers when my sink backs up and my toilets overflow. Next time I might pass up the handsome and articulate fellow for one who really knows his way around valves and joints. But if I vote for a politician who looks like – and perhaps once was – a movie idol or who is possessed of a mellifluous voice and an endless stock of bromides for all occasions, I shall never be presented with the necessity of reevaluating my principles of political selection. My vote has generated no outcome and even if similarly ill-informed votes did, in aggregate, elect a candidate of distinctly inappropriate qualifications, the costs thereby imposed are spread out over the entire citizenry rather than falling with distinctness on those who had voted with the reflective awareness of a kitten at play. The point is that while a p-preference may more accurately represent reflective preference already in place than does the corresponding m-preference, market processes are a far better *generator* of useful reflective preferences than are political processes. The argument for supplying merit goods through voting has its greatest appeal when presented as a purely ceteris paribus proposition; the dynamics of preference formation–dissolution and reinforcement–weakening lend strong support to the privatization of choice.

To recognize the importance of reflective preference as enhancing the abilities of individuals to comport themselves rationally is not to conclude that reflection serves equally well in all kinds of circumstances. In particular, it will usually be the case that individuals will reflect more attentively and intensely if much is riding on what will motivate them when they are called to act. When their own actions are likely to make no appreciable difference to what befalls them and others, reflection is apt to be perfunctory, if it is carried out at all. We take to heart (a variant of) Dr. Johnson's observation that the prospect of being hanged on the morrow wonderfully concentrates the mind. The prospect of acting decisively on the morrow for good or ill *also* concentrates one's mind wonderfully, and such decisiveness is omnipresent in the market but absent in the polling booth. In saying this we do not assume the role of the external evaluator urging individuals to get their motivational house into order; rather, we maintain that individuals themselves realize that they reflect more wisely over issues that they believe to be laden with portentous consequences and so have reason reflectively to judge – at a metalevel – that the trustworthiness of their r-preferences varies directly with the consequentiality with which they are imbued. If that is so, then they have reason to favor institutions that elicit reflective preferences by passing them through a "concentrated mind." Private activity provides such concentration far more reliably than does collective choice. Ulysses' reflections are more sharply focused than would have been the case had he been one of many Achaeans voting on a Siren-avoidance policy for public consumption. Sometimes the other side of inconsequentiality is detachment, but sometimes it is just plain inconsequentiality. The difference will largely lie in how direct the connection is between one's reflections in a cool, quiet moment and what will follow from one's activity when the chips are down.

A related consideration is that it will often be the case that one is not well situated to plan in advance of action how one should respond to eventualities that will then present themselves. Not all the facts will be known at an earlier stage, and thus reflective prescription of a determinate line of conduct will amount to an inadequate arbitration. Before going to the dinner party, the overindulgent diner may well know enough from prior experience the relevant costs and benefits of helping himself to a third serving of chocolate mousse and therefore will have sufficient reason to act in advance of the moment of decision to raise his propensity to decline that offer. Should he instead rely on his spontaneous judgment at the time to see him through, he will come to rue the excess calories added to his bulk. But to plan out in advance a strategy for dinner table conversation will be less useful, even if reflective preferences are entertained for some conversational lines over others. Because the invitee does not yet know what direction the interchange among the guests will take, he is ill-prepared to commit himself to a prescribed sequence of remarks. Guests who come to dinner knowing full well how they would like to steer the conversation and determined to do so are tedious. Relaxed spontaneity, following the conversation wheresoever it may lead, is apt to make for a better gathering, and because this is the case one does better to eschew predetermined strategies. The reflective preference then is to allow preferences over outcomes to emerge as they will. One may, of course, have reason not to adopt a policy of total spontaneity. If it is known that Mr. X regularly introduces religious pronouncements at which Mrs. Y takes offense, then it may be worthwhile to decide in advance to intercept Mr. X's declaration on the Pope's recent trip to South America with remarks about one's own holiday in Buenos Aires. The point is that sometimes one does well reflectively to anticipate future choices and sometimes one does not. We intend no general directives for dinner party success, a topic on which we plead lack of expertise.

All precommitment via reflective preference confronts the danger of judging from insufficient information. The magnitude of this danger will not be the same in all cases: The glutton or alcoholic fighting against his weakness of will can be virtually certain that no new fact will arise indicating that his interests will best be served by consuming the mousse or martini. Ulysses has excellent reason to believe that swimming after the Sirens will be disastrous for him, but it is *just possible* that the experience of actually hearing their magnificent melody would provide data indicating that the truly best course for him would be to swim to them after all. It is *risky* to bind oneself such that m-preferences cannot be translated into action when further information comes to hand, though it may well be the *lesser risk*.

The conclusion to be drawn is not that utilizing p-preferences to overrule m-preferences is never indicated, but that an inevitable cost of doing so is diminished flexibility in responding to new information. Within the market, agents can adjust to information as it presents itself; shifts in supply and demand schedules are directly reflected in relative prices. By contrast, political provision of merit goods involves a studied disregard of revealed m-preferences based on the reflective judgment that they mislead. However, by distancing oneself from *deceptive* m-preferences one also cuts oneself off from all the information that prompts them, information that may prove to be crucial in formulating a truly optimal course of activity. It is, therefore, a double-edged strategy. Judgments about which goods are merit goods are, when translated into political prescriptions, rendered less amenable to revision that further experience might call for.

Finally, it must be recognized that the term "self-paternalism" is, when applied to political determinations, always in part a misnomer. Individuals differ amongst themselves in their preferences over outcomes and also in their reflective preferences. We have employed stylized examples in which the assumption of a homogeneous electorate served to illustrate in an uncomplicated way the emergence of voter's dilemmas and the provision of merit goods through electoral processes. But electorates as we find them are decidedly nonhomogeneous. One man's merit good is another man's detested imposition of coercive authority. It is one thing to act in a private capacity to limit the range of one's own future choices, quite another to invoke the mechanisms of the state to restrict the choices of all, including those whose reflective preferences run counter to one's own. The former is consistent with liberal insistence that each person be afforded the liberty to direct her own activity according to her own lights while the latter is antithetical to it. Moreover, even if reflective preferences are homogeneous, political provision of merit goods in order to counter *akrasia* is likely to involve a forcible redistribution away from the morally continent toward the morally weak. What normative principle can be invoked to validate this redistributive practice? None comes readily to mind. Intuitively, it seems morally dubious to penalize the virtuous for the sake of the less virtuous. The costs of moral weakness are thereby socialized so that they do not fall on those who lack proper self-control but instead impinge on their neighbors who may be quite capable of controlling their own m-preferences and would prefer to do so themselves – either because they subscribe to a different standard of the good or for other reasons. Calvin's Geneva may have offered a structure of control reassuring the faithful that their abhorred propensity to backslide would be countered and chastened, but the "gifts" it extended to those outside the Calvinist fold were not quite so eagerly embraced.

In practice then, self-paternalism through political means devolves to paternalistic control exercised by a majority over themselves *and others*. It therefore does indeed run afoul of Mill's strictures in *On Liberty* concerning the domain within which the state may justifiably restrict the liberties of its mature citizens, *pace* the defense of political provision of merit goods advanced in the preceding section. Self-paternalism is not a benign instance of paternalism when its subject and object do not coincide. This conclusion does not, of course, rest on appeal to the authority of Mill; it is implicit in almost every recognizable version of liberalism. Coercive production and consumption of merit goods violates, we might say, the (liberal) *right* of dissenters to act on their own projects. Or, to employ Kantian language, to impose "merit goods" on those who reject that appellation is to treat them as mere means to the ends of the dominant majority rather than as ends in themselves. It is not possible in this compass to argue the case for liberal constraints on collective activity,[11] but we note that those constraints oppose the correction of exigencies of private choice through public means. Just as there exists a tradition commending the intrapersonal authority of reflective preference, so too does there exist a tradition that rejects the authority of one man's reflective preference over another.

Earlier in the chapter we contended that a necessary prerequisite in making institutional comparisons is a prior decision as to whether it is political preferences or market preferences that should be decisive; one may not simply assume that it is market preferences that are normatively authoritative. Accordingly, the preceding section was addressed to constructing as strong a case as can be made for the primacy of p-preferences in those cases where m-preferences and r-preferences diverge. Although that case is not inconsiderable, there is a great deal to be said on the other side. Certainly, we do not want to be seen as arguing that wherever m-preferences and p-preferences diverge, there is any kind of automatic presumption that p-preferences will be reflectively superior. It is one thing to argue that where m-preferences and r-preferences diverge, electoral processes may be a useful technology for securing outcomes that are r-preferred. It is another entirely to argue that p-preferences are likely to be reflectively preferred when we have no grounds for thinking m-preferences defective. As we have emphasized, p-preferences may – and in many cases will – diverge from m-preferences for reasons that provide no grounds for anxiety about the reflective status of market preference. That is exactly what the voter's dilemma in its simple face-value interpretation shows.

Moreover, it needs to be emphasized that markets themselves provide technologies for assisting agents to refrain from doing things they reflectively prefer not to do and, obversely, to cultivate a capacity to do things they reflectively want to. Health spas, diet clinics, give-up-smoking programs, cultural education institutions – these are all available on a decentralized, voluntary basis. There clearly is a demand for the services of such institutions/programs, and the market can apparently meet that demand in part. Perhaps in some cases political processes can fulfill those demands more extensively or more efficiently. But that is about as much as can reasonably be claimed – in some cases, perhaps.

Merit goods and public goods

Whatever its justification – or lack of same – we can expect that citizens in a democracy *will* vote for the provision of merit goods in appreciable quantities. Their doing so does not presuppose any sophisticated appraisal on their part of their own preferences and metapreferences; no more is required than the snap judgment "There ought to be more of x" and the transformation of that judgment into a vote.

It is essentially irrelevant in making that snap judgment whether or not x exhibits elements of publicness, or at least that is a matter that does not contribute *directly* to political viability. Of course, the judgment that there should be more x will reflect perceptions as to whether market provision is "adequate," and in that sense

---

[11] For such an argument, see Lomasky (1987).

the presence of significant market failure will tend to support political provision. It may perhaps be that this is what Musgrave had in mind when he suggested (1959, p. 13) that many merit goods have publicness dimensions, and vice versa. However, analytically speaking, the decision-theoretic structure of publicness and electoral support are quite distinct.

In order to draw the public good/merit good distinction more clearly, it may be useful to make appeal to a couple of strategic examples. The two examples we shall choose are first, the so-called greenhouse effects of carbon dioxide and methane emissions on world climate; and second, additions to the stock of knowledge via research. These examples are strategic because they are ones that clearly involve significant publicness in the Samuelsonian sense. We want to ask whether that publicness can explain government provision.

One of the notable features of recent political developments is the greening of political ideologies. Single-issue proenvironmental parties have sprung up throughout the Western democracies. The public economist will be tempted to identify such political pressure as consistent with recognition of the environment as a classic "public good" of the Samuelsonian kind. And this description is surely valid: We simply confront in modern environmental problems the familiar Pigovian factory–laundry interaction writ large. Yet it is a mistake to see the political provision of environmental policies as primarily explicable in public goods terms, because in many instances the public good being provided is a truly global one. This is so, specifically, in the case of the greenhouse effect generously associated with increasing carbon dioxide and methane concentrations in the atmosphere (currently a significant preoccupation for environmental prophets of all types). Let us presume for the purposes of the present argument that there is global warming going on, that the global warming is attributable to increased greenhouse-gas emissions, and that the net effects of such global warming are undesirable – all points that might conceivably be contested. It then follows that policies to reduce greenhouse-gas emissions, a Pigovian tax on CO_2 emissions perhaps, will be globally desirable. The greenhouse effect has, in this sense, been rightly described as a "global commons" problem (a clear reference to Garrett Hardin's famous "tragedy"). The emphasis in such a description is usually on the commons aspect. But here we focus on the global dimension. Precisely because the problem is global, it is not in any one nation's interests to do anything about it *unilaterally:* Each nation rationally free-rides on the others, just as individuals are presumed to do in all public goods cases. The nation state is by definition not a sufficiently large entity fully to internalize global externalities. To claim that it is rational for any one nation to impose, say, a Pigovian tax on its CO_2 emissions (for greenhouse reasons) is to deny the plausibility of the *n*-person prisoners' dilemma that underlies the case for any market failure at all. Yet no such niceties seem to concern the "greenies." Purely national political movements, dedicated to globally environmentally sound policies imposed purely at the national level, are now familiar. The electoral success of these movements cannot be rationalized in public goods terms: The policies are not to be seen as complex exchanges among citizens to secure mutually agreeable modifications in polluting behavior, because at the purely national level such modifications will generally impose more costs than benefits. For Australia, for example, to impose taxes sufficient to reduce CO_2 emissions by 50% would involve enormous costs on the citizenry without securing any noticeable change either in total CO_2 concentrations in the atmosphere or in any resultant greenhouse effect. And this is true for a significant range of environmental problems. In our view, environmentalism is to be seen primarily as a kind of religion, whose political expression simply demands its instantiation. And policies implemented as a result of environmental politics are to be seen as properly appealing to the merit goods, not the public goods, category.

A similar argument can be made in connection with additions to the stock of knowledge of a broad, conceptual kind. A specific case that might perhaps spring to mind is that of research into the theory of electoral preference. Economists often remark that such research exhibits important publicness characteristics – Newton and Einstein, for example, do not and cannot fully appropriate the benefits of their discoveries. [12] But in the case of "pure" research in which the publicness characteristics are most clear, the benefits are global not national. Any polity aiming to maximize national interests would simply free-ride on other nations' research findings. Of course, (global) utilitarians (and research scientists) would want to insist that national provision remains desirable, but only from a global viewpoint. If we assign *explanatory* power to the public goods concept – that is, if we try to explain government provision of such research in terms of public goods considerations – then we run afoul of an obvious paradox. Either individuals are altruistic, in which case we do not need governments to provide public goods, or they are not, in which case national polities will not unilaterally provide research funding. The resolution of this paradox involves jettisoning any significant explanatory role for the public goods concept in political processes. In our view, political process gives rise to research funding because research is a merit good – one that citizens regard as a "good thing" in itself and that engages thereby expressive support at the ballot box.

And so, in our view more generally, the degree to which public goods are supplied will largely be a function of the extent to which they have merit goods characteristics. There is some irony to this conclusion: The literature of public finance is much taken up with discussions of public goods but displays only the mildest interest in analyzing the merit goods concept. If our argument is correct, however, this is a case of the tail wagging the dog; merit goods much more than public goods show up on the political bottom line.

Merit goods and public provision

It is, at this point, important to emphasize that even where circumstances seem maximally congenial to the political provision of merit goods, the market outcome may yet be reflectively preferred to the political outcome by all individuals. Sup-

---

[12] An observation that is not sufficient to provide grounds for public subsidy, since human curiosity may generate enough such research *without* public intervention: The relevant externalities may be almost entirely "inframarginal," to use the appropriate jargon.

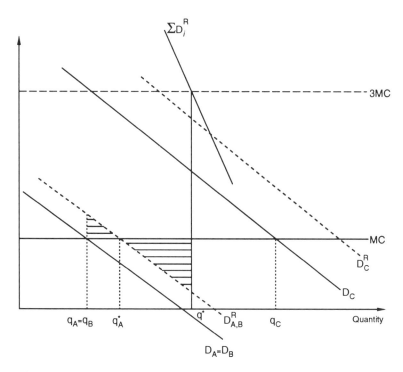

Figure 9.1

pose, for example, that the concept of a merit good is well-defined, p-preferences unerringly coincide with reflective preferences, and the good is a merit good for *all* individuals, in the sense that each recognizes on reflection that he himself consumes too little of it in the market. Specifically, consider the simple three-person example depicted in Figure 9.1. The three persons (groups) we designate as A, B, and C, and we shall for diagrammatic simplicity take A and B to be identical. The merit good we denote as X. The ordinary market demand curves for X are D_A, D_B, and D_C, and the consumption levels of X for the three individuals q_A, q_B, and q_C, under conditions of perfect competition. The reflective preferences for X, however, generate demands denoted by D_A^R, D_B^R, and D_C^R, with the corresponding reflectively preferred levels of consumption q_A^*, q_B^*, q_C^*. All persons believe that they "should" consume more of X than they do. Hence, X is a merit good, both in aggregate and for each individual separately. Suppose the political outcome that emerges reflects the Samuelsonian conditions for the reflectively preferred demand curves, D_i^R: This outcome is, in a straightforward sense, the reflectively preferred political ideal and occurs at q^*, where the vertical sum of the D_i^R cuts the line $3MC$ ($3MC$ because the political mechanism provides, by assumption, equal amounts of X to each individual). But note that q^* is reflectively worse for all individuals than the market arrangement: C gets less X than she would buy under market provision; and A and B get so much more that they would *reflectively* prefer that they would be *reflectively* better off at the market equilibrium (i.e., in Figure 9.1, the striped area below $D_{A,B}^R$ to the left of q_A^* is less than the striped area to the right). This result occurs because of the *technology* of public provision. The political outcome, though based on arguably superior preferences, is not, by reference to those preferences, superior to the outcome under decentralized markets.

This somewhat perverse result arises because the political arrangement is taken to impose uniformity of consumption. This uniformity is a common feature where the good is subject to both government production and allocation. However, alternative and probably preferable policy technologies for merit goods provision are available. In this case, for example, a Pigovian subsidy placed on consumption of X at some appropriate rate would at least ensure that all consumption levels moved in the right direction. More generally, however, X may be a merit good for some but not others – and the simple expedient of subsidizing rather than direct provision will not necessarily improve matters. Indeed, in the merit goods case there does seem to be some a priori justification for direct provision – for there is some presumption that the *largest* increase in consumption is appropriate for those consumers whose market consumption is least. Obversely, in the case of demerit goods it seems likely that the highest reflective preference for reduced consumption will be among those whose market consumption is highest. Uniform consumption ensures that outcome.

Conclusion

There is much more that could be said about the way in which merit goods considerations – and those that possess a similitude of merit goods but are not the bona fide article – play themselves out in the political arena. It is our hope that theorists will turn to such investigations. Heretofore, the dominant tendency within the public economics literature has been to downplay the importance of the merit goods concept. Either the concept has been considered semantically empty (following McLure) or institutionally irrelevant (following Head). In the latter case, the thought has been that even where consumer preferences can be meaningfully identified as wrong, there is no likelihood that political processes will correct such errors of preference.

We have disputed both those claims. That m-preferences can meaningfully be said to be mistaken is consistent with methodological subjectivism concerning values. And because voting strips away costs that, in the market, conduce toward *akrasia*, electoral processes can generate merit goods and often will do so. However, electoral processes can also generate spectacularly nonmeritorious outcomes. The argument presented in this chapter is not to be construed as a general justification for electoral decision making per se. But it can be interpreted as establishing the institutional relevance of merit goods and the logical necessity of taking account of merit goods arguments in any relevant comparison of possible institutional arrangements.

10 Toward a democratic morality

A phenomenon noticeable throughout history regardless of place or period is the pursuit by governments of policies contrary to their own interests. Mankind, it seems, makes a poorer performance of government than of almost any other human activity. In this sphere, wisdom — which may be defined as the exercise of judgment acting on experience, common sense and available information — is less operative and more frustrated than it should be. Why do holders of high office so often act contrary to the way reason points and enlightened self-interest suggests? Why does intelligent mental process seem so often not to function?

Barbara Tuchman, The March of Folly

By the people?

Democracy, so the popular maxim assures us, is government of the people, *by* the people, *for* the people — and it is unique among political regimes in being so. In this chapter we seek to interrogate that species of democratic piety. To be more precise, we shall question two-thirds of it. That democracy is government of the people is hardly to be denied. But this is not what makes democracy unique: All functioning political regimes govern "the people." It is rather democracy's status as rule *by* the people and *for* the people that is the distinctive core of the democrat's faith.

The two elements — the by-ness and for-ness — are not unrelated. Although government for the people by a beneficent elite is a conceptual possibility, it is a highly improbable one. Elites cannot be relied on to pursue individuals' interests with anything like the consistency or intensity that the individuals themselves regularly do: Benevolent despots are considerably more likely to remain despotic than benevolent. Moreover, effective benevolence requires that one determine what genuinely constitutes the interests of others, and such judgments are deeply problematic.[1] Even if the decision maker is sincerely motivated to pursue the good of others, identification of that good, almost inescapably, will be colored by his own views as to human flourishing. Accordingly, so the argument goes, government for the people enjoys some decent likelihood if government is by the people, and it is wildly unlikely otherwise.

The formulation of an appropriate morality of democracy begins, therefore, on the more or less straightforwardly consequentialist grounds that people tend to fare better in democratic regimes than they do under alternative political structures. The by-ness of democracy possesses instrumental value insofar as it promotes for-ness. If, as Tuchman argues, the history of political rule is a march of follies, then

---

[1] The difficulty of such judgments has been an important theme in the Austrian discussion of the feasibility of "socialist calculation." For a recent relevant statement, see Hayek (1988).

democracy is to be endorsed insofar as it breaks step. For two reasons, though, that is too slender a reed on which to construct a robust democratic faith. First, while democracies may slow down folly's march, sometimes they rush pell-mell along it. To wit, Tuchman's rendition of the American experience in Vietnam, public choice's lengthy catalog of the woes of collective decision making, and, indeed, the additions to that dispiriting catalog broached in the preceding chapters. Democratic procedures neither reliably elicit citizens' preferences over outcomes nor rationally aggregate the results of balloting. That other regimes typically do even worse may be true, but that observation hardly fires the imagination.

That democracy does have a capacity to fire the imagination, that individuals have been observed willing to fight and die under its banner, suggests the second deficiency of a purely instrumental account. Governance by the people is valued not only because it conduces to social welfare, but also because it is an intrinsic good. It matters to a person not only how well things go, but also who it is that is making them go. One might, for example, be convinced that arranged marriages are likely to enjoy more long-term success than those contracted independently and yet prefer a system in which people choose their own mates. "It's *my* marriage" may not only be a report of who the wedded party is to be, but an insistence on an entitlement to tend to the arranging oneself. Similarly, a colonial people may wish to strike out for independence even if the rule of the imperial government has been more efficient and fair minded than the indigenous alternative promises to be. On both the personal and political level we value self-determination, and not simply because we are convinced that we shall choose better for ourselves than others will do on our behalf. The capacity to make one's own mistakes may be a valued component of autonomy irrespective of any judgment as to whether some other person or group will make decisions for one that are less "mistaken" than one's own. To be treated as a cloistered minor is demeaning to one who has morally come of age.

It is, therefore, a central element of the democratic brief that the people genuinely have the status of responsible political actors if and only if they are self-governing. Accordingly, should the coherence of government by the people be at risk, then the notion of political responsibility will have to be rethought, and with it much in the lexicon of democratic civic morality: How should I vote? Should I vote at all? Why? And so on. And, as we shall argue, if the construction of a democratic civic morality is problematic, so is much that passes for justification of democratic institutions.

It is helpful to a normative analysis of the practice of democracy to distinguish between democratic "macroethics" and democratic "microethics." The former embraces questions of global institutional design: Are decisions of such and such kind to be made collectively or through decentralized individual choice? If collectively, are determinations to be made democratically or via some other procedure? If democratically, what should the voting rules be, and should they be constrained or unconstrained (e.g., by judicial review)? Who will be permitted/required to participate in elections? And so on. Microethical questions concern the performances of individual voters: Should I vote? If I do vote, how should I determine the direction of my ballot? How much investment should I make in securing political information? And so on.

In this chapter, we want to refocus the argument of the foregoing chapters on microethical issues specifically. The linchpin of the analysis is the concept of political responsibility, the alleged by-ness of democratic procedures. We shall argue in the upcoming section that that concept, as normally construed, is highly dubious. We thereafter ask whether the idea of democracy being for the people might nevertheless be rescued to some extent, and what would be required to make any such rescue operation successful. The following section constitutes the bulk of this chapter and is where we consider whether and how one might construct a civic morality that coherently engages individuals on the level of their particular voting performances. We argue that an expressively based understanding of voting not only does service as a positive theory of electoral phenomena, but also affords the most plausible grounding of democratic microethics that can be constructed. The final section builds on these results to show how one can effect a transition from judgments of individual voter responsibility to the global macroethical concern that democratic governance be reliably for the people. That, in turn, prepares the way for the book's final chapter in which we turn to macroethical democratic policy making.

The dubious status of "collective self-determination"

The proposition that democracy is government by the people and thus for the people depends, in its naive version, on a picture of democratic action as individual choice writ large. The intuition is that just as an individual chooses among options to produce intended results in the private arena, so all individuals, acting in concert, choose among social outcomes via explicit collective decision-making processes. When an individual chooses the maximally preferred set of achievable outcomes from among the alternatives open to her, she thereby acts rationally. Similarly, collective choice is rational insofar as "society" has evaluated alternatives and chooses from them those deemed best. This organic conception of society currently enjoys much less currency than it once did – an eclipse we applaud. Within the rational actor tradition with which we associate our own work, the organicist view embodies a gross conceptual confusion. As countless examples of the prisoners' dilemma attest, the processes through which individual actions are translated into social outcomes are complex and sometimes perverse. Any theory that treats social aggregates as choosing entities, much like individuals, sweeps away many of the most interesting intellectual questions in social analysis and many of the most pressing practical problems in social policy design.

Consider the simple analogy of the littered beach. The litter arises as a result of human action – we can plausibly say that the beach is littered *by* the people. But there can be no suggestion that the litter arises as a result of users' careful computations of alternative states of the beach and that the litter is there because the people prefer it. While there may be a natural presumption that a choice made by an individual is for that individual, no such presumption applies in the collective case. Even if there is an intelligible sense in which beach litter is by the people, that sense does not legitimate the inference that a littered beach is their preferred outcome, that it is expressive of their will – that the outcome brought about by the people is, therefore, *for* the people. Because the littered beach is not in any meaningful sense collectively *chosen* (or, for that matter, chosen by any one of the individual litterers), the sense in which the litter is by the people must be quite different from that involved in the individual case. Individual and collective choice are sharply disanalogous in this respect.

The robustness or lack of same of such analogies would matter little in practice if we could be sure that democratic procedures ruled out prisoners' dilemma problems. But this is what needs to be proved. And, of course, both public choice orthodoxy and the alternative theory developed in the preceding chapters emphasize the relevance of prisoners' dilemma problems to majoritarian decision-making procedures. Public choice orthodoxy focuses on the problems of revolving coalitions and political instability; our alternative emphasizes the disproportionate influence of expressive considerations at the ballot box. In the development of our central propositions in Chapter 2, we took particular care to stress the underlying prisoners' dilemma potential of the collective decision-making problem. Because of that potential, the fact that government is by the people does not necessarily mean that it is for the people – and we would expect that in a significant number of cases it will not be. The alleged connection between by-ness and for-ness, the fulcrum of the democratic faith, is severed.

A yet deeper question needs to be broached. Is there any significant sense in which democracy constitutes government by the people? It may seem that this must be so. In a democracy political outcomes do not merely *happen* but rather are the product – even if not a collectively chosen product – of the various voting acts of the citizenry. It is through their agency, and not some other thing, that outcomes are determined, and since they are, taken together, "the people," democratic governance – whatever its deviations from a hypothesized social welfare optimum – is government by them.

The conclusion is too quick, at least if there is to remain any link whatsoever between government by the people and citizens' political responsibility. To see that that is so, consider the following "electoral" setting. As with our elections, every two or four or some other number of years voters march to the polls and select levers to pull. As with our elections, the quantity of pulls determines the success of one of the standing candidates/policies/parties. Unlike the running of our elections, however, these levers are unmarked. No voter knows which lever-pulling action supports which candidate. Nonetheless, levers get pulled, totals cumulated, winners determined, and policies enacted. Do we have here an instance of government by the people?

Well, one could choose to *call* it such. But this is very cheap talk indeed. Clearly it is talk too impoverished to support any imputation of moral responsibility for what has been brought about "by" the voters. Government by unmarked levers is government by lottery. As with other (fair) lottery forms, it induces no attempt on the part of candidates to secure support. And voters will have no reason to pull one lever rather than another – or at least no reason connected with an intention to secure a particular political outcome. The role of levers is purely causal. But by-ness in this attenuated sense is palpably insufficient to sustain an argument that governance in a democracy is something that the people do, that it is something for which they bear moral responsibility (and not just causal responsibility in the way a lightning strike is causally responsible for the felling of the tree). If democratic governance is to be an activity of the people, we need not merely causation but also, at a minimum, *intent*. There lies the democrat's problem. In elections where the numbers are even modestly large, the political outcome is, for each and every voter, essentially incidental to his action – and that is so whether or not the levers are identified. That is, what presents itself for the voter's choice is not the political outcome, and any voter who believes otherwise must be deluded. One who intends through his vote to bring about the election of candidate X is on all fours with someone who steps on a crack with the intention thereby of breaking his grandmother's back. Irrespective of what they may believe they are doing, they are in fact not acting intentionally to secure favored outcomes. Each is in need of a patient course of instruction in the workings of the causal order. Conversely, undeluded X-voters are doing something other than intentionally choosing political outcomes. And when a large number of persons all engaged in doing something *else* produce as an incidental byproduct of their action a particular state of affairs, then the insinuation that this state of affairs is, in some meaningful sense, expressive of their *will* must be regarded as highly suspect.

We do not mean by this observation to imply that any state of affairs so generated will necessarily be the worse for being undesigned. It has been a familiar theme in political economy since Mandeville and Smith that benign outcomes may be produced by invisible hand mechanisms rather than via deliberate construction. Whether a possible invisible hand lurks nearby in this case is, however, a quite complex matter – as far as we know unargued in the literature on democracy, or at least unargued in any explicit way. Some such argument would, however, seem to be crucial to any reasoned defense of democracy, and so it is to that argument we now turn.

Quasi-invisible hands and public-interested voting

The most familiar picture of the operation of invisible hand institutions is that offered by Smith in his description of well-ordered markets, nowadays thoroughly absorbed (with some modification) into mainstream welfare economics. In this context, agents who are predominantly egoistic promote through their actions the interest of others. Competitive markets locate each actor in a network of what may be conceived as bribes – less pejoratively, prices – paid to the actor to modify her conduct in the interest of others.

The institutional structure is crucial here. In the absence of well-defined property rights and appropriate arrangements to enforce them, and without the possibility of enforceable contracts between agents, the alchemy of the idealized market cannot work. And it is worth emphasizing that this institutional structure is supported by a range of benign prisoners' dilemma interactions. It will often be in the interest of a subset of the community to coordinate behavior at the expense of nonmembers of that subset: This is precisely what happens when sellers of a commodity form a monopolistic cartel. However, any member of such a cartel can typically steal a personal advantage by free-riding on other members; and it is this free-riding behavior that inhibits the emergence of cartels, undermines those that do materialize, allows the freely competitive market to flourish, and empowers the invisible hand to shower its blessings on the multitude. The implication of the Smithian analysis is that there is no warrant for the assumption that prisoners' dilemma interactions are necessarily welfare diminishing for all affected parties. We must examine and assess the outcomes of such interactions as best we can on a case-by-case basis.

Does the democratic political process with electoral competition under majority rule constitute an incentive structure that induces political agents (specifically, political decision makers, whether politicians or bureaucrats) to act in the interests of citizens? Is politics like the market in this sense? The answer generally offered by public choice scholarship is no! Majority rule does not aggregate preferences in a determinate way, and in the absence of further restriction there is no bound on the political outcomes to which majority rule can give rise. To that difficulty, we insist, must be added another – namely, that the *inputs* to the majoritarian aggregation process are not of the right kind: They are not reflections of voter preferences over political outcomes.

Perhaps, though, the second difficulty *mitigates* rather than exacerbates the first. It will do so if voter inconsequentiality itself ("as if by an invisible hand") induces persons to forgo in some measure the political predation they would undertake were they to enjoy the capacity to act decisively. The suggestion carries credibility because inconsequentiality radically lowers the costs of indulging one's benign sentiments toward others. The preference aggregation that external institutional procedures are unable to effect may, then, occur internally in the minds of appropriately motivated individuals. Suppose specifically that citizen-voters are impelled not by self-interest but by a desire to express the public interest as they perceive it. If their perceptions are not too divergent, it seems plausible that the kinds of instability emphasized in public choice orthodoxy might be significantly moderated if not totally solved.[2] To majority rule would be left the modest role of sorting out minor differences in voter judgments of the public interest, rather than settling irreconcilable conflicts over whose particular interests are to be served.[3] This scenario may strike the economist (and political skeptics, cynics, and other low forms of life) as hopelessly quixotic. Nonetheless, other political theorists, notably

---

[2] Although the respective contexts differ markedly, this proposed solution to the problem of distilling a public interest from the interplay of private interests is interestingly reminiscent of Rousseau's project of extracting from citizens' particular judgments political outcomes that are authentically indicative of a general will.

[3] See Chapter 5 for a more detailed discussion of the implications of expressive voting for public choice orthodoxy.

those who situate themselves in the republican tradition,[4] do seriously entertain the likelihood of a vigorously public-spirited citizenry, and the expressive theory of electoral preference may buttress their hope that the propensities of democratic governance are fundamentally benign. That hypothesis now merits further attention.

The clear message of the redistribution example discussed at length in Chapter 3 is that the collective nature of voting does indeed lower the cost of "voting morally." Individuals who believe in the abstract that poverty ought to be relieved, that they have a strict duty to aid the poor, may in the arena of private action be observed to relinquish a very small percentage of their assets toward redistributive ends. This is hardly puzzling. Although aiding the poor is judged to be the morally right thing to do and therefore assigned a positive valuation in utility functions, a yet higher valuation is assigned to personal consumption. A dollar given away to the poor is a dollar's consumption forgone, and so the poor will fare quite badly. If, though, the cost of a dollar's worth of poverty alleviation dropped to a dime, to a fraction of a penny, then the poor might make out much better.

Because voting does lower the cost of acting on one's perceived moral duties, individuals will find it less onerous to vote morally than they would if they stood to bear the full costs of their actions. Self-interest, we might say, no longer blinds them from seeing where their moral duty lies, and weakness of will does not hobble them from carrying it out. The voter's dilemma of Table 3.1 is, from this perspective, altogether auspicious rather than symptomatic of some deep-seated pathology of democratic procedures. True, each voter gets the outcome he desires less, but it is nonetheless the outcome that he acknowledges to be the morally better one.[5] It can hardly be a damning indictment of democracy that voting substantially mutes the voracious acquisitive appetite that dominates market behavior and thereby amplifies the too often inaudible voice of conscience. In this vein, J. S. Mill says of the individual who participates in public functions:

He is called upon, while so engaged, to weigh interests not his own: to be guided, in case of conflicting claims, by another rule than his private partialities; to apply at every turn, principles and maxims which have for their reason of existence the common good. He is made to feel himself one of the public, and whatever is for their benefit to be for his benefit. (1958, p. 54)

By way of contrast, where citizens are generally excluded from political activity, Mill states:

Scarcely any sense is entertained that private persons, in no eminent social situation, owe any duties to society, except to obey the laws and submit to the government. There is no unselfish sentiment of identification with the public. Every thought or feeling, either of interest or of duty, is absorbed in the individual and in the family. The man never thinks of any collective interest, of any objects to be pursued jointly with others, but only in competition with them, and in some measure at their expense. Thus even private morality suffers, while public is actually extinct. (pp. 54–55)

---

[4] See, e.g., Pettit (1989) and Braithwaite and Pettit (1990).
[5] This argument receives more extended treatment in Chapter 8.

Mill is, of course, speaking of public participation extending beyond the mere exercise of the franchise, but his reasoning nicely fits the narrower case of voting. Society, he believes, is the recipient of substantial benefits when citizens actively involve themselves in the conduct of public business. Individuals have not only one persona but at least two: the practical but unlovely visage of homo economicus and a public-spirited self of greater comeliness but lamentable shyness. Mill, and exponents of democracy more generally, can present the following syllogism: Institutional structures that encourage a shift in concern away from the acquisitive, reflexively absorbed self toward the greater community merit support. Democratic institutions do encourage this shift. Therefore democratic institutions ought to be supported.

But we must be careful, not least because it would be so reassuring to be persuaded by the argument. Such reassurance, it seems to us, is precarious for at least three reasons. First, although voter inconsequentiality lowers the cost of voting one's moral principles, it also lowers the cost of voting on the basis of whim, fancy, or prejudice. That is, although public-interest considerations are among those that may drive individuals' expressive activities, expressive preferences can, as a pure matter of logic, take any content whatever. It is a pious hope to imagine otherwise. As was noted in Chapter 3, expressions of malice and/or envy no less than expressions of altruism are cheaper in the voting booth than in the market. A German voter who in 1933 cast a ballot for Hitler was able to indulge his antisemitic sentiments at much less cost than she would have borne by organizing a pogrom.

Second, there are grounds for fearing that voting, particularly voting under conditions of secrecy, favors more than does market activity the "darker side of the force." Because votes are anonymous, recipients of altruistic concern expressed through the voting act will be unable to identify and express gratitude toward their benefactors. If someone places value not only on *helping* other persons, but also on *being seen by them to have helped,* he will receive a greater return from a dollar of direct giving than from incurring an equal expense through his vote. Although voting remains a relative bargain for one prone to economize on the expression of altruism, there is at least some countervailing tendency for persons to channel their altruistic impulses into private giving rather than philanthropic ballots. The reverse is true with respect to malice. Here, anonymity stands to be a benefit rather than a cost because it insulates one from the reproach and reciprocation of one's victim. Admittedly, the sadistic and vengeful may not only desire to harm someone but also desire that their target know whence his harm comes. But this is surely the exception; more people will vote for capital punishment than will volunteer for duty in the firing squad, and many Germans noted with equanimity the disappearance of the Jewish population from their communities without desiring to become more deeply involved in the machinations of the Third Reich. Between altruism and malice, there is some grounds for anxiety that democratic procedures tend to favor the latter.[6] Consequently, an apology for democracy on the grounds that it encourages

---

[6] This argument was initially suggested to us by a reading of the account of sympathy in Adam Smith's *The Theory of Moral Sentiments* (1982), especially pp. 113–34. It is buttressed by Smith's reflections in

greater public-interestedness than would be observed in private transactions is in some jeopardy – at least under conditions of secret voting. Whether unveiling the vote might encourage increased "civic virtue" is a matter we take up in Chapter 11. The point to be made here is that because voting is virtually cost free, it is likely to prove conducive to extremes of expression, both altruistic and malicious and that at least under prevailing conditions of secrecy, the malicious extreme might be differentially encouraged.

Third, even if voting does engage the moral impulses of the citizenry, there can be no guarantee that these moral impulses will in fact generate social goods. We have already referred to the difficulty that some commentators, and most notably Hayek, have identified as attaching to judgments of others' interests. On this argument, even if voters were to *aim* at some internal analogue of the aggregation process that serves public interest in the market case, their success could not be assumed. Moreover, voters are far more likely to fasten onto emotionally vivid features of candidates and policy proposals as a vehicle for the identification and expression of their moral principles than onto broader and more subtle components of the public interest. Where the candidates stand on, say, abortion or South Africa may influence votes even though the office in question has virtually nothing to do with the formulation of policy in those areas. Political folklore informs us that kissing babies garners votes – and that kissing episodes that reach the front pages of the lurid tabloids sold in supermarkets do rather the opposite. Are moral impulses at work in these cases? No doubt. Do they reliably advance a public interest? That is considerably more dubious.

Responsibility and voter morality

If public-interest voting, or morally defensible voting more generally, is to predominate in large-scale settings, electoral conduct will have to be the subject of a prevailing civic morality, one that gives a satisfactory account of why individuals should exercise the franchise and why they should do so in a publicly interested way. As noted earlier, the inconsequentiality of individual votes seems to provide fertile soil in which such a civic morality might take root, since moral injunctions do not have to overcome the clamorous urgings of self-interest. And certainly there is no shortage of moral charges to the effect that, as citizens, we ought to vote, that we ought to do so in an informed and responsible manner, that one who takes the performance of voting lightly is derelict in civic duty, and so on. The question is, How can such injunctions be grounded? The very inconsequentiality of the individual vote – that which suggests the possible potency of electoral morality – also

The Wealth of Nations concerning the "man of low condition": "While he remains in a country village, his conduct may be attended to, and he may be obliged to attend to it himself. In this situation, and in this situation only, he may have what is called a character to lose. But as soon as he comes into a great city, he is sunk in obscurity and darkness. His conduct is observed and attended to by nobody, and he is therefore very likely to neglect it himself, and to abandon himself to every sort of low profligacy and vice" (1930, Bk. V p. 705). The parallel between the anonymity of urban existence and that of the voting booth is suggestive. A Smithian moral psychology is extremely congenial to our argument though not strictly presupposed by it. See Brennan and Lomasky (1985) for a fuller discussion.

seems to undermine the most natural route toward justification; for how can it be the case that a citizen can properly be blamed or praised for an action the performance or nonperformance of which almost certainly makes no difference? And for an action, moreover, that she *knows* will almost certainly make no difference? Unless some plausible account can be given, democratic macroethics will entirely lack an adequate microethical foundation.

To the question Why vote? there are broadly three kinds of answers. The first focuses on the *probability of being decisive*. It claims that it is wrong to suggest that a vote will "almost certainly" make no difference – that, in fact, there is a reasonable chance of exercising some effect. The second fastens instead on the *magnitude of the moral stakes* involved. It accepts that the chances of actually deciding the electoral outcome are extremely remote but argues that the consequences of generating the wrong electoral outcome are sufficiently grave most of the time to justify voting, and voting in the right way. The third focuses directly on the *content of expressive preferences*. It maintains that one is morally obligated to express one's views on significant political issues whether or not one is likely to have an impact on electoral outcomes, and that one is morally answerable for one's views as such (or for failing to have any) and for giving them expression in appropriate forums, as well as for the political (or other) outcomes that may result from such expression.

In what follows, we shall explore these three possibilities. And we explore them in relation to the two questions that we see as central in any democratic civic morality: Why should I vote, and how should I vote? The latter is ultimately the more salient because participation in elections would have no moral point but for the fact that voters' decisions about the direction in which to cast their ballots determines the quality of political outcomes. (Recall the example of the unmarked levers. Under such conditions could any sense be given to the proposition that to vote is better than to refrain from voting?) The interest in democratic microethics is, whatever its further ramifications, directed by a quest for a civic morality consistent with eliciting satisfactory electoral outcomes from democratic processes. That interest is more than theoretical because the preceding chapters' analysis of rational voter behavior indicates that large-scale elections have a propensity to produce political outcomes that the voters themselves do not want.

The exploration of issues in democratic microethics is, then, framed by macroethical concerns: Ultimately we are going to want to evaluate the particular performances of individual citizen-voters within a context of democratic institutions in which their actions give rise to outcomes that significantly affect their weal and woe. This is not, however, to presuppose that an adequate civic morality must be consequentialistic. For at least three reasons, no such implication follows. First, direct concern for consequences could be self-defeating. It may be that prevalence of an option-oriented or expressive civic morality makes democracy "work better" than would be the case if people were motivated exclusively by consequentialist considerations. Second, although democratic institutions would not exist if people did not care about their outcomes, to proceed forthwith to a consequentialist rendering of civic morality begs all the crucial questions in the debate between teleology and deontology in ethics. Consider the following analogy: There would be no practice of promise making if people had no concern for whether that which is promised will be forthcoming, and moral principles that adequately regulate the making and keeping of promises are predicated on that concern. It does not follow that one is morally obligated to keep (or make) some promise if and only if doing so yields the greatest utilitarian sum. Third, and this we will argue at length, ordinary consequentialism is unable to provide any cogent reasons why it is generally morally better to vote than not to vote, why individuals should invest time and resources in investigating the issues, or even why one who does vote is morally obligated to vote for the candidate whose victory would most advance overall well-being. These are central tenets of the democratic faith, yet a straightforward consequentialism leaves them embarrassingly vulnerable. The failure of consequentialism to ground a civic morality does not, however, entail the demise of democratic microethics. Although we stop short of categorically maintaining that individuals do have a duty to vote, do have a duty to investigate the issues, and do have a duty to cast ballots for the candidate/policy deemed best for the polity, we argue that these injunctions derive at least some prima facie support from an expressive ethics. To put it another way, if there does exist a well-grounded democratic microethics, its contours are expressive rather than directly consequentialist.

Why should I vote?

We take it as given that voting is costly, in both the objective and the opportunity cost sense. The fact that not all citizens vote (even in places like Australia where voting is nominally compulsory) and that *many* do not vote on some occasions in other places, indicates that citizens place positive value on alternative uses of their time and energy. Even if turnouts were total, the time and energy used up in voting would have alternative uses that may be deemed to be of higher value. Those California voters, for example, who voted in the Reagan and Bush elections when the outcomes were already known, could arguably have devoted their energies to more personally or socially productive activities than voting. To the extent that they voted out of civic duty, for example, an act utilitarian could argue that they behaved on the basis of a mistaken morality and that a correct utilitarian calculus would have indicated some other activity as more desirable.[7] If the satisfaction they derived from the act of voting was sufficiently great, then these ''irrelevant'' Californian voters do right to vote, but there is no basis for encouraging other citizens to follow their example. In any event, we take it to be nonaxiomatic that everyone ought to vote, that the optimal turnout is the entire set of enfranchised persons. Whether one ought to vote, whether one's responsibility to vote is a matter simply of getting the optimal turnout, and, if so, what that optimal turnout is are all matters to be determined.

We also take it to be nonaxiomatic that actual turnouts are necessarily suboptimal. One might argue that, although optimal turnouts may be less than 100%, the

---

[7] To avoid complexities not directly relevant to the issue under consideration, we note but do not further discuss the fact that those California ballots also contained local races and referenda. If, for one already at the polls, a further lever pull comes at virtually zero utility cost, then a presidential vote does not display a calculative error. Neither, though, is it, from a utilitarian perspective, morally preferable to abstention.

importance of a vibrant civic morality constitutes strong presumptive reason for be-lieving that turnouts in which a significant slice of the eligible citizenry fails to vote are suboptimal. However, once it is accepted that citizens may have reasons to go to the polls that are independent of moral duty, or that civic morality can be potent (and potentially excessively so) in promoting electoral activity, the possibility that turnouts may be too large cannot be ruled out: A less rather than more vigorous civic morality may be preferable. Interestingly, this possibility is virtually never mentioned in discussions of the subject. It is simply taken for granted that larger turnout is better than smaller, and that the aim of moral admonition is to increase political participation. We find this literature unpersuasive. Turnout can in princi-ple – and in fact – be too large as well as too small. Restricting ourselves for the moment to purely consequential considerations, the rule for optimal turnout is that the expected value from an additional vote (in whatever terms that value is speci-fied) should be equal to the cost of that vote. Accordingly, at optimal turnout we should be effectively morally indifferent as to whether one additional person votes or not. What that optimal turnout will be in any particular case is, of course, a function of the circumstances – how much is at stake in the election, how many others are voting, how those other voters are likely to vote, and so on – as well as any good consequences that derive from participation per se.

One possible source of the common intuition that more turnout is better than less lies in the prospect that there are good consequences deriving from participation over and above any influence on electoral outcomes. It can be argued, for example, that participation *legitimizes* the electoral outcome to participants, and that in-creased legitimation promotes wider voluntary compliance with public decrees and, more generally, enhanced political stability. Or one might join Mill in main-taining that voting incorporates a contemplation of the public interest, the effects of which spill over into other arenas of conduct that are consequential (e.g., private provision of public goods). Such arguments provide presumptive reason for pre-ferring larger turnouts to smaller. Or, they do at least in those cases where the elec-toral outcomes are appropriately satisfactory: One might doubt whether it is a desirable thing to have citizens regard as legitimate outcomes that are truly disas-trous (such as undertaking horrendously destructive wars; see Tuchman, 1984, for further details). And, returning to the central question of this chapter, one might doubt whether legitimacy does properly attach to outcomes that are not truly cho-sen by the people in the relevant sense. In other words, the alleged benefits of in-creased participation are dependent on how people vote and whether the resultant outcomes correspond tolerably well to citizen preferences over them. And even supposing that, other things (and specifically the quality of collective decisions) being equal, benefits from increased turnout tend to be positive, the magnitude of these positive externalities may well in any large-scale election be dwarfed by the costs to a reluctant voter of an unwanted trip to the polls. If these factors support a consequentialist case for increased political participation, they do so only at the periphery. Accordingly, we turn to the central microethical justificatory routes.

The influence factor. Consider the three alternative foci for morally based admonitions to vote: the probability of influence, the magnitude of the stakes, and the moral content of expressive preferences as such. As a representative example of the first genre, we offer the following editorial comment, fortuitously encountered by one of us (invisible hand?), while trying to break the boredom of travel, in the October 1982 issue of United Airlines' in-flight magazine and penned by its CEO at the time, Richard J. Ferris:

Why do so many Americans take for granted the right to vote? Perhaps it's because they are politically apathetic, distrustful of the system, unwilling to take the time, unbending in their belief that their vote can't possibly have an impact on the outcome of an election. How wrong and how wasteful. By voting, *a person chooses leaders, endows them with power, and holds them accountable.* (Emphasis added)

Heartening though it is to find among our great corporate executives such abiding respect for the political potency of the average (non)voter, the central empirical claims here are just plain wrong. A person does not, in fact, choose leaders; his influence on their power is asymptotically negligible; and since he cannot unilaterally bundle them out, it is hard to see how *he* can hold them accountable. *Pace* Mr. Ferris, the belief that a single voter is extremely unlikely to have an impact on the outcome of an election is true. Perhaps to assert otherwise is a noble lie, but it is a lie just the same.

But is it even noble? Suppose that the Ferris strategy worked, that voters came to believe that the probability of being decisive was considerable. Then individuals would presumably be encouraged to vote as they act in other arenas where they are decisive – that is, according to private outcome-oriented interest. Such private interest would, incidentally, be unlikely to be congruent with United's or Mr. Ferris's interests, which supports the suspicion that Ferris himself does not actually believe the propositions he is urging. More to the point for our purposes, all the traditional anxieties troubling an interest-based voting system, familiar from orthodox public choice, would reemerge. Suppose next, for the sake of argument, that Ferris is right, that one who does not vote would have a significant chance of affecting electoral outcomes if she did vote. Then it follows that democracy as it actually works, and in particular with the levels of turnout that actually prevail, generates electoral outcomes that we would expect to be very different if turnouts were larger. What authority then do the actual outcomes have? What confidence can we have that emergent outcomes reflect any reliable measure of the public interest? Surely the Ferris depiction is an *indictment* of American democracy as a process of collective decision making! To be sure, nondemocratic processes may be yet worse; but it must be sobering news for the democraphile that electoral outcomes are so arbitrary.

Our own view, as we said, is that Ferris is wrong on this matter. We may have grounds for anxiety about democratic outcomes, but sensitivity to small changes in voter turnout is not among them. There is, though, one qualification to be entered. Individuals may en masse refrain from voting as a means of expressing lack of support for the current incarnation of a traditionally favored party. A seasoned Democrat who finds it impossible to vote for the Republican candidate however much she detests her own party's candidate may simply stay away from the polls. If she is one among many such, the electoral outcome will respond – but the response

Table 10.1. *The egoistic calculus*

Each	All others		
	Majority for *A*	Majority for *B*	Tie
Votes for *A*	7	107	7
Votes for *B*	0	100	100

is not arbitrary, and one presumably would not want to insist that such a non-voter should vote. Nonvoting is precisely the means whereby her preference is given effect.

The stakes. The second route to civic morality is to accept that each voter has a minute probability of being decisive, but to emphasize the magnitude of the stakes involved. Brian Barry (1979) pursues this consequentialist line in the voting context specifically:

If an act-utilitarian really gives full weight to the consequences for *everyone* that he expects will be affected, this will normally provide an adequate reason for voting. If I think that one party will increase the GNP by ¼ per cent over five years more than the other party, that for a utilitarian is a big aggregate difference. Are there *really* so many more beneficial things one could do with fifteen minutes! (p. 39)

On the more general issue of the moral grounds for taking account of small chances, Derek Parfit (1984) has this to say:

It may be objected that it is *irrational* to consider very tiny chances. When our acts cannot affect more than a few people, this may be so. But this is because the stakes are here comparatively low. Consider the risks of causing accidental death. It may be irrational to give any thought to a one-in-a-million chance of killing one person. But if I was a nuclear engineer, would I be irrational to give any thought to the same chance of killing a million people? This is what most of us believe. . . . When the stakes are very high, no chance, however small, should be ignored. (pp. 74–5)

Barry and Parfit concede, in effect, that from a perspective of self-interested prudence, investment in a trip to the polls is irrational. The individual does not stand to gain enough *for himself.* However, when the relevant stake is the sum of benefits to the citizenry at large, calculations are radically transformed. And it is, of course, the overall social good on which the utilitarian fastens. So far so good. Those who maintain on consequentialist grounds that there is a moral duty to vote surely do not mean to say that the balance of advantage accrues exclusively or primarily to the individual voter. Such self-derived benefits are incidental. Their claim is that voting is a public good, and that an adequate civic morality bids us each to supply that good to our fellows.

Is the utilitarian ideal, then, a citizenry in which all participate at the polls? That question cannot be answered as it stands; for here, as elsewhere, what it is that I should do to produce the best overall consequences crucially depends on what

Table 10.2. *The utilitarian calculus*

Each	Majority for A	Majority for B	Tie
Votes for A	7	$100n + 7(S + 1)$	$7 + 7n/2$
Votes for B	$7m$	$100n + 7S$	$100n + 7n/2$

Note: m is the number of (other) voters for A when A wins, S is the number of (other) voters for A when B wins, and n is total citizen population (all of whom are assumed to vote).

others will do. Barry and Parfit fail to address the various possibilities; we now do so by exploring variants of the voter's dilemma introduced in Chapter 3.

The standard "egoistic" version is depicted in Table 10.1. Recalling that each voter's valuations are taken to be identical, the *total* cost of outcome A is not a benefit of 100 forgone but a benefit of 100 to each citizen-voter – that is, a total benefit of $100n$ (where n is the number of citizen-voters). Thus the matrix relevant to a utilitarian is the one depicted in Table 10.2. An expected payoff calculation will require the agent to weigh the benefit (7) of voting for A against the benefit ($100n$) of voting for B. All that seems required to induce the agent to vote is a probability of being decisive larger than $7/100n$. With citizens numbering in the millions, this requirement seems a weak one.[8] So, one might conclude, each person should vote, and each should vote for B over A.

But this is too quick. One may not ignore what others are doing. So let us begin by universalizing Table 10.2. Suppose that the utilitarian argument is a compelling one, and all voters can be relied on to vote for B over A. Then we should need only *one* voter to secure the preferred electoral outcome. To have n votes for B is to have $(n - 1)$ too many. Resources are being squandered that could be employed elsewhere to generate utility.

Less restrictively, we can allow for mistakes in pulling levers and errors of judgment, but unless the probability of a representative individual supplying the correct vote is very close to one-half,[9] the proportion of the electorate required to vote in order to ensure that the right outcome emerges is very small. For example, the probability of my being decisive if 100 other voters vote for B with a probability of .9 is (using Equation (4.6)) 3.6×10^{-24}. If there are 100 million citizens (or otherwise affected parties), then the payoff *to each* would have to be of the order of 10 thousand trillion (10^{12}) dollars in order for it to be worth a forgone \$3.60 for the 101st person to vote. In other words, in a community composed entirely of individuals who are motivated by concern for the general weal and whose judgment of where the weal lies is fairly reliable, the turnout required to generate the correct

---

[8] It is weaker still if, as will often be the case, benefits extend to individuals beyond the polity's boundaries. Recurring to Barry's example, if America's GNP increases by 0.25%, the consequences for those who trade with Americans will also be positive. Should it be an issue of war or peace on which the election turns, such external effects will be yet more pronounced.

[9] If that probability is less than .5, then the *smaller* the turnout, the greater the likelihood of the correct outcome. If that probability is more than slightly greater than .5, larger turnouts are wasteful of resources.

outcome is quite small – only a tiny fraction of the enfranchised group. Of course, as we noted above, one would have to allow here for any benefits of increased legitimacy or compliance (whether soundly grounded or not) that flowed from electoral participation; if such benefits exceed the cost of voting for some or all voters, then turnout should be larger on that account. But such considerations do not seem to be connected to the stakes at issue in any election and are certainly not what Parfit and Barry have in mind, so we shall set them aside. There is, however, a further complication that is relevant to the utilitarian calculus. Note that there is an expressive return to the individual from going to the polls and *voting for A*. Since the probability for the 100th voter of doing any harm by voting for *A* when the other 99 all vote for *B* with probability .9 is truly negligible, it increases overall preference satisfaction for that voter to go to the polls and cast a ballot *against* the utilitarian-preferred candidate. Suppose we set aside the problem of mistakes. Then the true utilitarian ideal will not necessarily be where one person votes for *B* and no one else votes, but may instead be where everyone votes, with a simple majority of exactly one voter for *B*. This will be so if the expressive benefit from voting for *A* is at least *twice* the cost of voting, because for each additional *A*-voter we allow we must admit an additional *B*-voter to ensure that the correct outcome is assured. Of course, no such outcome is really feasible unless there is an appropriate coordination mechanism in place. If each must vote for *A* or *B* probabilistically, because she does not know deterministically how others will vote, then the ideal stochastic outcome will be one in which *B* defeats *A* (on average) but in which each votes for *A* with sufficient probability that the expected expressive benefit from voting exceeds the cost.

If we drop the assumption of identical voters, we can suppose that some will derive smaller expressive benefits from voting for *A* than will others. It is the former group that should vote for *B*, if indeed they should vote at all. And among the latter group, it may well be that some of them should not vote, even though it is individually rational for them to do so, because their voting in the "wrong way" requires that someone else may have to vote in the "right way" to ensure that getting the desired outcome is appropriately likely. Actual turnout could indeed be too large.

All this may seem like an excessively elaborate way of making the following simple point: Once expressive considerations are allowed for, what each ought to do depends critically on what all others do, even if the merits of the competing electoral contenders are unambiguous and even if all citizens are moved by concern for the public interest. That is, it may be best for me to vote for *A*, to vote for *B*, or not to vote at all, depending on what I think others are going to do. And this is so even if the stakes involved in the electoral success of *B* over *A* are quite large.

But how plausible is it to suppose, given assumptions of general public-spiritedness and reliable judgment, that the stakes are substantial? In that envisioned world, any forces of electoral competition that are operative will force parties to adopt policy platforms that are perceived by voters to aim at the overall social good. Thus, if the appeal to the public interest is compelling and parties respond to electoral demands, they will converge on roughly the same point in electoral space.[10] The electoral landscape simply will not exhibit contests such as those in Table 10.2 in which there is a clear and significant consequentialist demarcation between the contending parties. Differences will be almost entirely matters of "style," alternate paths to the political summum bonum, rather than differences of substance. Insofar as individuals accrue greater or lesser or negligible expressive returns from one of these paths, they will rationally vote for *A*, vote for *B*, or not vote at all. But the claim that each is morally obligated to vote in virtue of the gravity of the stakes evaporates.

Barry and Parfit could protest that the preceding analysis is beside the point. We do not, alas, live in a world in which each intends the public interest. If we did live in such a world, all the prisoners' dilemma problems on which so much of welfare economics and political philosophy hang would be solved. Provision of public goods would no longer be a problem that required for its solution large-scale collective action. To be sure, coordination problems of various kinds might still arise, and so anarchy would not necessarily provide the optimal level of spending on public goods, but the standard cases of internal and external defense provision, littered beaches, excessive greenhouse-gas emissions, and so on would be removed. But this is a pipe dream. The average level of benevolence we in fact experience is distinctly subutopian, and there is considerable variance around that mean. We do better, therefore, to take Barry and Parfit to be prescribing for the actual world and its near neighbors rather than an envisioned utilitarian paradise. Specifically, we can take them to be assuming that many individuals will not vote even if there would be a nonnegligible public benefit to their exercise of the franchise, and that many of those who do bestir themselves to vote will be moved by a private interest that diverges from the public interest. Moreover, the argument will not be directed toward the moral saints, of whom there are too few within electoral precincts to have any discernible impact, but rather toward men and women who can be induced to do the moral thing if the costs are not too great and if they perceive that benefits to the general public are substantial. This revised scenario is analytically messy. Eschewing as it does any neatly simplifying hypothesis about what "all others" will do, it is indeterminate. Still, we can say something about it – and we had better if we hope to assess the consequentialist argument as it applies to the actual world.

The question then becomes: In a world where special interest as well as whim, malice, and ideology are dominant electoral forces, should I vote? And if I do vote, should I cast my ballot for the candidate whose election I judge would maximize the utilitarian sum? We take Barry and Parfit to be answering in the affirmative to them both, explicitly concerning the former and implicitly with regard to the latter. Both answers, we contend, are undersupported by consequentialist considerations.

Consider first the claim that voting is morally preferable to not voting (or, yet stronger, that voting is a moral duty). There are at least four points to be noted against this version of the utilitarian argument. First, as noted previously, the argument rests on the assumption that it is not generally compelling. If it were a

---

[10] Note that this analysis, unlike those assuming predominantly egoistic voters, is not sensitive to the number of contending parties.

compelling argument, then the "moral equilibrium" would be one in which we should be morally indifferent as to whether turnout was marginally larger or not, and the political equilibrium would be one in which differences in policy platforms would be small in utilitarian terms. The more the argument persuades, the less inherently persuasive it becomes.

Second, since we are being called on to assume that we are located a long way from any such moral equilibrium, it follows that collective decision making produced under real-world democratic situations is likely to be extremely inadequate. If the stakes are sufficiently high that individuals are morally obligated to vote even though the probability of being decisive is very low, then the expected cost of getting the "wrong outcome" must also be high enough to cause alarm. In other words, there are echoes here of the implication of Ferris's argument on turnout: If it is so manifestly clear that one ought to vote in the kinds of electoral situations that actually prevail (whether because one is likely to be decisive or because the stakes are so high), prevailing electoral situations must be held to be highly defective. The democrat's faith has, then, a distinctly otherworldly tenor.

Third, the Barry–Parfit "real-world" consequentialist analysis is itself infected by a disabling unrealism. Barry stylizes the electoral choice as one for or against higher GNP; Parfit analogizes it to a nuclear accident in which one million perish. Can one imagine any actual electoral contests being waged under such banners? Party platforms do not declare, "We promise exactly what our opponents do – except that we will give you less economic growth or nuclear safety." (The electoral prospects of any such platform would merit derision rather than disquiet.) A realistic construal of political competition in democracies will instead recognize that all credible candidates insist that it is through enactment of *their* platforms that the public interest will be best served, that they endeavor through their public actions to render this claim persuasive to a skeptical electorate, that they adopt policies that can never be known with anything approaching certainty to be efficacious in achieving their declared ends, and that they must necessarily endorse trading off more of one good for less of another, the net balancing of which is excruciatingly difficult. So instead of a transparently facile choice between more or less GNP, more or less nuclear safety, an electorate will instead confront the alternative of slightly more economic growth versus slightly lower inflation, increased safety but higher energy costs. How clear is it in these cases where the utility balance lies?

Let us then reformulate Barry's calculus. Suppose one judges that the victory of party B will result in a 0.25% increase in GNP compared with what would result from the victory of A. Performing the straightforward utilitarian calculation of multiplying the probability that one's vote will be decisive times the utility of such an increase in GNP will be justified only if one *knows* with a certainty approaching 1.0 that those consequences have been estimated correctly. But political life simply does not admit of such certainty. So one must bring into one's accounting a whole host of additional considerations: the likelihood that party B will indeed, should it gain power, pursue the policy that it says it will; the likelihood that one's theory about the determinants of GNP is correct; the likelihood that party A would, if elected, pursue a less optimific policy; the adequacy of one's judgment that a heightened GNP will produce more aggregate well-being than the alternative under which, perhaps, the inflation rate would be a percentage point lower; and a host of ceteris paribus conditions.

Voters are prone to claim great prodigies of knowledge and insight for themselves, and many will contend that they do indeed know such relevant facts.[11] We confess ourselves guilty of such hubris from time to time. A more accurate epistemic test, then, might be to ask what degree of confidence one has that one's neighbor (political affiliation unknown) has the degree of knowledge and moral motivation required for the expected payoff to his vote to be strongly positive. We believe it is not implausible to maintain that if political prejudices are recognized for what they are and appropriately discounted, it will generally be the case that the likelihood that any given voter will hit on the utility-enhancing line is not appreciably greater than the chance that he will select the one that is utility diminishing. It is the difference between these two possibilities that gives the net expected payoff to a vote. When that sharply reduced sum is multiplied by the probability of being decisive, the utilitarian rationale for a vote becomes exceedingly problematic.

Fourth, individuals are not homogeneous with regard to their ability to assess accurately the effects of political policies. Some are more easily gulled by sharp-talking political operatives; some have a greater understanding of what genuinely comprises the public interest. It follows that a blanket consequentialist endorsement of voting is unjustifiable. If electoral participation is a serious business, then it ought to be consigned to those with the expertise to conduct it most responsibly. A consequentialist argument that properly attends to voter heterogeneity, therefore, does not extend to the general electorate; it is, rather, addressed to the Wise and the Good. Persons who lack a full quota of wisdom and moral motivation do better not to vote at all. Their ballots add "noise" (that is at best random) to the total electoral outpouring, thus making it more likely that those best equipped to ascertain the common good will find themselves among the overall minority. Rather than an argument for democracy, the argument becomes a curiously backhanded brief for a reign of philosopher-kings.

The upshot is, then, that we can find no good utilitarian case for increased turnout as such. Expressive returns to the individual voter aside, it is very likely that one could do better for overall utility by doing something else. A perhaps surprising corollary of this result is that there is no good utilitarian reason why one who does vote should cast a ballot for the candidate whose election it is judged would be

---

[11] Why, in the face of a multitude of factors that should incline one toward caution, do individuals tend to be so obdurately convinced of the soundness of their political judgments? Although we disclaim expertise in political psychology, two explanations suggest themselves. First, it is the business of political parties and candidates to sell unquestioning conviction. True believers vote more reliably than do those who profess Socratic ignorance, and so it is to the creation of true belief and the destruction of doubts that political actors bend their efforts. Political evangelism is, in this regard, very much akin to religious evangelism. Second, expressive returns will usually be an increasing function of strength of conviction. We can presume that the fans who cheer most vociferously and unyieldingly are the ones who most enjoy themselves. To delight in following the shifting fortunes of the Yankees is incompatible with persistently questioning whether they deserve one's support. For the political analogue, substitute, for Yankees, Republicans or Democrats.

most conducive to the greatest good of the greatest number. Given the minute chance of being decisive and the imponderables surrounding political prognostication, little stands to be gained through so directing a ballot. If, however, the individual can accrue significant expressive returns through a vote for some one of the (nonutilitarian preferred) candidates, then a concern for consequences dictates that she snatch the bird in the hand rather than stalk utility in a bush that is almost certainly unreachable and that may not even exist. Ordinary standard consequentialism, we therefore conclude, cannot sustain a robust democratic faith.

The expressive domain. To this point the quest for an adequate democratic microethics has been unavailing. This suggests that it may be a mistake to construe the moral significance of voting as a matter of achieving "optimal turnout" and wrong to think of voters as bearing responsibility for their electoral behavior only insofar as it affects, or seems likely to affect, electoral outcomes. Suppose that in an election involving two outcomes *A* and *B,* it is a foregone conclusion that *A* will win. Clearly, a vote for either option will not alter the probabilities in any nonnegligible way. Nonetheless, we might want to say that the *A*-voters bear responsibility for their candidate's victory, and that they bear it no less fully when the preelection polls indicate a 70–30% margin for *A* than they would if the polls had indicated the election too close to call. To approach the point from a slightly different direction, it seems intuitively acceptable to hold up to reproach someone who voted for the Ku Klux Klan party candidate for president even though the Klandidate was not listed on the ballots of enough states to comprise a majority of the Electoral College, and hence could never win. One who registers himself as supporting the thoroughly unsavory is culpable irrespective of the tendency that such expression has to generate the repugnant state of affairs. Why that should be so deserves a closer look.

To cast a Klan ballot is to *identify oneself* in a morally significant way with the racist policies that the organization espouses. One thereby lays oneself open to associated moral liability whether that candidate has a small, large, or zero probability of gaining victory, and whether or not one's own vote has an appreciable likelihood of affecting the election result. Even stronger, to express such support in a forum in which no outcomes will be decided, such as in casual conversation or in response to a survey, is also odious. That is not, of course, to deny that any influence on electoral outcomes is morally relevant: To express support for *A* and to bring about the victory of *A* is worse than merely to express support for *A*. The point is not that effects on political outcomes do not matter, but they are not all that matters.

It may be that outcome considerations enter not so much into the choice of action as in assessing the significance of the context within which the expression of one's views takes place. If one cheers as the lion devours a Christian, the act is laden with more significance than is cheering at a football game in which the Lions are devouring the Bears; the moral stakes are higher. Nothing in this necessarily commits one to a view of cheering as a means to bring about a preferred result. Neither, importantly, does it entail an outcome-oriented account of why cheering one way or another merits commendation.

One who writes a letter to a newspaper in which it is contended that Hitler's assumption of the chancellorship was a good thing, as were the events that followed therefrom, throws oneself open to rebuke. The grounds for criticism are not simply that one has made an intellectual error – for which correction and not castigation would be the appropriate response – nor any alleged tendency of one's public expression to influence others to build a Fourth Reich that resembles the Third. Even assuming that such manifestos have any discernible public impact at all, they cannot be assumed more likely to generate increased bigotry than to renew vigilance against bigotry. But we need not indulge in such far-fetched causal speculations to identify sufficient grounds for moral disapproval. Persons are morally responsible not only for what they *bring about,* what they *intend* to bring about, and what they help to bring about; they are also responsible for what they *endorse* and for that with which they choose to *identify themselves.*

One might indeed go further and maintain that persons bear responsibility for their characters and attitudes whether or not they choose to give them expression. An antisemite who never expresses her loathing for the Jews may still be accounted morally defective, and this whether she refrains from public expression because she judges it to be imprudent or because she herself recognizes and loathes the bigotry to which she finds herself chained. If that is correct, then persons are responsible not only for that which they voluntarily perform, but for that which, quite nonvoluntarily, they are.[12] This reflection matches common intuitions and would, we believe, be seen more widely as plausible were it not for the continuing grip of philosophical theories insisting that the connection between willing and responsibility must be universal. There is nothing unusual or paradoxical about esteeming someone who is unreflectively and instinctively kind and compassionate toward others despite querulous Kantian suggestions that benevolent states resulting from natural inclination merit no moral credit. It would be extravagant to push this line of argument further. Whether or not individuals bear responsibility for their characters and attitudes, all we need to maintain for present purposes is that they are accountable for that which they choose to express.

There is, then, a logic of moral discourse appropriate to expressive activity. It is impossible here to do more than to begin to sketch its contours, but no involved exercise in cartography is needed to render its likeness familiar; our ordinary activity richly exemplifies the play of normative considerations underlying expressive

---

[12] Some will object that a person can be morally accountable for her attitudes and character only to the extent that she acted to *produce* them in herself or to the extent that it is now up to her whether to *change* them. The contention is that individuals are responsible only so far as their voluntary agency extends. We do not find it obvious that that is so. Indeed, the claim is especially questionable in the first-person case. To recognize in oneself a vice, and to recognize it *as a vice*, is, we think, incompatible with taking the trait to be a matter of utter moral indifference. What of third-person ascriptions? Again, we find it implausible that the nonvoluntary is necessarily immune from moral categorization. There may be no point to *blaming* or *punishing* someone for that which is not within her voluntary control, but other moral stances (e.g., scorn, contempt) may nonetheless be appropriate.

acts. When we sympathize with a sick friend (or are left cold by someone "too busy" to do so), mourn the irretrievably lost, and bristle at injustice, our activity is laden with moral significance. These entirely familiar performances are, in the first instance, expressive. They may be indirectly consequential for good or ill, but that is not their point. Similarly explicable as expressively based are versions of the frequently voiced claim that citizens in a democracy have a *duty* to vote. Such appeals reach a crescendo in the flurry of media pronouncements preceding national elections. One who turns on a television set will be regaled with emotive messages about patriots who have done their part by defending the nation at the cost of their lives. One is solemnly informed that the least an ordinary citizen can do to fulfill his end of the social compact is to exercise the franchise. In Australia this sentiment is given legal force via a requirement backed up by fines that all adult citizens able to vote do so. And many of those who do not recognize the existence of a strict duty to vote will nonetheless concede that it is a good thing that citizens vote, that voting is an act to the individual's moral credit.

As we have noted, these pronouncements are often buttressed with strained claims about the chances of being decisive or the magnitude of the stakes involved. No such claims, even where plausible, seem to be required. What is wrong with abstention does not need to be tied to any effect on outcomes: The wrong inheres in the apathy thereby displayed.[13] In great national elections or referenda, principles of undeniable moral salience are at stake. Political parties prepare lengthy platforms stating their positions on the major issues of the day, and candidates contend with each other concerning the ends to which the nation ought to devote itself and the appropriateness of rival means to those ends. What is done and how burdens and benefits come to be assigned will depend on who gets in and who is tossed out. This is the stuff of which serious commitment is made. By the stand one takes, one displays to oneself and to others what sort of person one is.

Or rather, one who takes some stand or other does so. But the individual who declines to get involved, who is so unmoved by the debate before her that she will not give up a few minutes of her time to register her views in the electoral precincts provided for that purpose can present the appearance of a political neuter. She is too diffident or too detached from events of great moment to bestir herself. In showing herself unmoved by that to which her fellow citizens assign considerable weight, she displays an insensitivity for which they can reasonably take her to task.

We believe that this is, in embryo, the strongest argument that can be made for the claim that individuals do wrong by not voting. Is it compelling? To adjudicate

---

[13] Conscientious abstention is, on this reading, to be accounted very differently, though the effect, if any, on electoral outcomes is the same. Indeed, this observation exposes one strength of the expressive account – that it not only provides a case for why individuals typically ought to vote but also enables one to draw moral distinctions between different reasons for nonvoting. Consider someone who declines to vote not out of apathy or inertia but as a principled protest against the grounds on which the election is fought or because he believes the political process of which it is a part to be corrupt. We might disagree with the substantive position taken by this person, but we could hardly contend that his abstention on grounds of principle is dereliction of an obligation to take a stand on momentous issues. On strictly outcome-related grounds, however, the efficacy of a lazy abstention and a principled one are exactly the same.

that point we would have to develop a full-fledged normative theory of expression, and that is beyond our current aspirations. What we claim here for the expressive argument is not conclusiveness but intrinsic cogency. It is a *contender* as an account of why citizens ought to vote, while consequentialist arguments that one should vote because the chance of being decisive is substantial or because the magnitude of the stakes mandates a trip to the polls are summarily dismissible.

How ought I vote?

The question of which considerations should weigh in deciding how to vote is, in our view, a more significant one than persuading persons to go to the polls, at least in Western democracies as they actually function. Whether because they are impelled by a civic morality of electoral participation or for other reasons, voters turn out for significant elections in sufficient numbers to make the possibility of excessive influence by any one voter suitably remote and to confer on electoral verdicts whatever legitimacy may be forthcoming from the vox populi. The important macroethical consideration is to secure tolerable outcomes, not merely to get more voters to the polls. And in that process, the critical thing is to induce voters to vote in an appropriate way.

As we have emphasized, the question of *how* I should vote is closely connected with the question of *whether* I should vote, and much of the foregoing discussion is obviously germane. We can therefore be brief in discussing this second question.

Directly consequentialist considerations are, except in the most exceptional circumstances, mute. Virtually nothing (in the relevant expected sense) pertaining to political outcomes hinges on how the individual chooses to direct his ballot. So he might as well – indeed, he *must* if he is to give due weight to his own utility – vote as he prefers. Whether these preferences are egoistic or other-directed, well considered or whimsical, is immaterial. For a consistent consequentialism, voting behavior is the procurement of consumer goods from which externalities are almost entirely absent. *De gustibus non est disputandum.*

An expressively grounded theory of democratic microethics will have rather more to say. If the quality of expressive acts matters, it is not enough merely to go to the polls and vote any old how. Unless the act of voting is performed with the requisite preparation and attentiveness, it will not satisfy canons of good citizenship. Certainly this view accords with the message of common morality. Merely to vote, we are told, is insufficient; one who goes to the polls only vaguely aware of who the candidates are and what they stand for, and who pulls the lever closest to his hand so that he can be done with the business and return to his couch and television, stands hardly, if at all, higher than one who never left the couch. That is in part because one who votes in so desultory and absent-minded a fashion is not to be credited with taking a stand on anything. One may also fault the voter who knows well enough what he favors but does not have any good reason for favoring it. He has voted the straight Republican ticket in every election since he came of age, and his mother and father did so before him; therefore, he will vote the Republican ticket again in this election. The phenomenon may be common, but nonetheless can be judged an inadequate performance. One who votes should know the issues, scrutinize candidates' statements, and make up one's mind after weighing all the facts: This is how the voter's duty is often expressed.

It is often observed that the return to voters' expenditures of time and resources in the pursuit of political information is minuscule. When the probability of the direction of one's vote being improved by more information is multiplied by the probability that one's vote will be decisive, an investment in political information seems to be one of the lowest return ventures one might undertake. In the light of such demonstrations of the irrationality of the exercise, it might seem utterly incongruous that "knowing the issues" is so widely endorsed by common democratic morality. However, that incongruity dissolves once we drop the assumptions that voting behavior is to be justified on the basis of effects on outcomes and that the basis for evaluating the pursuit of political information is derived from such effects. The proposition that individuals ought to take a principled stand on issues of great moment includes the notion that they ought to do so *intelligently*. If expressive activity matters in its own right, then high-quality expression is valuable irrespective of its causal product. A utilitarian calculus exhibits little difference with respect to overall optimization between an ignorant voter and one who is well informed (and none at all should they happen to support the same candidates), but a normative theory of expressive discourse can present such voters as sharply separated.

Again, what we claim for that theory is considerable congruence with the dictates of common morality. That is not to insist on its truth. But it is to locate the position within the wider framework common morality affords. One who comes down on the "right side" of an issue but does so for largely irrelevant and ill-informed reasons can be held up to criticism. This is so with respect to voting decisions but also holds, and for essentially the same reasons, for other expressive acts. An ignorant and poorly reasoned letter to the editor is disreputable for much the same reasons as is an ignorant ballot. To express disdain for the Nazis because they swaggered a lot, made interminable speeches, and wore those horridly unstylish brown shirts is simply to get the grounds for disapproval wrong. Both inside and outside voting booths, it matters what one stands for and why one stands for it.

The upshot of these considerations is this: Sense can be made of the assertion that individuals in a democracy are responsible for how and whether they vote. Even though an individual ballot is causally inefficacious, people are nonetheless morally answerable for their electoral conduct. To be sure, consequences up the moral ante. Moral deeds do speak louder than mere words. And in contexts where an agent acts to bring about a particular outcome, its characteristics will be a central part of any moral appraisal. So one can understand the temptation to construe civic morality as outcome oriented. But the standard arguments advanced in this connection are, upon analysis, found to be unpersuasive.

A more promising line focuses on the expressive dimension of voting. The object of an expressive civic morality is to inculcate an ethic of well-informed, responsible political participation more or less for its own sake. It directs attention to the character of the citizen rather than to the alternative electoral outcomes that the citizen might leave in her wake. Whether such an ethic can ultimately be vindicated and, if it can, whether it will be supportive of a satisfactory democratic macroethics must be left here as somewhat open questions. We can, though, offer a conditional judgment: If the democratic faith in government by a politically responsible people is sustainable, that faith will hinge on the potency of a largely expressive ethic of political conduct among citizen-voters.

Excursus: the "thrown-away" vote argument

One encounters claims that one should not "throw away one's vote," where what is meant thereby is that one should not vote for a third- (or fourth-, or seventh-) party candidate who stands no chance of winning. Rather, if one has any preference at all between the candidates who have a realistic chance of capturing the election, then one should vote for the more preferred major party candidate instead of the candidate preferred overall. A vote for the third-party candidate is a vote thrown away, while a vote cast for one of the legitimate contenders is a vote well spent.

Paul Meehl (1977) provides in "The Selfish Voter Paradox and the Thrown-Away Vote Argument" a clever and illuminating examination of this argument. Presenting the argument as a dialogue between SOP, a protagonist of one of the Standard Old Parties, and FEV, a Flat Earth Vegetarian advocate, Meehl denies that the latter can be given any good reason to reject voting for his most preferred candidate and instead back one of the two major-party contenders. A vote for either of the major-party candidates stands virtually the same (i.e., nil) chance of affecting outcomes as does an FEV vote, and therefore, if a third party vote is thrown away, so too is a vote for the first or second party. From this Meehl (or his surrogate, FEV) concludes that electoral participation cannot be defended as rational on economic grounds: "You can't get anybody to go 'rationally' to the polls, unless you introduce some sort of quasi-Kantian principle with a distinctly ethical content. Political participation theories that omit 'ethical' premises are all radically defective for this reason (p. 13). Meehl declines to endorse any one such principle but says that whichever principle does rationally motivate voting must be "axionomic" (not intended as instrumental with respect to outcomes) and "sociotropic" (assigning value to the interests of other members of the polity). He concludes that whatever renders it rational for an individual to go to the polls at all also renders it rational for that person to vote for the candidate he most prefers.

There are obvious affinities between Meehl's statement and the line that we take. Both point up the incoherence in orthodox public choice analysis of a narrowly self-interested rationale for political participation, and both maintain that an adequate substitute will reject modeling voters as insistently outcome oriented. Meehl maintains that voting becomes rational for an individual only if he subscribes to some quasi-Kantian moral principle, while we have argued that an individual's pursuit of expressive gains (which may but need not hinge on the acceptance of any particular moral views) renders voting rational. This disagreement is significant, but it extends only to the positive theory of voting behavior. We agree with Meehl that an adequate normative theory of democracy must incorporate nonconsequentialist principles, though we demur at labeling them "quasi-Kantian."

Consequentialists might argue against Meehl that though the probability of decisiveness if one votes for a major party is small, it is many times greater, indeed infinitely greater, than if one votes for an outcome-irrelevant party. To squander what little decisiveness one might enjoy is profligate: thus the force of the thrown-away vote argument. That response, though, represents neither competent consequentialist analysis nor an adequate statement of what is being criticized. Suppose that B is the utilitarian-preferred major party. (If we have no basis for identifying either of the contending major parties as utilitarian preferable, then there is no consequentialist case to be made at all.) Then what is to be recommended is not merely some grasping or other for decisiveness, but rather decisiveness specifically with regard to enhancing B's electoral chances. For the consequentialist, then, votes are arrayed: B>FEV>A, where ">" is interpreted "has a greater expected payoff than." To vote for the minor party is to do less well than one might, but it is to do better than casting a ballot for A. What the thrown-away vote argument maintains, though, is that to vote for *either* of the major parties is morally reputable in a way that a vote for the minor party is not. There is no obvious way to render this intuition viable within a utilitarian framework.[14]

Does an expressive theory help here? Or does it simply endorse Meehl's assessment of the thrown-away vote argument as fundamentally confused? It seems on first blush that the latter conclusion is indicated. An FEV vote is as inherently expressive as a vote for the Republican or Democrat. Each represents the individual as taking a stand on what is good and proper for her society, each can be backed by greater or lesser attention to the issues, and each can reflect full moral seriousness on the part of the voter. Therefore, it would seem that because the opportunity to accrue expressive returns is not functionally dependent on the likelihood that one's favored candidate will emerge victorious, no suitably motivated vote is thrown away. Alternatively, every vote is thrown away if only instrumental considerations are allowed to count.

Nonetheless, it does not seem to us that this reconstruction does full justice to the thrown-away vote argument, and it entirely fails to explain how that argument can have the intuitive force that it manifestly does. Meehl suggests that its appeal is a hangover from the erroneous belief that major-party voters enjoy a degree of decisiveness that does not fall to supporters of a minor party. While confusion on this score may account for some of the attractiveness of the argument, we question whether any argument of the thrown-away vote genre must appeal to outcome-oriented considerations.

The case against the minor-party voter could, we suggest, be put along the following lines. In an electoral system such as that of the United States, it is a foregone conclusion that one of the two major-party candidates will gain victory. Which of them it is will have a substantial impact on the course the nation takes, and responsible citizens ought to compare their platforms and come to a considered

---

[14] We do not deny that *some* convoluted utilitarian rationale might be forthcoming. One of the charms/liabilities of the theory is the wondrous way in which it can be twisted and turned to justify one's pretheoretical opinions, whatever they may be.

decision as to which would be more conducive to the common good. Moreover, one should not only *have* an opinion on such matters but should *express* it in an appropriate forum. The principle to which appeal is made is that while one is under no obligation to express or even entertain an opinion on every issue that might arise, one should, in the exercise of one's citizenship, take a stand on issues of considerable importance to the polity.

What is wrong about voting for a third-party candidate is not that one has displayed enthusiasm for, say, Flat Earth Vegetarianism, but that to do so in the context of voting is, ipso facto, to abstain from endorsing one of the two major parties as preferable to the other. That, however, is *the overwhelming significant practical issue* confronting the electorate. Next to it, questions about the merits or lack of the same of the FEV platform fade to insignificance. At least that is the way it is in the actual world; whether in some envisioned utopia the FEV program would galvanize public attention and would then call for deeply considered expressive activity is another, and peripheral, question. Things as they are, to vote for the third party is to abdicate one's responsibility to take a stand on the matter of greatest practical moment. It is along these lines, we suggest, that a reasonable statement of the thrown-away vote argument can be constructed. It would be better, though, to rename the argument: Its gravamen is not so much that the vote is thrown away but that it is *frivolous,* a sort of *self-indulgence.* It contends that one who so votes has failed to take advantage of an opportunity to declare oneself on something truly important and has instead opted to gratify one's own idiosyncratic expressive tastes. The indulgence is, then, a sort of vanity. What the public has presented through its political institutions as the portentous issue on which citizens are asked to take a position is set aside in favor of a purely personal expression of some eccentric and essentially irrelevant whim.

While we describe this as a reasonable reformulation of the thrown-away vote argument, we do not maintain that it is thoroughly compelling. Although a vote for a third-party candidate might be frivolously motivated (compare write-in votes for Mickey Mouse), it need not be. The voter may care deeply about the national welfare and may judge that the most fitting expression he can give to this care is by voting for the third-party candidate. His vote then is principled, much as an abstention from voting might be, and it can reflect serious attention to the question of what sort of stand he ought to take. Since it is not possible for him to express through his vote both which of the major candidates he prefers and which among the total list of candidates he prefers, he opts to do the latter. Even if this decision is criticized as mistaken, it does not seem inherently to exemplify lack of political seriousness.

The dilemma for the supporter of the minor party is, of course, due to the nature of the voting procedure being used. A person can avail herself of only one expressive act, but that is not enough both to pronounce on the relative merits of the Republican and Democrat and to indicate her overall preference. There is, then, an alternative to criticizing or exonerating the minor-party voter: It is to fault the voting system for presenting the dilemma in the first place. Requiring voters to select only one candidate when several are running is a procedure too ingrained to provide adequate opportunity for individuals to express all the significant preferences they hold. Some form of preferential voting would obviate much of the thrown-away-vote malaise. Such schemes have been endorsed by theorists as more accurate devices for generating collective determinations from a pool of purely outcome-oriented voters than is simple "first-preference" voting. It is interesting that an account of voting as a fundamentally expressive activity lends support to the same recommendation.

The evaluation of democratic determinations

Any normative evaluation of democratic procedures must include some judgment as to the quality of the *inputs* to those procedures – the quality, that is, of the votes that citizens cast over the electoral options that face them. That quality, we have argued, is not to be taken for granted. We cannot rely on the evolved instincts of each to seek his own good – on what we might call "natural prudence" – to secure outcomes that are preferred by the citizenry, even where majority rule aggregates satisfactorily. Such natural prudence does protect against folly in choice contexts where individual agents are decisive and where the consequences of action are a discipline on how the chooser chooses. But this protection is absent in the large-scale elections characteristic of contemporary democratic rule. In this sense, we have provided in the foregoing argument of this book an explanation of the phenomenon on which Barbara Tuchman remarks in the epigraph to this chapter and that she sees as a conspicuous feature of the entire political history of mankind, democracy included. Perhaps the obvious question to be posed to our diagnosis is whether any limits can be set to the dimensions of such folly. That is, the issue is not so much why collective folly emerges on enough occasions to be notable, at least to Ms. Tuchman's eye, but rather why collective folly is not universal.

There are two kinds of answer to this challenge. One is that collective decision making may be buttressed by various kinds of institutional protection that serve to filter out many of the more spectacular absurdities that might otherwise arise. (What institutional devices commend themselves in this regard will be the subject of our final chapter.) The other possible answer lies in the existence of widespread civic morality – attitudes on the part of voters that substantially limit the whimsy, apathy, or sheer malice that might otherwise infect their behavior. In its most optimistic version, such a civic morality may stimulate a kind of "public-interested" voting on the part of each citizen that more or less replicates the ideal aggregation of individual preferences performed by a perfect market at the level of private choice.

We have tried to argue in the preceding sections of this chapter that the most promising ground in which to root such a civic morality lies in an expressive, input-oriented prescription, rather than an outcome-oriented one. It has been argued that the outcome-oriented line cannot be rendered coherent at the level of the individual voter. We shall not attempt now to add to those arguments. Instead we focus on their implications for the evaluation of democratic arrangements.

At the most obvious level, the coherence of any normative theory of voter conduct presumably plays some role in the capacity of that normative theory to motivate. Specifically, if voters cannot be held to be morally (or in any other way) *responsible* for the electoral outcomes they collectively generate, then it is difficult to see how moral considerations could induce the kind of public-interested voting that is ideally required. Such moral responsibility can, we have argued, be more plausibly validated by appeal to expressive considerations than by recourse to far-fetched effects on electoral outcomes.

Moreover, as we have mentioned, the cases in which an outcome-oriented argument is most persuasive are precisely those in which democratic processes are, in fact, most deficient. If the expected benefit from voting is large, the prevailing political equilibrium must be such that either the voter is likely to be decisive or that the moral stakes are very considerable. In such an event, collective decision making is likely to give rise to ethically disastrous outcomes. It cannot be the case both that the abstentions of nonvoters are consequentially important and that electoral democracy as it currently operates dependably yields satisfactory outcomes. Accordingly, any civic morality grounded in outcome-oriented considerations must be deeply critical of real-world democratic outcomes and the institutional structures that make them operative. Of course, such criticism is not necessarily decisive. The economist's insistence that all normative evaluation be conducted in full comparative mode is well taken. Democracy may be the least bad of feasible alternatives. If so, that lends added point to Tuchman's observations, since her purview covers an experience only a small part of which has been democratic in the modern sense.

But does a plausible civic morality for democracy require us to take such a dismal view? We think not. Under the expressive account, a voter's responsibility to vote and to vote intelligently, seriously, and in a publicly defensible manner is not tied to the chance that she herself will make a difference to the electoral outcome. We presume that that chance is indeed negligible. But she should vote anyway because major elections are a venue in which she has both an opportunity and an obligation to express her political views. Voting responsibly is something the responsible citizen does. If this argument is inadequate to motivate public-interested voting – or, more modestly, to suppress voter flippancy and voter malice – then democracy is indeed in some trouble. At least the heroic versions of democracy as an institutionalization of some version of government "of, by, and for the people" seem seriously misconceived.

But such heroic versions do not exhaust all that is to be said in democracy's favor. If democracy is not government by the people, it is at least not government by some other person or persons. Citizens will remain subject to electoral determinations, and though the resultant outcomes do not reliably reflect citizens' interests (or preferences), neither do they reliably reflect the interests of some subset of society. There is a particular objectionableness to being the instrument of some other agent's purposes, and this objectionableness is something that democracy manages to avoid more than do alternative forms of government. If freedom can be properly understood not as control of one's environment but rather as the absence of deliberate control by others, then citizens in a democracy enjoy conspicuously more freedom than do citizens of other regimes.

Scant praise, perhaps. On this line, democratic outcomes would have no more to be said for them than outcomes selected by flipping a coin, since that procedure would also ensure such weak autonomy. A freedom that amounts to being buffeted about by the vagaries of an electoral system in which no one is in charge is, so the critic might contend, not a very valuable kind of freedom. Perhaps. But chance is not the worst of rulers. The Athenians, no slouches when it came to management of a democratic regime, used lots to fill various offices. Random selection is currently employed to select pools of jurors and, until recently, was used to conscript American armies. One might be prepared to endorse it more generally if one could indeed be *sure* that the procedures were genuinely random – which procedures may well not be if the options are selected by some agent with an interest in the outcomes. The essential point is that the relevant comparison is not that between random selection and some conceivable *ideal* decision procedure, but rather the comparison between various distinctly nonideal means through which collective outcomes can be determined. To one who surveys the history of blunders, outrages, and enormities perpetrated by political authorities acting in accord with some quite deliberate design – not least those that have checkered the twentieth century – genuinely random selection of officeholders perhaps does not come off looking too shabby.

Even if democracy were little better than a random outcome-generating machine, it might still be preferable to explicit randomization. Voting does not only generate outcomes, but it also affords to citizens an opportunity for the expression of sentiments in the same venue in which those outcomes are produced. Referenda and elections provide a structured mechanism through which burdens and benefits are distributed to assignable classes of persons; that is, in large measure, the *point* of the exercise. One who votes can do so in the consciousness that one is a participant in a process that is genuinely significant, even though the direction in which one casts one's own ballot is almost certainly inconsequential. A rich symbolism has grown up around the election process, endowing it with a portentousness to which few other avenues for expressive activity aspire. One can, for this reason, take seriously one's own vote, as the rhetoric that precedes Election Day continuously urges. And because so many people do go to some trouble to vote in spite of the negligible probability that their individual votes will be decisive, we can infer that the particular expressive possibility afforded them by voting is positively valued.

In the same way, we can predict that citizens in a democracy will also tend to "invest" in the exercise of the franchise – or, at least, invest more than is consistent with the homo economicus model of standard public choice theory. It is both tempting and easy to decry the egregiously limited political information that voters carry to the polls, and indeed it is undeniable that the representative voter is no rival to Walter Lippmann for political sagacity. However, once again the relevant appraisal is, compared with what? Electors devote far more of their resources to securing political information than can be explained by the expected payoff to them of a better informed vote. Just as expression provides a direct return, so too do acts preparatory to expression. Watching candidates perform in televised debates, reading journals of opinion, and poring through the newspapers for accounts of the latest scandal all have entertainment value for many citizens and result in their votes being better informed. Reverting to an earlier analogy, the most vociferous baseball fans also tend to be the ones best informed concerning the makeup of the roster, batting averages, and so on. In the same way, outcomes that emerge through voting reflect more and better information than is predicted by standard public choice analysis and, a fortiori, more than does decision by random selection.

It cannot be established as a matter of logic that aggregation of relatively knowledgeable votes will generate outcomes better than those arrived at through random selection or, much the same, from the aggregation of votes cast in impenetrable ignorance, but it seems reasonable to believe that this is so. Admittedly, we carry with us a certain residual prejudice on this score. We are in the business of trying to create and disseminate knowledge and so are professionally inclined to the belief that more knowledge is better than less. We hope that this is not an *entirely* groundless prejudice – or if it is, that it is a prejudice that the readers of this book are likely to share.

Moreover, although voters do not infallibly express preferences over outcomes, it would be foolish to deny the existence of any association. As was argued in Chapter 3, people's natural affections for themselves lead them to regard favorably candidates and policies that further their own interests. There is psychic economy to be had by establishing harmony between the principles one endorses and the path along which interest lies. To the extent that such harmony is achieved, one can both "do the right thing" and advance one's own ends. Moreover, we have seen that there is reason for believing that internal ethical considerations induce some individuals to vote much of the time according to their judgments of the public interest. The cost in terms of private interest forgone is negligible and, as we have argued in this chapter, an expressively based civic morality that endorses public-interest voting comports with common intuitions and is, at a minimum, better attested than rival microethical accounts. We do not deny that public-interested voting can and does go awry. The judgments it incorporates may be incomplete, ill-considered, and infected by other expressively potent motives.[15] Nonetheless, some modest reliance on the generally salutary effects of voting tempered by a civic morality seems indicated.

We do not take this residue of morality to safeguard against the voter's dilemma: Democracy is flawed as a mechanism for making social decisions and, on occasions, may produce genuinely disastrous outcomes. We ought to design our democratic institutions to make disastrous outcomes less likely, and one such prospect may lie in stimulating the right kind of civic morality. However, even with the best institutional structure for democracy, there must be a strong presumptive case in favor of making social decisions through decentralized arrangements in which in-

---

[15] Voter enthusiasm for the Reagan–Bush "war on drugs" is a current example of public concern run amok.

dividuals are characteristically decisive. In other words, the domain of collective decision making should be drawn rather restrictively. Nevertheless, that domain must necessarily be quite extensive: The institutional apparatus of markets is itself "public" in nature, and in at least some cases externalities will be sufficiently pronounced to require explicitly collective intervention. Where decision making cannot feasibly be decentralized, democracy seems likely to be superior to other forms of collective decision making. For the democratic enthusiast this distinctly modified rapture over the virtues of democracy will seem thin and feeble. But that is, in the light of our analysis, the best that can be said; and at the practical level of choice among alternative political forms, it is enough.

11 Constitutional implications

What should governments be allowed to do? What is the appropriate sphere of political action? How large a share of national product should be available for political disposition? What sort of political decision structures should be adopted at the constitutional stage? Under what conditions and to what extent should individuals be franchised?

These questions and many others like them clearly depend for answers on some positive, predictive analysis of how different political institutions will operate. An informed and meaningful theory of constitutions cannot be constructed until and unless there exists some theory of the operation of alternative political rules.

James Buchanan, *"Politics Without Romance"*

The normative dimension

How extended should the domain of politics be? Should democracy be representative or direct? What is the case for a federal as opposed to a centralized polity? How should power be distributed among the various parts of the state apparatus? What are the pros and cons of bicameralism?

Such questions are the very stuff of political theory, whether in the public choice variant or in the more traditional form familiar from political science and political philosophy. Whatever other ambitions it may have, political theory aspires to provide the resources for evaluating alternative ways of organizing political life.

Of course, public choice – and more generally political theory in the rational actor tradition – goes about its normative theorizing in a distinctive way. It imports from economics an attempted dichotomy between "positive" and "normative" analysis, and it embodies that dichotomy in a kind of two-stage procedure for normative theorizing. At the first stage, the analyst isolates the different worlds that would prevail under the various political arrangements to be normatively assessed. At the second stage, normative criteria are introduced to evaluate the feasible worlds so isolated, and thereby the particular political arrangements that give rise to those worlds. The justification offered for this procedure is that it draws attention to crucial feasibility considerations in political ethics; it ensures that the diagnosis of the disease (if any) is right before treatment commences. Equally, public choice scholars tend to be critical of traditional political theory, which they see as mixing descriptive analysis with evaluation in a manner altogether too cavalier, and as focusing too much on the specification and refinement of values (and too little on how alternative political arrangements actually work). In public choice eyes, traditional political theory is too preoccupied with ideal worlds, too little concerned with feasible ones.

As we have emphasized throughout the book, we believe that the public choice account of how electoral politics operates is seriously flawed. However, we endorse

199

in general terms the public choice method of normative political theorizing. We agree that understanding the way the world works is a crucial prerequisite to understanding how it can be made to work better; and we agree that general abstract reasoning, together with a lively sense of the "facts," is helpful in developing such understanding. We also agree that much traditional political theory is rather weak in providing proper analytical foundations for recommendations.

In some measure, however, we see our theory of expressive electoral politics as supplying some of that analytical foundation. Many of the concerns of traditional political theory – the nature of civic religion, the possibility of moral education, the values that alternative institutional arrangements instantiate (as well as the political consequences of such institutions) – emerge as salient matters in our theory of rational voter behavior.

In this connection, two aspects are worth specific emphasis. First, because ethical considerations weigh significantly in voter behavior, there is a wider array of mechanisms by which institutional arrangements can influence social phenomena. Standard public choice models focus exclusively on the use of invisible hand mechanisms of the kind exemplified by the idealized market in the famous Smithian account. Such mechanisms seek to secure desirable outcomes by operating on agents' *interests:* The object is to set in place incentive structures that so transform agents' interests that each agent operates in the interests of others. Our conception of electoral politics allows for another kind of mechanism, one that operates by supporting or encouraging behavior endorsed by some behaviorally relevant norm. We have, for example, already argued in the previous chapter that democracy is likely to work better on average if supported by a civic morality that encourages public-interested voting. If such a morality exists, what mechanisms might be used to encourage it? How do mechanisms introduced for other reasons bear on the potency of that civic morality? These questions that our approach invites are essentially overlooked (or assumed away) in the standard public choice account.[1] We shall want to look at them briefly here.

Second, it is noteworthy that the two-stage procedure for normative theorizing that public choice insists on and that we have endorsed naturally leads to a consequentialist mode of evaluation. Political institutions are evaluated in terms of the characteristics of the alternative worlds to which they give rise. In evaluating democracy as a form of political decision making, for example, the critical concern is the nature of the political decisions actually made and the effects those decisions have on the persons affected by them. But democracy may also be seen to "stand for" certain values in itself. The principle of "one person, one vote" may be seen to instantiate notions of equality and collective self-determination, even if the distributional outcomes thereby generated are likely to be quite unequal[2] or the idea of collective self-determination is deeply problematic (as we have argued in Chapter

---

[1] In another place and in a different collaboration, one of the authors has attempted to provide a more general account of such mechanisms and contrast them with invisible hand alternatives. See Pettit and Brennan (1991).

[2] For an argument suggesting that this may be a genuine anxiety under democratic procedures with simple majority rule, see Brennan and Buchanan (1985), chap. 8.

10). If choice of political institutions is itself part of the language by which citizens express their political values, then what political institutions *stand for* is potentially ethically and electorally relevant, independently of what those institutions actually produce. Moreover, if those institutions not only express but also stimulate certain ethical values, then choice of one institution rather than another might well influence the kind of behavior that agents adopt under its operation.

Consider, for example, the operation of the free market system. Economists from Adam Smith onward have focused attention on the outcomes that emerge under that system – on the implications of "the system of natural liberty" for "the wealth of nations," to use Smith's terminology. But one who accepted those implications might nevertheless be concerned to repudiate the values one sees the system to instantiate – cupidity, aggression, rivalry, wealth as an index of worth, and so on. One may be anxious that the market economy may differentially favor, and ultimately produce, persons with aggressively egoistic, competitive characteristics – and anxious about the long-term consequences of such character changes in the community at large. There is, of course, a strand of promarket thinking that disputes such claims and that upholds as one of the prime virtues of commercial society the "softness" that it produces in its members.[3] The point here is not whether such arguments are correct or not: It is that they are arguments that intellectual habits within contemporary economics either ignore or claim to be irrelevant. We make two observations. First, that the charge of irrelevance is itself an ethical claim and one that is difficult to sustain even within a utilitarian frame. Second, that whatever their ethical significance, the values articulated by an institution are likely to be of considerable *electoral* relevance and therefore play a proper role in the descriptive theory of the choice among alternative political institutions (as distinct, that is, from the normative theory of choice among institutions). Neither of these observations is to deny the importance of the traditional economist's defense of markets. But we do wish to draw attention to dimensions of evaluation that are typically neglected by economists (and by extension, public choice theorists) – ones that are more commonly part of traditional political theory and for which our account of electoral politics allows extended scope.

With all this as background, we turn to the specific institutional questions we began with. What insights does our analysis provide in understanding how salient pieces of the political-institutional fabric work and how they might work "better"? The particular pieces of institutional apparatus we shall focus on here include representative as against direct democracy, bicameral as against unicameral systems of organizing the legislature, the division of powers, the secret as against the open ballot, federal as against central systems of government and direct constitutional restrictions on the domain of public activity.

Our reasons for discussing these matters are twofold – first, because they are matters of enormous significance and intellectual interest in their own right; second, because discussion of them allows us to show how an expressive conception of voting behavior might color one's understanding of familiar liberal institutions. In

---

[3] See Hirschman (1982) for an interesting and elegant exposition.

accordance with this second purpose, we shall try to show how justification based on our expressive voting theory differs from other possible accounts: We shall emphasize how our line is distinctive. The discussion is necessarily brief. We have aimed to be suggestive rather than definitive. There are many loose ends, and much more needs to be said on all these matters. We hope we may ourselves say some of that "more" on some future occasion. For the time being, however, we seek only to offer a sketch.

In framing our discussion, we shall take it that a primary objective of democratic political arrangements is to secure political outcomes that reflect the will of the governed.[4] This norm places our treatment squarely within the liberal tradition of political thought, which is where we would seek to locate ourselves. It also goes naturally with our subject matter: It is difficult to see how concern with the nature of electoral process could arise in a context where citizens' preferences were taken to carry no normative weight.[5]

The domain of government action

We begin with two of Buchanan's questions cited as the epigraph to this chapter: What is the appropriate sphere of political action? And what claim on total resources is proper for that sphere? In its simplest terms, these questions could be construed as a single one – how "big" should government be? But the simpler single-operation version is clearly ambiguous, since it might refer either to the number of areas that government seeks to control, or the share of GDP that government appropriates for public use.

In what follows, we shall isolate four answers to our questions: the welfare economist's, the public choice theorist's, traditional political theory's, and that which emerges from our treatment of electoral preference.

The welfare economist's answer

Standard welfare economics offers a suitable point of departure for engaging the domain issue because questions of the appropriate sphere and extent of government activity are central ones in its purview. These questions are posed in the context of an understanding of the operation of perfectly competitive markets in which, under certain idealized conditions, market agents fully exploit all mutual gains from

---

[4] It is worth noting that our theory of electoral preference creates some interesting problems in the interpretation of that liberal principle, specifically whether "will" should be understood in terms of preference values or interests. Standard public choice thinking conflates those concepts into a single category – call it "preference" simpliciter – that is revealed in actual choice. We want to preserve those distinctions. And since action is context dependent in our theory, no behavioristically inspired retreat into action as the unique indicator of preference is available. We think there are some interesting issues at stake here, but we will not pursue them at this point.

[5] Difficult, but not impossible. The ritual of voting might serve the function of establishing a patina of legitimacy around state activities and thereby keep the masses quiet, while the real decision making goes on elsewhere and by reference to independent ethical criteria. Such a "normative theory of democratic politics" would treat electoral procedures as a *practical* constraint, but not an ethical one.

trade. The role of government is, on this reading, a threefold one: first, to establish and maintain the institutional structure within which markets can operate; second, to implement any redistributions that distributive justice requires; and third, where the required "idealized conditions" break down, to intervene so that all possible mutual benefits are appropriated. (Intervention here may take the form of direct provision or differential taxation/subsidization.) Although the first two roles are potentially important and may involve government in quite extensive activity (e.g., the definition and protection of personal and property rights, and the provision of enforcement machinery for contracts that citizens enter into freely), it is the third role on which welfare economists have focused all their analytic firepower. Here, attention has focused on developing a theory of "market failure" – a kind of taxonomy of all those circumstances under which the market equilibrium will leave mutual gains for appropriation. The appropriate polar concept here is that of Samuelsonian "publicness"[6] – a good is "public" if it is consumed equally and totally by all consumers (like an outdoor fireworks display) – because "publicness" seems to represent a distillation of all those characteristics of goods that might be sources of market failure. With this apparatus, the welfare economist could answer the two domain questions clearly: First, government should provide all "public goods," so understood, and leave all "private goods"[7] to be provided through the market; and second, these public goods should be produced up to the point where the total benefit to all persons from an additional unit of the good equals the cost of that unit.

The public choice amendment

A central element in the public choice agenda has been to amend the conclusions of the welfare economists' market failure model. Demonstration of market failure might remove any automatic presumption in favor of market provision, but as the public choice theorist properly insists, such demonstration is not sufficient to establish a case in favor of government provision. Perhaps there will be "government failure" of a magnitude greater than the market failure that government is supposed to correct. Nothing less than a piece of comparative institutional analysis can properly decide the question of what government should do, and any such analysis requires a formal treatment of political process and its "welfare" properties exactly analogous to the formal "economics" theory of the operation of markets.

Public choice theory purports to provide just such a formal treatment. And the message of that treatment is, at best, highly skeptical of political performance. As we noted in Chapter 5, though the median-voter model would, under suitably restrictive conditions, generate political equilibria that are proximately efficient, the circumstances under which the median-voter outcome is stable are sufficiently remote that not much confidence can be placed in this result. Instead, political equilibrium will either reflect the preferences of the strategic agenda setter – in which

---

[6] The classic treatment here is Samuelson (1955).
[7] Ones that have to be parceled out among consumers so that more for one means less for others, and for which property rights can be enforced.

case the outcome would be stable but dictatorial – or would wander more or less randomly through policy space. Moreover, even if something like the median-voter result did emerge in electoral politics, the differential potency of small well-organized lobbies could well produce redistributions away from the citizenry at large toward special interests.[8] And an exactly analogous anxiety arises on the question of redistributive justice. It is not enough for the welfare economist to identify the market distribution as nonideal: It is necessary also to show that government can on average be relied on to redistribute in the ethically approved direction.[9] Otherwise, the market distribution may be the best among those actually feasible.

It is worth noting here that at the purely ethical level – the level, that is, of evaluative procedures – public choice more or less accepts the relevance of the ethical categories that welfare economics isolates.[10] In particular, public choice orthodoxy accepts the normative relevance of the private goods/public goods distinction and of the particular conception of institutional "failure" as embodied in the market failure concept. Such acceptance is perhaps to be expected: Economists have been the principal audience for public choice theory, and in any event, public choice theorists have seen their primary contribution as lying in providing an appropriate "positive, predictive analysis," not in ethical theory as such. The general message that emerges from public choice theory is that governments should provide those goods where the extent of publicness and the degree of market failure is large enough, and otherwise leave goods to the market system. It is in this sense that public choice can be conceived as an "amendment" to welfare economics, significant though that amendment is. As to the levels of provision of such public goods, these simply emerge from the ongoing play of electoral politics: If there is any role at all for cost–benefit analysis and the "optimal conditions" for public goods provision that preoccupied welfare economists through the sixties and early seventies, that role is an entirely peripheral one. Virtually no reliance can be placed on either the authority of such normative judgments[11] or their independent political relevance.[12]

It should be noted that public choice theory does not suppose that in-period electoral politics can be relied on to set appropriate limits to its sphere of activities: On the contrary, all kinds of electoral pressures will be present to encourage expansion of government activity into areas where that activity cannot be normatively justi-

[8] See Peter Aranson's paper in Brennan and Lomasky (1989) for a useful discussion of these results.
[9] Again, orthodox public choice gives us reason to be anxious on this matter. See Brennan and Buchanan (1985), chap. 8, for relevant argument.
[10] Though the approach is often rather different. Our discussion of the role of unanimity in Paretian welfare economics in Chapter 8 illustrates one aspect of that difference.
[11] Because the truly relevant information about preferences is almost invariably inaccessible from the standard sources (i.e., agents' choices).
[12] Cost–benefit analysis may have a role to play in calculating the payoffs to politically relevant *groups*, and hence in assessing the likely success of alternative policies. But the conclusions do not represent for public choice theorists an independent, morally derived guide to action as they do for ordinary welfare economists.

fied. Pure public goods are not the most efficient instrument for securing transfers to decisive majority coalitions, and provision of these public goods will therefore predictably be reduced in favor of goods with the politically relevant redistributive characteristics (redistributive characteristics that have nothing to do in general with distributive justice). Accordingly, specification of the proper domain of government activity is an explicitly *constitutional* task. And we can have some confidence that properly informed citizens will exercise the right constitutional decisions because each is uncertain as to the comparison of future majority coalitions.[13]

Traditional political theory's perspective

To attribute a substantive position to traditional political theory – one to set against that of welfare economics, either as amended by public choice theory or not – is necessarily to do violence to an extraordinary variety of writings, all of which have their own richness and subtlety. Therefore, what we say here necessarily has to be general, impressionistic, and vague. We are not intellectual historians, which is probably as well, since if we were we would be unable to do the violence to political thought that we will doubtless do here. But with such disclaimers, it does seem to us that the kinds of concerns in much traditional political theory are different from those in welfare economics/public choice. For one thing, whereas welfare economics/public choice isolates those goods that governments legitimately *should* supply, traditional political theory has been rather more concerned with those that governments should not – and by this we do not mean to refer to the kind of blanket "all-else-to-the-market" requirement that public choice theory offers, but a more specific "here be dangers" kind of instruction. Liberal political thought has been explicit in carving out from the sphere of government provision, even of government influence, certain goods that, in preliberal times, government had been very much in the habit of providing: established religion, approved political doctrine, strictures for the conduct of personal morality, and so on. Liberal regimes in the traditional conception are concerned to protect such "private" areas of conduct from day-to-day politics by constitutional rules (doctrines of separation of church and state, say) or via "bills of rights" or in some other fashion. Compared with such concerns, the issues of what goods governments should provide or regulate and how much should be expended from the nation's resources on such goods are assigned second-order significance. But what makes activities like religion, political doctrine, and private morality "special"? Partly, clearly, in that they are constitutive of personhood in a way that the choice of doctor or of radio and television program[14] are not; but partly also perhaps in that they are areas to which political fingers are ineluctably drawn and which require special protection on that account. At least, we conjecture that this may be so. And our model of electoral politics has implications that fit quite naturally with the conjecture.

---

[13] The fundamental treatment of these ideas is in Buchanan and Tullock (1962) and Buchanan (1975).

[14] Both areas in the provision of which putatively "liberal" regimes have intervened.

Table 11.1. *Expressive values in electoral politics*

	Low expressive value	High expressive value
Private	1	3
Public	4	2

The expressive theory's response

The expressive theory of electoral politics, unlike the orthodox public choice account, emphasizes a distinction that is conceptually independent of the public good/ private good divide. According to our theory, electoral pressure will encourage governments to provide those goods that are highly valued expressively and to underprovide those goods that are of low expressive benefit. In specifying the domain of politics, therefore, there is fourfold classification that becomes relevant, which we can for simplification represent in matrix form as in Table 11.1. The row classification is the familiar public–private divide, which we retain because we accept its normative relevance. The column classification is between those goods that have little expressive value and those that have much, and follows the thrust of our discussion in the preceding chapters. Those goods with low expressive value will tend to be driven out of policy platforms in favor of those with high expressive value. Goods that generate substantial *negative* expressive returns will appear in party platforms in their negative form. For example, if pollution is negatively valued expressively, it will appear as "pollution abatement" in our matrix in the right-hand column.

The normative significance of the four categories can be described as follows:

Category 1. These are goods about which specifications of the domain of politics can reasonably, safely remain silent. It is desirable that these goods be provided in the market, but there is no electoral advantage in involving them in the party platform and, to that extent, little danger that they will be provided politically.[15]

Category 2. These are goods that should be and will tend to be politically provided. Defense, welfare payments, and environmental protection are obvious examples that we have discussed earlier. Goods in this category and Category 1 are relatively unproblematic, in the sense that they will naturally tend to find their way under the appropriate institutional umbrella. Of course, output may not be optimal. Provision may be grossly deficient or grossly excessive depending on the precise nature and volatility of the expressive benefits generated. Excessive xenophobia or imprudent pacifism may equally overturn calculations of "optimal" defense spending, for example. But at least one can rely on defense issues being politically addressed.

Category 3. These are goods for which political provision should be expressively prohibited. Although essentially private in character, and hence produced approx-

---

[15] If political provision affords large rents to small, concentrated groups, then other nonelectoral mechanisms come into play that may well secure political intervention.

imately optimally under decentralized market-like arrangements, there will be much pressure for competitive political parties to provide them. The most obvious example here perhaps is religion and related services. Although undoubtedly redolent with expressive significance, religion is, we believe, best provided under noncoercive institutional arrangements, either because to provide it otherwise is extremely dangerous to civic stability or because coercion (other than self-imposed, and with full rights of "secession") is self-defeating for the spiritual enterprise. More controversially perhaps, areas like the arts, sports, possibly higher education, and national airlines operating internationally are examples of this category. Their expressive significance is considerable, but they all seem to be examples of "private goods" in the technical Samuelsonian sense. Failure to restrict the domain of the public sector will tend to lead to these goods being publicly provided – with attendant inefficiencies. More controversially still, perhaps, are cases such as racial policies. It is not that racial discrimination may not emerge in market institutions: It is rather that political expressions of racial prejudice (either pro or con) are likely to be potent sources of electoral support and, hence, that political intervention in racial issues may well generate more rather than less discriminatory behavior.

Category 4. This category is problematic for precisely opposite reasons from those relevant for Category 2. These are goods that are technically public but that generate little in the way of expressive benefits. Sewerage and similar public health activities probably provide one example; possibly certain kinds of public information are another.[16] If such goods are provided by governments, they will tend to be underexpanded, and may require special institutional encouragement. (For example, decisions about their provision may be decentralized to "technical experts" whose affection for their own brainchildren may ensure adequate resources in the face of electoral unpopularity.)

It could, of course, be argued that the categorization in Table 11.1 is misleading in that it encourages too static a view of the expressive dimension. In particular, that table and the surrounding discussion presupposes that expressive properties inhere in the goods or activities under consideration. Such a view is too static. To some extent, expressive returns are a function of associations that are created by political entrepreneurs or that arise in the course of ongoing history and are then mobilized for electoral purposes by those entrepreneurs. Political rhetoric may not be mere advertising (an equivalence we reject in Chapter 6), but the two activities do have some features in common, including an important creative dimension. Nevertheless, for the purposes of specifying the proper domain of government, it is necessary to attach categories to activities or goods that are constitutionally specifiable, and we reckon this can be done along the lines indicated reasonably enough.

What is interesting about the categorization is that it embodies a notable gesture toward the specific concerns about inappropriate governmental obtrusiveness that

---

[16] Price indexes, balance of payments data, GNP estimates, and the like have assumed a certain public profile in the relatively recent past and acquired a corresponding expressive value. In this sense, corrections to last year's GNP estimates may be a better example.

we see as one feature of traditional political theory – the feature that bears most particularly on domain questions. The categorization also alerts us to another possible problem area – that where technical properties of publicness argue for political provision, but where low expressive significance suggests that, in fact, politics is unlikely to get involved. Such areas may require not only explicit constitutional reference as a public responsibility, but also additional forms of institutional protection.

Representative and direct democracy

The question of whether democracy should be direct or representative is clearly a major question in constitutional political analysis. And the fact that virtually all modern democracies have settled on the representative form should not be seen to diminish the significance of the question: In political life we cannot assume that practice makes perfect.

We shall approach the question, as in the domain case, by isolating three possible lines of argument – three conceptions (or models) of how electoral politics works or might be made to work. We shall begin, as before, with the orthodox public choice line.

The public choice line

What account of representative as opposed to direct democracy can conventional public choice scholarship offer? On the face of things, direct democracy seems naturally to be preferred: The mediation of "representatives" between policy decision and voter preference seems only to invite the possible misrepresentation of citizens' preferences. Problems of majority cycling and agenda setting may arise under direct democracy but do not seem to be in any way moderated by the device of representation: Indeed, by making the business of coalition formation and reformation easier, representation seems more conducive rather than less to ever present problems of majoritarian instability. There can be no sense made of any conception of parliamentary process as promoting discussion and argument with an eye to coming to a common mind. Citizens have well-defined interests on which policies may bear and which determine their voting behavior: The only scope for interaction lies in bargaining over the share of the spoils. Representation may facilitate that bargaining, but as public choice assures us, the bargaining process is itself unstable and any outcome (including truly disastrous ones) can emerge.

What positive arguments for representation might be offered? There are two, neither of them particularly persuasive. One is simply to appeal to the purely technical difficulties of organizing the entire polity to vote directly on all the issues, given the numbers of voters and the number of issues involved. But such difficulties would seem to be rendered obsolete by possibilities such as telephone or electronic voting.

The second, more promising line involves an appeal to Downsian rational ignorance. Direct voting is not feasible because voters would not have an incentive to be properly informed about the true effects of policies and, further, would be ill-equipped to isolate which information provided is actually correct. Within a representative assembly, however, rational ignorance is a much smaller problem: The probability of being decisive in an assembly of 200, and a fortiori in a committee of 15, is relatively significant. Accordingly, representation can significantly reduce problems of rational ignorance and expressive preferences. However, it is important to note the nature of the representation at stake here. The "representative" cannot be cast as the agent of some group whose interests she represents, because the same rational ignorance problem arises in the selection of the agent. Representation does not offer a solution to the rational ignorance problem in that sense. Rather, representatives should be freed entirely from any constraints and simply be allowed to pursue their own private interests in any assembly vote. Assembly members are "representative" of particular interests only to the extent that they vote as would any member of the group of citizens whose interests that members' interests happen to resemble. The role of the larger electoral process is, on this view, to secure an appropriate sample of the total polity. In that way rational ignorance and expressive preference problems can be significantly moderated by representation. This model of the representative assembly is what might be called a "jury" model, in contrast with a "conduit" model, in which representatives are conceived as conduits for the representation of the interests of their constituents.

Three comments arise. First, this line automatically invites the Burnheim suggestion[17] of random sampling as a superior mechanism for selection of representatives. Such a procedure, possibly buttressed by stratification to ensure the presence of interests that are significantly distinct, seems certain to produce a more representative sample than popular elections of candidates: Elections can only introduce unwanted distortion. Second, an assembly of this kind would surely be susceptible to all the standard public choice problems of majoritarian instability: Even if preferences were adequately sampled, the outcome would not reliably reflect them. And third, there must always be an anxiety that the assembly members, or some subset, would combine to exploit the citizenry at large: In a world of purely private interest and (some) private goods, there is no limit to the coalitions that can form, and a coalition of assembly members as such seems an obvious and dangerous possibility.

In short then, representation can moderate problems of rational ignorance – but only at the probable cost of exacerbating much more serious problems of instability under majoritarian cycling. If instability is not a problem (for reasons that are independent of matters under consideration here), then the proper procedures for representation would seem to be random sampling, not election: Voting would be relevant only at the level of assembly decision making. And more generally, representative institutions would have to be set against other possible techniques of providing politically relevant information reliably, such as public subsidy of genuinely independent sources of information. Direct democracy with subsidized information may well be the better course. On balance, then, the standard public

---

[17] Set out in Burnheim (1985) particularly sec. 3, pp. 82–105.

choice line offers rather little in terms of persuasive arguments for representative institutions.

Political talk

One of the reasons why public choice orthodoxy provides no immediate presumption in favor of representative democracy is that the theory provides no place for talk. Processes of argument, discussion, persuasion, and finally coming to a mind – processes that were arguably central to the Athenian ideal and that receive considerable contemporary support in the works of Jurgen Habermas – are entirely otiose in a view of politics as an exercise in sheer self-interest. If, however, talk is seen to play an important role in democratic process, then some form of representative democracy seems obligatory. There may be no difficulty in organizing millions of persons to indicate yes or no. There would be enormous difficulty in organizing an intelligent debate involving a mere hundred participants: By the time the ninety-ninth rose to speak, the first would have long since ceased to listen.

Isolating a central place for talk in democratic politics seems, then, to be one way of establishing a case for representation. And as we have argued in Chapter 6, the expressive theory of electoral behavior does isolate such a place. However, in the Habermas/Athenian account of the role of talk in the assembly, no obviously critical role is afforded by the election of representatives. In the Habermas account, participants in assembly debate are constrained by the requirement to persuade each other: Each is taken to be obliged by the context to address himself to the public or general interest, and it is in the process of debate that each sufficiently refines his sense of what the common interest is to be able to reach agreement with others. On this view, the assembly is rather like the academic seminar, in which appropriately intelligent and informed persons can be expected to reach agreement on whether a particular argument is right or not. And for this purpose, the Athenian ballot has as much justification in selecting assembly members as does any other process.

The expressive account

In our theory, however, it is the nature of expressive benefits that constrains candidates to a public-interest rhetoric – or a rhetoric, at least, cast in terms of some expressively potent line. The claim that a policy is "good for me" is not likely to gain electoral support; more to the point, it is often enough not sufficient to claim that a policy is "good for you." Policies must be "good" simpliciter or good for some group for whom a critical number of voters wish to express support. The individual voter may herself be a member of that group, but she equally may not. Interests may reappear in the electoral picture, but they certainly need not.

Representative democracy works, in our view, mainly because an individual candidate or set of candidates (as in a party) persuade a sufficient fraction of the electorate that that candidate (or set) merits support. It is in demonstrating a conception of the public good, or in projecting an image of competence and general worthiness, that such support is garnered. Representative democracy differs from direct democracy in that direct democracy is driven by expressive characteristics of specific *proposals,* whereas representative democracy is driven by the expressive characteristics of specific candidates or parties. What then is the argument for representative democracy?

First, as we have emphasized, the expressive characteristics of specific proposals can lead to policies being implemented that do great violence to citizens' interests, and that virtually no citizen would be predicted to choose if decisive. If proposals can be mediated by persons who are enrolled to execute the public interest or who are chosen by reference to independent personal characteristics – integrity, competence, and so on – then the scope for perverse policies will be moderated. Of course, some association between expressively valued policies and expressively valued candidates/parties can be expected: If xenophobic policies generate larger expressive return, candidates who support those policies will tend to be elected. But the mediation of persons between voters and policies does make a difference; for parties/persons are elected to govern, not to be mere ciphers of voter preferences. And they are evaluated in terms of their expected capacity to do that job of government. Their support of specific policy platforms is instrumental in showing what sort of values they have, and if those values (and associated policies) turn out to be destructive or disastrous, the candidate/party will be held responsible. Parties themselves will then seek to exercise an independent judgment as to whether policies are likely to be destructive, and hence whether a "stand" on some salient issue is a wise strategy. The overall party commitment to its stated conception of the public interest becomes a kind of filter in which voters' dilemmas will tend to be washed out.

There are two further reasons why representative democracy may be better than direct democracy. The first relates to political participation. It seems plausible to suppose that voters are more likely to be induced to express support for persons than for policies per se. The reasons are psychological: The term "human interest" does have real content, and electoral races that teem with such human interest seem more likely to engage the passions of voters than a contest among specific policies or abstract political philosophies. To the extent that increased participation is desirable, a presumption that features in most discussions of participation (though one on which we would, as in Chapter 10, want to retain an open mind), representative democracy is to be preferred.

The second observation is that, on the whole, people are better judges of other people than they are of rival policies. People need to develop a good sense of the trustworthiness and competence of others to function satisfactorily in arenas of life where they are decisive. Arguably, humanity has evolved to have well-attuned skills in this domain. But outside the set of social scientists, philosophers, and the highly trained,[18] few have the skills to evaluate the implications of alternative policies. That skill is not something we have been "selected for": Failure to possess it is virtually costless to the individual who fails. Besides, as every economist knows, policies often have profoundly counterintuitive consequences too elusive even for

[18] And by no means all of that set.

most (other) economists. If so, we can expect better voter choices among rival *candidates* than among rival policies. It may have made some sense therefore for Mr. Edmund Burke to appeal to the voters of Bristol in terms of his own personal qualities. The fact that Burke's appeal was more successful in saga creation than in securing his own political success should not, perhaps, disturb us too much. We do not hold that proclaiming the truth is necessarily electorally rewarding: And in any event it seems likely that some statement of "policy" is necessary to persuade voters of commitment, reliability, and seriousness of purpose.

The general point here is, however, that representative government alters the domain of expressive support (toward persons away from policies) and restricts policy decision to the smaller arena of parliament (or party room) where expressive considerations are likely to be less potent. We do not believe that the institution of representation will overcome the risk of political perversity: We do think representation will reduce that risk, and hence is to be preferred.

Optimal electoral constraints

How binding should electoral constraints be? What should electoral constraints apply to? And where, in the set of possible mechanisms for constraining political outcomes, should the weight primarily be placed – on elections or elsewhere?

Part of this array of questions we have already addressed in the preceding section. We think electoral constraints are better applied to candidates or parties and their expressed conceptions of the "public good" rather than to specific policies. The abstraction from specific issues that representation affords we think to be a good thing: Public choice orthodoxy probably comes down on the other side of that issue.[19] This difference in prescription arises from a rather different diagnosis of the central problems of democratic governance. Public choice theory emphasizes the problem of majoritarian instability, of inefficient redistributions to strategic majorities, and of possible excessive monopoly rent creation for politicians, bureaucrats, or party institutions. We are inclined to see such problems as less significant, at least, the former two. In our view, the chief problem lies in the possibility of occasional perverse outcomes, ones that leave virtually everyone worse off. These are the outcomes that Barbara Tuchman refers to as "follies"[20] and that we have here diagnosed as instances of the voter's dilemma. As we see it, there is always the prospect of genuine electoral enthusiasm for policies that would be truly disastrous for the citizenry – enormously costly and manifestly unwinnable wars, for example, or massive and totally unrealistic social programs.[21] The task then in institutional design is to seek an optimal balance between two competing considerations: We seek to ensure that electoral enthusiasms can be checked in relevant cases and, at the same time, that political agents cannot behave in a fashion that promotes

---

[19] Witness, e.g., the literature on general fund financing as opposed to earmarking. In the public choice literature emphasis is placed on the costs of bundling large numbers of policy matters together, with an appeal to the welfare economic analysis of bundling in monopoly provision of marketed goods.

[20] See the epigraph to Chapter 10.

[21] The rhetoric involved in the two spheres can be interestingly similar – the Johnsonian "war on poverty" was arguably little better conceived than the war in Vietnam.

their interests at the expense of the citizenry at large. Neither the electorate nor political agents can be fully trusted. The objective of optimal balance seems to argue for imposition of appropriately loose constraints: constraints that are defined fairly abstractly and over a variety of policies, but that become operative only when there is a perceived major net cost to the public interest in the offing. The institutions of representation we see as one form of such constraint: The shift from direct electoral determination of specific policies to electoral assessment of general declarations of a philosophy of public interest, to which candidates/parties can be held accountable, seems to us a shift in the right direction. But there are other dimensions in which electoral constraints can be more or less binding, and other mechanisms by which various fail-safe mechanisms can be built into the political system; these deserve some mention here. The discussion is necessarily sketchy, but we hope it is suggestive.

Terms of office

It is clear that one means of insulating political outcomes from electoral pressure is to increase the length of term of office. What case is there for longer rather than shorter terms, beyond the benefit of reducing the purely administrative cost of additional elections? Lengthening terms seems simply to increase the scope for the play of officeholders' private interests. And so it does, but in our view this is not necessarily a decisive count against longer terms. Officeholders' private interests, to the extent that they roughly mirror the interests of the community at large, should come into play whenever disaster – or plain silliness – looms. Moreover, we want to replace representatives in a context where the electoral rhetoric makes sense – where notions of electoral trust and promises of faithful pursuit of national interest can be taken seriously: Elections that are too frequent seem likely to undermine the sense of occasion that voting should carry with it and to introduce a presumption in favor of direct electoral determination on contentious issues. Often when arguments against shorter terms are made (usually by politicians themselves), those arguments have an air of special pleading: We believe such arguments are not without merit, even though we accept the dangers of looser reins on politicians' interests.

Two additional points arise. The first is that the *effective* term has to be distinguished from the nominal. There is, in particular, considerable evidence in political experience of a significant incumbency advantage – the simple approximation in the U.S. Congress, for example, seems to be that incumbents *retire*, but are never defeated. Given this, representatives, once elected, would seem to be significantly insulated from electoral forces, even where nominal terms of office are quite short: Everyone appears to be elected more or less to retirement, notwithstanding periodic elections between times.[22]

---

[22] In fact, however, this issue of incumbency effects is interestingly complex. In a rational actor view, e.g., any incumbency advantage would be exploited by the incumbent's behavior on other margins (accepting bribes to vote in ways that will lose constituent support, voting her own views, etc.) and could in the limit be totally used up in this way. (Accordingly, perceived incumbency advantage – measured, say, in terms of the empirical relation between probability of reelection and number of previous terms –

There is a second issue at stake here, related not so much to the length but to the sequencing of terms. An example may illustrate what we have in mind here. Suppose all candidates have terms of four years. Suppose further that half the candidates are elected (for their four-year term) every two years, so that no more than half are elected at any time. Then any particular whim that happened to be widespread within the electorate at any one time could not dominate the representative chamber: No candidate would be any less responsible to voters than with simultaneous terms, but the sensitivity of political judgment to current electoral preference would be modified. We think there is much to be said for overlapping terms.

Bicameralism

One means of limiting the risk of disastrous outcomes is to require that policies must be subject to multiple filters. To the extent that these filters are independent – for example, involve representatives elected under different arrangements, or indeed involve some participation by entirely nonelected persons – then the prospect of genuinely disastrous outcomes must surely be diminished. There are three obvious possibilities here. One is the bicameral system. Usually lower and upper houses of Parliament are organized with the explicit object of representing different constituencies, or representing the same aggregate constituency in systematically different ways. This is often rationalized on the grounds that particular ''interests'' need to be politically represented in special ways: The requirement, for example, that the Senate explicitly represent the states in the Australian and American federations is traditionally rationalized on the grounds that historically the states qua states played a particular role in the creation of the federation/union. Assigning the state machinery a specific voice was, so the argument might go, the price that had to be paid to induce states (particularly the less populous ones) to surrender some of their preexisting powers. But bicameral arrangements exist in polities where no special representative function is to be served. The British House of Lords, for example, has no obvious rationale in democratic principle: The lords are not elected. But ''upper'' houses, even in such cases, can be justified as a protection against electoral excesses, if the notion of electoral excess is admitted as a logical possibility. A party swept to power on a wave of popular sentiment for bellicosity (or for that matter, perhaps, servile passivity) will not have an unfettered hand in responding to the sentiment that secured their victory. If the policies are genuinely disastrous, there is surely some prospect that the pure self-interest of the upper house

is always an understatement of the actual advantage, some of which has been predictably traded for other benefits.) Moreover, it will always pay the incumbent to exploit voters totally in her last term before retirement. However, knowing this, voters if rational will not vote for a candidate likely to retire in the current term. Hence, the rational politician will rationally defect in her next to last term; so she will not be elected then either. And so on, back to the present. Her rational strategy is then to bind herself never to defect. And voters rationally will only vote for a candidate who has so bound herself, supposing of course that such binding is feasible. But what binding methods are available? One possibility is a commitment to a morality of nondefection. Another (not mutually exclusive) is to join a coalition of candidates who will jointly determine the incumbent's behavior, and for whom the expected costs of defection always exceed group benefits. With a coalition of candidates most of whom are appropriately distant from retirement, defection will never be observed by any.

itself will intervene. Of course, it may be argued that the upper house role will be better performed and will be less of an affront to liberal principle if its composition is determined via an explicitly random process, in the same manner as for jury services, for example. It might be expected, or at least hoped, that the role of the upper house would be a minimal one, called into effect only on relatively rare occasions. However, as for all genuine insurance facilities, the protective role is an important one and worth paying something to secure.[23]

Division of powers

A second application of the multiple filters notion lies in the division/separation of powers. This latter notion has traditionally been argued to be a central one in democratic constitutions and claims a lineage from the Roman jurists through Montesquieu (*Esprit des Lois*) to Madison (*Federalist Papers*, No. 47). Precisely what is the analytic foundation for the sort of creative ambiguity that the separation of powers is supposed to secure is unclear in both modern democratic theory and in public choice analysis. Some public choice scholars have seen the fact that the president is the sole agent actually voted on by the nation as a whole as suppressing some of the role of special regional interests and resultant logrolling inefficiencies that are seen to dominate congressional decision making. These scholars then tend to argue in favor of shifting the distribution of power in a presidential direction: The presidential line-item veto, for example, becomes on such grounds a critical measure. Such arguments for such redistribution of political power make appeal to the inherent superiority of some electoral arrangements over others rather than to the separation and balance of powers. There appear to be some (implicit) inconsistencies, moreover, in the treatment of institutions for which constraints are absent. An independent bureaucracy, for example, generally comes in for lively criticism in public choice circles. In the absence of constraints, bureaucrats are presumed to serve their own interests, which typically involves increasing the size of their various bureaucratic empires (see Niskanen, 1971). However, an independent judiciary is normally assumed to be totally reliable in enforcing the law – and even in maximizing "economic efficiency" in rendering their judgments – without any very clear analytic account of why it would be in their interests to do so.[24]

Presumably, a conventional public choice scholar might defend the separation of powers along the lines that the simultaneous application of overlapping coalitions of interests renders the problems of agenda setting and revolving majorities less intractable. If, for example, a policy proposal must sustain the approval of three overlapping domains of authority (the legislative, executive, and judicial; or, for that matter, three chambers of a legislature), and if the relevant majority coalitions are randomly related, then the probability that any individual will be in an unrepresented minority falls from one-half to one-eighth (supposing the probability of being in the minority for any one level to be asymptotically one-half – that is, all

---

[23] For a very different account of the virtues of certain forms of bicameral structure, see Brennan and Hamlin (forthcoming). A similar argument is set out in Hammond and Miller (1987).

[24] For a discussion of this matter, see Cooter and Rubinfeld (1989), particularly sec. 3, pp. 1091–4.

majorities are minimal). There may, of course, be reasons why the relevant majority coalitions will not be randomly related; powerful interests can expect to exert their influences in more than one arena. Even so, it does seem clear, on this reading, that the effect of the division/separation of powers is to increase the de facto decision rule necessary for policy approval and, thereby, to inhibit majoritarian cycling and the power of any residual agenda setter. For this argument to go through, however, it seems necessary to have the various "powers" subject to independent electoral constraint: If, for example, one necessary power is vested in a single individual group, *unconstrained* by electoral considerations, then this individual group could be predicted simply to adopt the agenda-setting role, or to split the proceeds with the agenda setter – as, for example, some public choice theories of bureaucracy assume.

Under our theory of voting behavior, majoritarian cycling and agenda setting are not the conspicuous problems they appear to be in conventional public choice theory (though they may still be present in modified form). Given our alternative diagnosis of democratic problems, the requirement that *all* the relevant divided powers be *elected,* with somewhat different constituencies, is much less strong. An independent bureaucracy, for example, even if somewhat self-serving, might be relied upon to inhibit electoral enthusiasm for policies contrary to general interests.

A simple example may be useful here. We have noted earlier that diffuse malice toward the rich may lead parties to promote redistributive programs whose effect is to push marginal tax rates at the upper income levels beyond the revenue-maximizing point. The outcome here is one that no citizen would choose if decisive: There are potential gains from exchange when the fisc is placed on the backward-bending portion of the Laffer curve. Electoral competition cannot in this case exploit such potential gains: But the bureaucracy might be expected to oppose confiscatory tax rates. Bureaucrats, in most familiar models, are postulated to be revenue seekers, either because they have a high own-demand for public programs or because of empire-building instincts of a more self-serving kind. Accordingly, the bureaucratic interest will stand against revenue-reducing progressive tax arrangements; and the division of powers – and specifically, the assignment of genuine discretionary power to the bureaucracy – will limit fiscal perversity of this kind. Within more conventional public choice models, such assignment of power beyond the ambit of electoral constraints seems decidedly more problematic.

Restrictive decision rules

The notion that decision rules more restrictive than simple majority might be exploited to limit political "inefficiency" has been a familiar one since Wicksell (1896/1964), Lindahl (1919), and Buchanan and Tullock (1962). Indeed, in *The Calculus of Consent,* more restrictive decision rules are the primary mechanism for ensuring that the "external costs" imposed by political process do not become excessive. That analysis is predicated on the notion that voters vote their interests, as are Wicksell's and Lindahl's earlier treatments. The central problem in politics is seen to be the provision of special-benefit expenditures out of general taxes, leading to a systematic overexpansion of those expenditures (and, with distorting taxes, a corresponding relative underexpansion of genuinely public goods of a national kind).

It should be clear that the problem of nondecisiveness, with its possible consequent distortion of electoral preference, is not significantly diminished by changing the decision rule. Indeed, as we have shown in Chapter 8, the same problem arises even under complete unanimity. What the more restrictive decision rule does, of course, is to restrict parties to those policies that secure expressive support from a larger proportion of the electorate. This means that fewer policies will be implemented: But since the status quo will necessarily reflect the distorted preferences of previous supramajorities, it is not clear that the status quo is to be preferred. Certainly, the sort of mechanism envisaged by Buchanan and Tullock, based as it is on a market-like cost–benefit calculus by individual voters, does not go through in our model of voter behavior. Compared, for example, with explicit restrictions on the domain of government activity and the other kinds of safeguards (bicameralism, division of powers, etc.) that we have here canvassed, more restrictive decision rules seem somewhat peripheral to the problem.

However, more restrictive rules for particular kinds of decisions (say, for constitutional changes) may be a way to isolate particular decisions for special expressive significance: Greater restrictiveness in voting procedures may serve to mark off particular issues as matters of greater seriousness. To enter the supramajoritarian realm in electoral matters is, it may be argued, a little like walking into church: To express whimsy or malice in such a setting is sacrilege. In this way, the decision rule might exercise an effect on the expressive dimension of choice, not via the decision-theoretic structure, but via an exploitation of the expressive considerations to which that decision-theoretic structure gives rise. It seems unlikely that any case could be mounted on such grounds for a *general* increase in the restrictiveness of decision rules, since the argument hinges on supramajoritarian procedures being "special." But as a means of filtering out trivia and mobilizing residues of "deeper" expressive concerns in the context of more momentous decisions, special voting rules may have something to commend them.

The secret ballot: monitoring the vote

As we have argued, the chief dangers in the electoral process are, first, that voters may vote frivolously, or with inadequate understanding and, second, that the sorts of considerations that they may seek to express may be based on highly dubious passions such as malice, envy, xenophobia, racial prejudice, and the like. It is arguable that such dangers are much reduced in an environment of open voting, that the secret ballot (or Australian ballot, as it is sometimes known) makes it more likely on balance that such ethically dubious behavior will emerge.[25] Of course,

---

[25] In any joint work there are bound to be matters on which the authors disagree. In this book, there are remarkably few. This section is, however, one of them. There is no disagreement that the argument is interesting or that it illustrates an application of a distinctive kind of mechanism – one that operates indirectly on voters' motives rather than directly on political options (as in the domain case) or on the

given current democratic mythology, any such claim is bound to seem unnecessarily provocative. The secret ballot is commonly seen as a triumph of democratic principle, almost a sine qua non of the liberal order. There are, therefore, two points that need to be made at the outset.

First, we readily concede that, in some contexts, open voting will not be desirable. Wherever the law and social custom are incapable of preventing individuals from being intimidated or blackmailed into voting a particular way, then secrecy may be a necessary protection: Nazi Germany or modern-day Northern Ireland do not suggest themselves as suitable locations for an experiment in open voting. But neither are Nazi Germany or Northern Ireland the norm. In large-number democracies with well-established traditions of civil liberties, the danger of bribery, blackmail, or systematic persecution in the electoral context seems small. Even under secret ballot the political-ideological affections of some individuals are well known: Yet those persons do not appear to be objects of victimization. We do not, in other words, depend on *secrecy* for our political liberties, and it would be a sad state of affairs if we did.

Second, it should not be thought that open voting comes with no tradition in political theory, or that the success of the secret ballot historically represented the triumph of *principle* over the vested interests of the political establishment. The debate at the time when the issue was a live one (on both sides of the Atlantic during the nineteenth century) was largely one of political principle – not, it would seem, veiled self-interest. The case for the open vote was put strongly, for example, by John Stuart Mill (1861/1964), in an interesting reversal of a previously held opinion. As Mill put it:

Thirty years ago it was still true that in the election of members of Parliament the main evil to be guarded against was that which the ballot would exclude – coercion by landlords, employers and customers. At present, I conceive, a much greater source of evil is the selfishness or the selfish partialities of the voter himself. A base and mischievous vote is now, I am convinced, much oftener given from the voter's personal interest, or class interest, or some mean feeling in his own mind, than from any fear of consequences at the hands of others; and to these influences the ballot would enable him to yield himself up, free from all sense of shame or responsibility. (p. 302)

Essentially what we do in the argument that follows is to restate and adumbrate Mill's claim. The point of departure for our argument is to note that the present enthusiasm for the secret ballot proceeds without any theory of what it is exactly that people do when they vote – indeed, the affection for the secret ballot seems almost pretheoretical.[26] Within the orthodox public choice view, the argument is, presumably, that secrecy frees the agent to express *true* preference over political outcomes. In this view, the relation between vote and preference is unproblematic, and social pressure, whatever its influence, can only divert the agent from an as-

---

role of alternative mechanisms (as in the bicameralism case). But Brennan is more persuaded of the cogency of this argument for open voting than Lomasky is. The argument is developed at greater length in Brennan and Pettit (1990).

[26] It is congruent with the mythology of secrecy that what agents actually do inside the ballot box is not to be questioned, but this can be no defense of *analytical* silence on the matter.

sumed genuine statement of preference. One would have grounds to worry about how such preferences would be aggregated via party competition under majority rule, and these worries might make one wonder whether the expression of true preference rather than something else was so much to be preferred – but any case *against* secrecy seems, at best, quite beside the point. In our view, however, that conclusion follows only once the relevant ''point'' has been assumed away. Once the revealed preference theory of voting is seen to be incoherent, and the normative authority of the individual vote is up for grabs, the case for secrecy is far from self-evident. What one seeks in ideal electoral institutions is some mechanism that will tend to filter out meanness, malice, and flippancy. It is surely arguable that the constraints of public scrutiny tend to do this. To vote publicly is to be *answerable* for one's vote. One invites the possibility of being called to account, and one had better have on hand an array of publicly acceptable reasons to justify one's action. Such reasons include, conspicuously, judgments of the public interest and appeal to matters of political principle. In general, hatred of others or naked self-interest are unlikely to satisfy the acceptability test.

There is perhaps more to this than insisting that persons be able to excuse their conduct. The institution of the secret ballot clothes the individual's political views in a shroud of ''privacy'': To ask a person in a dinner party conversation how she voted at the last elections or intends to vote in the next is sometimes taken as tantamount to inquiries about favorite positions for sexual intercourse, and met with blank amazement, steely silence, or outrage. The secret ballot encourages a cult of popular political secrecy. The secrecy suggests that political debate is acceptable within the parliamentary assemblies, on the pages of newspapers, or on the television screen, but that this debate should be pursued by ''experts'' (politicians, journalists, academics) and not as part of the normal converse of ordinary citizens. In this way, the business of formulating an intelligible political position is left to political parties and/or (very) public figures: This state of affairs amounts to an effective party-establishment *monopoly* on offering ideological alternatives. The necessity for each voter to come to a mind about the issues of the day – not merely for the purposes of making an entirely private choice on Election Day, but rather as a systematic part of functioning in the community – wrests that monopoly control out of the party-journalistic establishment. Open voting encourages freedom of entry into the creation and popularization of political ideas. Open voting would, on this view, also encourage citizens to be politically informed, though not in the kind of way relevant to ''rational ignorance'' as Downs conceives it. Citizens would have no particular incentive to find out the precise incidence of alternative policies or how any given platform happens to impinge on their individual incomes. Rather, they acquire political information of a kind that enables them to converse intelligently among their fellows and to provide a defensible account of their own electoral actions.

The claim should not be too heroically cast. We do not believe that the open ballot can instantly and of itself create a popular political culture, however unpropitious the soil. Rather, we hold that the secret ballot may well inhibit such a culture. And should this seem implausible, it is worth noting that the introduction of the secret ballot seems to have reduced voter turnout significantly wherever it was introduced. Arguably, some of the point went out of voting once voting ceased to involve an open declaration of one's political convictions.[27]

It is interesting here to consider other contexts in which persons vote, and in which there is a clear expectation of voting in the light of publicly defensible criteria. An obvious example, familiar to many readers, is the academic appointments committee. In this setting, members are expected not to vote their interests but their *judgments* of candidates' quality. They are expected to provide *reasons* for those judgments, which explicitly exclude spurious considerations such as appearance, accent, race, sex, and so on. In this setting, the standard practice is for voting to be open. Members are required to indicate their preference over candidates openly and to provide relevant grounds for the preference. The process of collective deliberation is designed to *move* members' views in the light of the salient considerations brought forward. To insist on secrecy of voting in this setting seems bound to subvert the purposes of the committee. If voting were secret, collective deliberation would become a sham: Members could *argue* according to the relevant grounds, but the institution of secrecy at the voting stage effectively admits the legitimacy of other considerations (though ones that the voters do not seek to confess to). Of course, it may be the case that members are, in this setting, subject to various kinds of undesirable pressure: Junior staff may feel at risk in a variety of ways if they disagree with more senior staff, and there is little doubt that they may well indeed be vulnerable. Yet this fact rarely induces us to retreat from the ideal of open debate. And not merely because we believe that better decisions will be made in each case. Rather we recognize that academic values need to be rehearsed if they are to be promoted: The exercise of academic judgment as a public activity is an important ingredient in sustaining the academic culture, and appointments/promotions committees are important contexts for such an exercise. The effect of the secret ballot in this setting must surely inhibit both good judgment and the culture within which good judgment is fostered.[28]

It could, of course, be argued that the academic setting and the more general electoral setting are totally disanalogous. Within the academic setting, there is a generally agreed culture and a set of shared values that makes the conception of voting as judgment meaningful. In an environment where such values are not shared, agreement is limited to a set of procedures for simply getting political business done, and some very basic differences will have to be brokered along the way. Perhaps. But our ambitions for open voting in general elections are quite limited

---

[27] There is, of course, an alternative explanation – that politicians gave up bribing voters to vote for them once the obvious possibility of monitoring the voter's performance disappeared. That bribery was pursued on such an enormous scale in quite large nineteenth-century electorates we find somewhat unlikely.

[28] We acknowledge that such committees' deliberations are never *totally* public. Candidates themselves are not party to the debate about them. And indeed, secrecy is practiced elsewhere in academic contexts. Referees of papers submitted for journal publication are typically anonymous, as sometimes are the authors. But in the refereeing context we have other arrangements in place to monitor the behavior of referees: the provision of written reports "justifying" the referees' judgments and the scrutiny of academically distinguished editors.

ones. We do not require any Habermasian consensus on political outcomes or even on relevant dimensions of evaluation of outcomes: All we seek is a procedure that tends to filter out the worst cases of whimsy, prejudice, malice, and unreflective voting. Equally, we do not seek to encourage a culture in which the only legitimate topics of dinner party conversation would be political. We do, however, wonder whether our political culture would be better served by having political discussion a more common or garden affair.

The general point is, in any event, clear. There may well be countervailing reasons why secrecy may be desirable in certain settings. But there is plenty to be said on the other side. In many choice contexts, individual agents are accountable for their actions because they have to live with the consequences their actions bring about. In collective choice contexts like voting, individuals are not naturally accountable in this way, and we might look to institutional arrangements by which individual accountability can be, in some measure, restored. Making agents act under public scrutiny is one possible arrangement, and it deserves more consideration than it currently receives. The open vote invites public scrutiny: The secret ballot does not. Arguments against open voting on the grounds of increased susceptibility to blackmail and intimidation, though valid in principle, can easily be exaggerated. And even where those arguments apply and are decisive, we ought at least agree to this – that secrecy at the polls seems a major retreat from the ideal of vigorous participatory democracy. It is not at all obvious how secrecy can properly be seen as an intrinsic *component* of that ideal, as it currently seems to be.

Federalization: the Tiebout alternative

In what way, if at all, does our theory of electoral behavior bear on the choice between federalized, as opposed to centralized, political structures? There are two ways. First and most obviously, there is the point that ceteris paribus the smaller the decision-making unit, the greater the probability of being decisive and hence the smaller the bias toward expressive considerations in voting. Accordingly, interests will play a larger role in smaller polities, though the effects of interests will remain tiny. Whether this increased role for interests is a desirable thing depends in part on whether one believes the public interest version of expressive democratic politics is at all plausible and on whether an increased role for interests does not serve simply to reestablish traditional public choice concerns. If one sees the primary political problem to be the voters' dilemma problem we have focused on in this chapter, then there must be some presumptive virtue in more federal structures, simply because the expressive role is diminished. If that presumption is accepted, then several aspects of the federalism required are worth emphasizing: first, that the federalism in question must be *political* – the mere decentralization of administrative functions of government, perhaps with some autonomy assigned to lower levels, will not suffice;[29] second, that the argument does not depend in any way on the existence of

---

[29] It is worth making this point because much of the discussion of the "economics" of federalism emphasizes the efficacy advantages of regional variations in the supply of particular services, but allows

regional diversity – the argument would apply equally well if all individuals were exactly identical.[30]

However, we want to advance here an alternative argument for a federal structure, not because the argument is unfamiliar, but because the mechanism for its success is not vulnerable to the voters' dilemma at all. The argument is the mobility constraint argument originally advanced by Tiebout (1956). Here we want to emphasize the two distinct strands of that argument. First, there is a "pure-demand" strand that emphasizes the lower costs of "secession" individuals face in a federal polity. Individual citizens can choose among alternative locations on the basis of the package of public services (among other things) that different locations offer. Even if different local governments choose public policies randomly, the presence of alternative locations limits the extent to which citizens can be harmed by those public policies. Citizens can always "vote with their feet," as the familiar expression has it. Yet the expression is misleading in one sense that we find crucial: Location choice is not like voting, because in location choice the chooser is actually decisive. Expressive considerations play no disproportionate role in location decisions.

In the demand-side strand, there is no "producer" response to citizen choice as such. It may be that the process of citizen relocation will leave some localities citizenless, and in that sense certain local public sector arrangements will be filtered out, but there is no adjustment on the part of locality managers. In the supply-side strand, by contrast, local governments are taken to *respond* to the mobility possibility. That is, local governments actively compete for citizens, both to retain current residents and to attract residents of other jurisdictions.[31] There is at stake here a substantive assumption about the motivations of local politicians – that they are population maximizers or revenue maximizers. In general, it seems to us an empirically reasonable assumption. Local governments do, presumably, have general interest in expansion of the local fiscal base, and residents are usually attached to tax resources. However, welfare recipients and others who are a net drain on fiscal capacity will, on this reading, be much less worth attracting or holding.

Given this assumption about the motivations of subnational governments, the threat of net citizen loss becomes a constraint on subnational government behavior – a constraint that is independent of the electoral mechanism and that operates via the aggregation of market-like (decisive) choices. That is, these mobility constraints have no disproportionate expressive context: They are not victim to voters' dilemma problems. They may raise other problems – specifically they may encourage redistribution of benefits toward (and taxes away from) more mobile sectors of the economy/polity. However, on balance, we believe the forces of interjurisdictional competition to be benign.

---

for such regional variation to be imposed from above. No specifically political decentralization is required. In our argument, however, *political* decentralization is crucial.

[30] And it is worth making this point because some commentators seem to believe that the absence of regional diversity undermines any case for federalism – and hence that an appropriate normative test for the advantages of federalism is, say, whether the patterns of public spending differ among regions/states/provinces.

[31] A more complete account of such a model is provided in Brennan and Buchanan (1980).

In particular, such competition infuses local government decisions with an interest-based discipline that stands as an important corrective to possible voters' dilemmas. The shrewd local politician will be one who can minimize the conflict between citizens' expressive and instrumental preferences, who can manage to render expressively salient matters that are congruent with citizens' interests. We see this double discipline as being highly desirable and reckon it to establish a strong presumptive case in favor of federal systems.

Constitutional *choice?*

In the foregoing sections of this chapter, we have analyzed various important dimensions of democratic institutional fabric in the light of our expressive theory of electoral behavior. There is much more to be said about these matters, of course, and about other dimensions of democratic organization that we have not discussed – for example, whether voting should be compulsory (as in Australia), whether proportional representation is superior to a system of single-member electorates, whether preferential voting systems are desirable, and so on. The way the expressive theory of voting bears on such issues will have to wait other occasions and, perhaps, other commentators.

We want to conclude the discussion in this chapter with a more general point – namely, that expressive considerations will themselves intrude every bit as much at the constitutional level of collective choice as at the in-period level. Accordingly, although the foregoing arguments (and others like them) might be taken to show which institutions would be most likely to produce political outcomes in the public interest (i.e., they show which institutions are normatively approved), it is not necessarily the case that those institutions will actually be constitutionally chosen. As we noted in Chapter 8, *unanimity* does not obliterate the voter's dilemma, so even if unanimity were applied at the constitutional level, there could be no guarantee that expressive considerations would evaporate. Moreover, the kinds of issues at stake in constitutional choice – issues of how we shall order our political life – seem to be precisely those most likely to summon up expressive wellsprings: Deeply held identifications with ideological positions of all kinds will be engaged, and the hope either of consensus at all or of consensus on the "best" institutions must seem a rather pious one.

This conclusion is strikingly at variance with that which modern political theory tends to endorse. Both in the Buchanan strand of public choice scholarship and the influential Rawlsian account of justice as fairness, the shift from ordinary politics to the constitutional level of choice, where each individual is appropriately ignorant of her own future position, involves a radical shift of focus. Citizens afflicted in ordinary politics by an inevitable war of interests come at the constitutional level to a common mind on desirable institutions both because their particular interests are washed out of constitutional deliberations and because they have nothing other than interests to guide them.

Our view of electoral choice rather downplays the constitutional–in-period divide and raises questions about the unique normative authority of decisions at the constitutional level. Large-number electoral decisions at the level of ordinary politics are rather like idealized constitutional choices in the standard Rawls–Buchanan schemes. In both constitutional choice and in-period electoral choice, the individual's particular interests are irrelevant: The "veil of insignificance" characteristic of the electoral setting has this feature in common with the "veil of ignorance." But in practice, constitutional and in-period electoral decisions both involve large numbers and absence of individual decisiveness, and hence expressive considerations seem likely to obtrude in both.

It is, of course, possible to remove the veil of insignificance while holding the veil of ignorance in place. One does this by entrusting constitutional decisions to a small number of randomly chosen, or otherwise representative, "founding parents." Because of the small numbers, these decision makers are, individually, close to being decisive; but, by virtue of the veil of ignorance, they can be relied on to refrain from decisions that reflect their *particular* interests – or so the argument would go. The cost of such a procedure is that the constitutional decisions so made lack the explicit popular endorsement that liberal thinking would seem to require. To enroll larger numbers in the ultimate decision procedure is, however, to encourage the emergence of expressive "noise": It is to shift criteria of evaluation away from dull pragmatic considerations to considerations vibrant with expressive/symbolic value. That shift is not necessarily neutral among institutions. As we suggested in our discussion in the opening section, institutions like democracy itself or like the market system tend to be evaluated by reference to the values they are seen to stand for, as much as they are by reference to the outcomes they generate. Moreover, it is not obvious to us that *normative evaluation* should ignore such considerations. In other words, the veil of insignificance may have some normatively attractive features that the veil of ignorance lacks: In-period politics may be somewhat more defensible normatively, and constitutional politics somewhat less, than current habits of political thinking encourage us to believe.

Reflecting more broadly over the expressive account of electoral politics and its implications both for understanding the way various possible political institutions might work and for the choices among possible institutional arrangements actually made by functioning democratic communities, we find ourselves faced with an ineluctable moral ambiguity. On the one hand, we recognize that the moral element in politics is necessary to get it to work at all well. Without various kinds of moral imperatives, voters would either not vote at all, leaving decisions to the will of the few, or would vote in whimsical, malicious, or divisive ways. Without those moral imperatives, politicians and other public officers would be clandestinely corrupt, judges self-serving, bureaucrats uniformly open to quiet bribe. In brief, the presence of moral behavior in politics is to be valued, and on our argument democratic electoral process has a critical role to play in encouraging that moral behavior.

On the other hand, it is in stimulating a more vibrantly *moral* mode of political life that democracy magnifies the heroic aspirations of politics, aspirations we deeply mistrust. There is, to be sure, a long and respected tradition of political idealism, at least as old as the Aristotelian idea that politics is the highest calling to which a free person may lend herself. But our affections incline us toward a more mundane view of politics, in which the language is prose not poetry, and in which the conception of the task is rather more like bricklaying or dentistry than priest-craft. To be sure, bricklaying is a worthy skill: It can be done better or worse, and having it done better is a matter of some consequence. But bricklaying does not have the capacity to define who we are, to give our lives meaning and significance, to become the locus of our highest and noblest ambitions. To see bricklaying in such terms is merely silly. To see politics in such terms strikes us not merely as silly but also as highly dangerous.

In fact, public choice orthodoxy has done much to hose down such heroic no-tions. It has put abroad the idea that politics is all just a scramble for self-interest, after all; that the high-flown rhetoric is pretense; and that any elevated conception of politics as a search for the ''good'' or the ''true'' is romantic delusion. Public choice theory has done this, however, by appeal to a model that effectively assumes the problems away. How could any halfway sensible or perceptive person believe in a politics of romance if the public choice account told the whole story?

We believe – partly on empirical grounds, partly on logical decision-theoretic ones – that, at least in *electoral* politics, the standard public choice account is nothing like the whole story and is actually rather a small part. Our alternative account leaves scope for the self-aggrandizing character of politics: It suggests how it might be that democratic politics could ''get above itself.'' It also explains how democratic politics might work tolerably well over a wide range of matters for much of the time. What seems critical in achieving the latter prospect is a civic morality that falls well short of idealism.

Somewhere between the total amorality of the public choice line and the moral hubris of the heroic one, there is some middle ground – one where responsible civic conduct is sustained, but where no one sees that civic performance as more than a small part of moral life. The question is whether electoral politics can remain in this middle ground. Politics as bricklaying may be the right image, but it is not obviously an image that will win the most enthusiastic support. In liberal democ-racies, the chief problem may not be so much to identify good institutions as to implement them and keep them.

Bibliography

Abrams, Burton, and Russell Settle. (1976). "A Modest Proposal for Election Reform." *Public Choice* 28:37–54.

Aitkin, Don, ed. (1985). *Surveys of Australian Political Science.* Sydney: Allen & Unwin.

Alchian, Armen. (1950). "Uncertainty, Evolution and Economic Theory." *Journal of Political Economy* 58:211–21.

Alt, James, and Ken Shepsle. (1990). *Perspectives on Positive Political Economy.* Cambridge University Press.

Aranson, P. (1989). "The Democratic Order and Public Choice." In G. Brennan and L. Lomasky, eds., *Politics and Process: New Essays in Democratic Theory,* pp. 97–148. Cambridge University Press.

Ashenfelter, Orley, and Stan Kelly. (1975). "Determinants of Participation in Presidential Elections." *Journal of Law and Economics* 18:695–733.

Barry, B. (1970). *Sociologists, Economics and Democracy.* London: Collier-Macmillan.
   (1978). "Comment." In S. Benn, ed., *Political Participation,* pp. 37–48, cited p. 39. Canberra: ANU Press.

Barzel, Yoram, and Eugene Silberberg. (1973). "Is the Act of Voting Rational?" *Public Choice* 16:51–8.

Beck, N. (1975). "A Note on the Probability of a Tied Election. *Public Choice* 18:75–80.

Bennett, James, and Thomas Di Lorenzo. (1982). "The Political Economy of Political Philosophy: Discretionary Spending by Senators on Staff." *American Economic Review* 72(no. 5):1153–61.

Bergstrom, Theodore, and Robert Goodman (1973). "Private Demands for Public Goods." *American Economic Review* 63(no. 3):280–96.

Black, D. (1958). *The Theory of Committees and Elections.* Cambridge University Press.

Bloom, Howard. (1979). "Public Choice and Private Interest: Explaining the Vote for Property Tax Classification in Massachusetts." *National Tax Journal* 32:527–34.

Borcherding, Thomas, and Robert Deacon. (1972). "The Demand for Services of Non-Federal Governments." *American Economic Review* 62(no. 4):891–901.

Bowen, Howard. (1943). "The Interpretation of Voting in the Allocation of Economic Resources." *The Quarterly Journal of Economics* 58(no. 1):27–48.

Braithwaite, J., and P. Pettit. (1990). *Not Just Deserts: A Republican Theory of Criminal Justice.* Oxford: Oxford University Press.

Brennan, G., C. Bohanen, and R. Carter. (1984). "Public Finance and Public Prices: Towards a Reconstruction of Tax Theory." *Public Finance/Finance Publiques* 39:157–81.

Brennan, G., and J. M. Buchanan. (1980). *The Power to Tax.* Cambridge University Press.
   (1981). "The Normative Purpose of Economic Science." *International Review of Law & Economics* 1:155–66.
   (1984). "Voter Choice: Evaluating Political Alternatives." *American Behavioral Scientist* 28:185–201.
   (1985). *The Reason of Rules: Constitutional Political Economy.* Cambridge University Press.

Brennan, G., and A. Hamlin. (Forthcoming). "Bicameralism and Stability." *Public Choice.*

226

Brennan, G., and L. Lomasky. (1984). "Inefficient Unanimity." *Journal of Applied Philosophy* 1:151–63.

(1985). "The Impartial Spectator Goes to Washington: Towards a Smithian Model of Electoral Politics." *Economics and Philosophy* 1(no. 2):189–212.

(1989). *Politics and Process: New Essays In Democratic Theory.* Cambridge University Press.

Brennan, G., and P. Pettit. (1990). "Unveiling the Vote." *British Journal of Political Science* 20:311–33.

(Forthcoming). "Invisible and Intangible Hands." *Synthese.*

Brennan, G., and C. Walsh, eds. (1990). *Rationality, Individualism and Public Policy.* Canberra: Australian National University – Centre for Research on Federal Financial Relations.

Browning, E. (1975). "Why the Social Security System Is Too Large in a Democracy." *Economic Inquiry* 13:373–88.

(1979). "The Politics of Social Security Reform." In C. Campbell, ed., *Financing Social Security,* pp. 187–207. Washington, D.C.: American Enterprise Institute.

Buchanan, J. M. (1967). *Public Finance in Democratic Process.* 2d ed. Chapel Hill: University of North Carolina Press.

(1975). *The Limits of Liberty: Between Anarchy and Leviathan.* Chicago: University of Chicago Press.

(1977). *Freedom in Constitutional Contract: Perspectives of a Political Economist.* College Station: Texas A & M University Press.

(1984). "Politics Without Romance: A Sketch of Positive Public Choice Theory and Its Normative Implications." In J. M. Buchanan and R. D. Tollison, eds., *The Theory of Public Choice,* vol. 2, pp. 11–22. Ann Arbor: University of Michigan Press.

(1979). *What Should Economists Do?* Indianapolis: Liberty Press.

Buchanan, J. M., and Dwight Lee. (1982). "Politics, Time and Laffer Curve." *Journal of Political Economy* 90:816–19.

Buchanan, J. M., and R. D. Tollison. eds. (1984). *The Theory of Public Choice,* vol. 2. Ann Arbor: University of Michigan Press.

Buchanan. J. M., and G. Tullock. (1962). *The Calculus of Consent.* Ann Arbor: University of Michigan Press.

Burnheim, J. (1985). *Is Democracy Possible?* Cambridge: Polity Press.

Campbell, Angus. (1960). *The American Voter.* New York: Wiley.

Campbell, A., P. Converse, W. Miller, and D. Stokes. (1964). *The American Voter.* Research Center, University of Michigan, New York: Wiley.

Campbell, C. D. (1979). *Financing Social Security Reform.* Washington, D.C.: American Enterprise Institute.

Clarke, E. (1971). "Multipart Pricing of Public Goods." *Public Choice* 11:177–233.

Colm, Gerhard. (1965). "National Goals Analysis and Marginal Utility Economics." *Finanzarchiv* 24(no. 2):210–22.

Converse, P., W. Miller, J. Rusk, and A. Wolfe (1969). "Continuity and Change in American Politics, Parties and Issues in the 1968 Election." *American Political Science Review* 63 (no. 4):1083–105.

Cooke, Alistair. "Letter from America." October 1986.

Cooter, R., and D. Rubinfeld. (1989). "Economic Analysis of Legal Disputes." *Journal of Economic Literature* 27:1067–97.

Coughlin, Peter. (1982). "Pareto Optimality of Policy Proposals with Probabilistic Voting." *Public Choice* 39:427–34.

Coughlin, Peter, and Shmuel Nitzan. (1981). "Electoral Outcomes with Probabilistic Voting and Nash Social Welfare Maxima." *Journal of Public Economics* 15:113–21.

Downs, A. (1957). *An Economic Theory of Democracy.* New York: Harper & Row.

Elster, Jon. (1979). *Ulysses and the Sirens: Studies in Rationality and Irrationality.* Cambridge University Press (see also rev. ed. 1984).

——— (1983). *Sour Grapes.* Cambridge University Press.

Enelow, James, and Melvin Hinich. (1984). *The Spatial Theory of Voting.* Cambridge University Press.

Etzioni, Amitai. (1988). *The Moral Dimension.* New York: Free Press.

Fair, Ray. (1978). "The Effects of Economic Events on Votes for President." *Review of Economics and Statistics* 60(no. 2):159–73.

Faith, Roger, and Robert Tollison. (1990). "Expressive versus Economic Voting." In Mark Crane and Robert Tollison, eds., *Predicting Politics*, pp. 231–44. Ann Arbor: University of Michigan Press.

Frank, Robert H. (1988). *Passions Within Reason: The Strategic Role of the Emotions.* New York: Norton.

Friedman, M. (1953). "The Methodology of Positive Economics." In *Essays in Positive Economics*, pp. 3–43. Chicago: University of Chicago Press.

Frohlich, N., J. Oppenheimer, J. Smith, and O. Young. (1978). "A Test of Downsian Voter Rationality: 1964 Presidential Voting." *American Political Science Review* 72:178–97.

Gatlin, D., M. Giles, and F. Cataldo. (1978). "Policy Support within a Target Group: The Case of School Desegregation." *American Political Science Review* 72:985–95.

Gauthier, David. (1986). *Morals by Agreement.* Oxford: Oxford University Press.

Goodin, Robert, and Kevin Roberts. (1975). "The Ethical Voter." *American Political Science Review* 69:926–8.

Grofman, Bernard. (1983). "Models of Voter Turnout: A Brief Idiosyncratic Review." *Public Choice* 41(no. 1):55–61.

Groves, T., and J. Ledyard. (1977). "Optimal Allocation of Public Goods: A Solution to the 'Free Rider' Problem." *Econometrica* 45:783–809.

Hammond, T., and G. Miller. (1987). "The Core of the Constitution." *American Political Science Review* 81(no. 4):1155–74.

Hawthorne, M., and J. Jackson. (1987). "The Individual Political Economy of Federal Tax Policy." *American Political Science Review.* 81(no. 3):757–74.

Hayek, Friedrich. (1978). *New Studies in Philosophy, Politics, Economics and the History of Ideas.* London: Routledge & Kegan Paul.

——— (1988). *The Fatal Conceit: The Errors of Socialism.* Chicago: University of Chicago Press.

Head, J. G. (1966). "On Merit Goods." *Finanzarchiv* 25(no. 1):1–29.

——— (1969). "Merit Goods Revisited." *Finanzarchiv* 28(no. 2):214–25.

——— (1974). *Public Goods and Public Welfare.* Durham, N.C.: Duke University Press.

Hicks, John. (1940). "The Valuation of Social Income." *Economics* 7:105–24.

Himmelfarb, Gertrude. (1974). *On Liberty and Liberalism: The Case of John Stuart Mill.* 1st ed. New York: Knopf.

Hirschman, A. O. (1982). "Rival Interpretations of Market Society." *Journal of Economic Literature* 20(no. 4):1463–84.

Kaldor, Nicholas. (1939). "Welfare Propositions of Economics and Interpersonal Comparisons of Utility." *Economic Journal.* 49:549–52.

Kalt, Joseph. (1981). *The Economics and Politics of Oil Price Regulation.* Cambridge, Mass.: MIT Press.

Kalt, Joseph, and Mark Zupan. (1984). "Capture and Ideology in the Economic Theory of Politics." *American Economic Review.* 74(pt. 1):279–300.

Kant, Immanuel. 1913. *Gundlegung zur Metaphysik der Sitten* vol. 4. In Kant's *Gesammelte Schriften.* Berlin: Preussidre Akademic de Wissenschafter.

Kau, James, and Paul Rubin. (1976). "The Electoral College and the Rational Vote." *Public Choice* 27:101–7.

(1982). *Congressmen, Constituents and Contributors: Determinants of Roll Call Voting in the House of Representatives.* Boston: Martinus-Nijhoff.

Kelman, Mark. (1988). "On Democracy-Bashing: A Skeptical Look at the Theoretical and 'Empirical' Practice of the Public Choice Movement." *Virginia Law Review* Symposium on the Theory of Public Choice, 74(no. 2):199–273.

Kelman, Steven. (1987). "Public Choice and Public Spirit." *Public Interest* (87:80–94).

Kinder, Donald, and Roderick Kiewiet. (1979). "Economic Grievances and Political Behaviour: The Role of Personal Discontents and Collective Judgements in Congressional Voting." *American Journal of Political Science* 23:495–527.

(1981). "Sociotropic Politics: The American Case." *British Journal of Political Science* 11:129–61.

Knight, Frank. (1923). "The Ethics of Competition." *Quarterly Journal of Economics* 37:579–624.

Kramer, Gerry. 1971. "Short-term Fluctuations in US Voting Behaviour: 1896–1964." *American Political Science Review.* 65:131–43.

(1983). "The Ecological Fallacy Revisited: Aggregate versus Individual Level Findings on Economics and Elections, and Socio-Tropic Voting." *American Political Science Review* 77(no. 1):92–107.

Lindahl, Erik. 1919. *Die Gerechtigkeit der Besteurung.* Lund: Gleerupska.

Little, Ian M. D. 1950. *A Critique of Welfare Economics.* Oxford: Oxford University Press.

Locke, John. (1960). *Second Treatise of Government.* Ed. by P. Laslett. Section 119. Cambridge University Press.

Lomasky, Loren. (1987). *Persons, Rights, and the Moral Community.* New York: Oxford University Press.

Margolis, Howard. (1982). *Selfishness, Altruism and Rationality: A Theory of Social Choice.* Cambridge University Press.

Margolis, Michael. (1977). "From Confusion to Confusion: Issues and the American Voter (1956–1972)." *American Political Science Review* 71:31–43.

Markus, Gregory (1988). "The Impact of Personal and National Economic Conditions on the Presidential Vote." *American Journal of Political Science* 32, 137–54.

McKelvey, Richard. (1976). "Intransitivities in Multidimensional Voting Models and Some Implications for Agenda Control." *Journal of Economic Theory* 12:472–82.

McLure, C. E., Jr. (1968). "Merit Wants: A Normatively Empty Box." *Finanzarchiv* 27(no. 3):474–83.

Meehl, Paul. (1977). "The Selfish Voter Paradox and the Thrown-Away Vote Argument." *American Political Science Review* 71:11–39.

Meltzer, Alan, and Scott Richard. (1981). "A Rational Theory of the Size of Government." *Journal of Political Economy.* 89:914–27.

Mill, J. (1957). *Utilitarianism.* Ed. by O. Piest. Indianapolis: Bobbs-Merrill.

(1958). *Considerations of Representative Government.* New York: Bobbs-Merrill.

(1974). *On Liberty.* Ed. by G. Himmelfarb. Harmondsworth: Penguin.

Miller, A., M. Watterberg, and O. Malachuk. (1986). "Schematic Assessments of Residential Candidates." *American Political Science Review* 80(no. 2):521–40.

Mitchell, W. C. (1977). *The Popularity of Social Security: A Paradox in Public Choice.* Washington: American Enterprise Institute.

Mueller, Dennis. (1979). *Public Choice.* Cambridge University Press.

(1987). "The Voting Paradox." In Charles Rowley, ed., *Democracy and Public Choice: Essays in Honor of Gordon Tullock,* pp. 77–99. Oxford: Blackwell Publisher.

Musgrave, R. A. (1959). *The Theory of Public Finance.* New York: McGraw Hill.

Niskanen, W. (1971). *Bureaucracy and Representative Government.* Chicago: Aldine.

Owen, G., and B. Grofman, (1984). "To Vote or Not to Vote." *Public Choice* 42(no. 3):311–25.

Palfrey, T. R., and H. Rosenthal. (1983). "A Strategic Calculus of Voting." *Public Choice* 41(no. 1:7–53.

(1984). "Participation and the Provision of Discrete Public Goods: A Strategic Analysis." *Journal of Public Economics* 24(no. 2):171–93.

Parfit, D. (1984). *Reasons and Persons.* Oxford: Oxford University Press.

Patton, C. V. (1977). "The Politics of Social Security." In M. H. Boskin, ed., *The Crisis in Social Security.* San Francisco: Institute for Contemporary Studies.

Peltzman, Sam. (1984). "Constituent Interest and Congressional Voting." *Journal of Law and Economics* 27:181–210.

Pettit, P. (1989). "The Freedom of the City: A Republican Ideal." In A. Hamlin and P. Pettit, *The Good Polity,* pp. 141–68. Oxford: Blackwell Publishers.

Pincus, Jonathon. (1977). *Pressure Groups and Politics in Antebellum Tariffs.* New York: Columbia University Press.

Plott, Charles. (1967). "A Nation of Equilibrium and its Possibility under Majority Rule." *American Economic Review* 57(no. 4):787–806.

Popkin, Samuel, J. Gorman, C. Phillips, and J. Smith (1976). "What Have You Done For Me Lately? Towards an Investment Theory of Voting." *American Political Science Review* 70:779–805.

Quine, W. V., and J. S. Ullian. (1978). *The Web of Belief.* 2d ed. New York: Random House.

Rawls, J. (1971). *A Theory of Justice.* Cambridge, Mass.: Harvard University Press.

Riker, William, and Peter Ordeshook. (1968). "A Theory of the Calculus of Voting." *American Political Science Review* 62:25–42.

Robbins, Lionel. (1932). *An Essay on the Nature and Significance of Economic Science.* London, Macmillan Press.

Robertson, Dennis. (1956). "What Does the Economist Maximize?" In D. Robertson, *Economic Commentaries,* pp. 147–55. London: Staples Press.

Rorty, Amelie, ed. (1976). *The Identities of Persons.* Berkeley & Los Angeles: University of California Press.

Samuelson, Paul A. (1955). "Diagrammatic Exposition of a Theory of Public Expenditure." *Review of Economics & Statistics.* 37:350–6.

Schuman, Howard, and M. Johnson. (1976). "Attitudes and Behaviour." *Annual Review of Sociology* 2:161–207.

Schumpeter, Joseph. (1950). *Capitalism, Socialism and Democracy.* New York: Harper & Row.

Sears, D., C. Hensler, and L. Speer. (1979). "Whites' Opposition to Busing: Self-Interest or Symbolic Politics?" *American Political Science Review* 73(no. 2):369–84.

Sears, D., R. Lau, T. Tyler, and H. Allen. (1980). "Self-Interest vs Symbolic Politics in Policy Attitudes and Presidential Voting." *American Political Science Review.* 74:670–84.

Sears, D., T. Tyler, J. Citrin, and D. Kinder. (1978). "Political System Support and Public Response to the Energy Crisis." *American Journal of Political Science* 22:56–82.

Sen, Amartya. (1970). *Collective Choice and Social Welfare.* San Francisco: Holden-Day.

(1987). *On Ethics and Economics.* Oxford: Blackwell Publishers.

Silberman, John, and Gary Durden. (1975). "The Rational Behavior Theory of Voter Participation." *Public Choice* 23:101–8.

Silver, Morris. (1973). "A Demand Analysis of Voting Costs and Voting Participation." *Social Science Research* 2–3:111–24.

Smith, Adam. (1930). *An Inquiry into the Nature and Causes of the Wealth of Nations.* 5th ed. London: Methuen & Co.

(1978). *Lectures on Jurisprudence.* Ed. by R. L. Meek, D. D. Raphael, and P. G. Stein. Oxford: Oxford University Press.

(1982). *The Theory of Moral Sentiments.* Ed. by D. Raphael and A. MacFie. Oxford: Oxford University Press.

Smith, Jeffrey. (1975). "A Clear Test of Rational Voting." *Public Choice* 23:55–67.

Stigler, G. (1972). "Economic Competition and Political Competition." *Public Choice.* 13:91–106.

(1973). "General Economic Conditions and Natural Elections." *American Economic Review* 63:160–7.

(1981). "The Economist as Preacher." Tanner Lectures, Harvard University, Cambridge, Mass.

Stokes, Donald. (1966). "Dynamic Elements of Contests for the Presidency." *American Political Science Review* 60:19–28.

Ten, C. L. (1981). *Mill on Liberty.* Oxford: Oxford University Press.

Thompson, Fred. (1982). "Closeness Counts in Horseshoes and Dancing . . . and Elections." *Public Choice* 38(no. 3):305–16.

Tideman, T. N., and Gordon Tullock. "A New and Superior Process for Making Social Choices." *Journal of Political Economy* 84:1145–59.

Tiebout, Charles M. (1956). "A Pure Theory of Local Expenditures." *Journal of Political Economy.* 60:415–24.

Tollison, R. D., and T. D. Willet. (1973). "Some Simple Economics of Voting and Not Voting." *Public Choice* 16:59–71.

Tuchman, Barbara. (1984). *The March of Folly: From Troy to Vietnam.* Worcester, Mass.: Billing.

Tufte, Edward. (1975). "Determinants of the Outcomes of Midterm Congressional Elections." *American Political Science Review.* 69:812–26.

Tullock, Gordon. (1971). "The Clarity of the Uncharitable." *Western Economic Journal.* 9:379–92.

(1981). "Why So Much Stability." *Public Choice* 37:189–205.

Weaver, Carolyn. (1982). "The Long-Term Outlook for Social Security." Mimeo. Public Choice Center, George Mason University.

Wicksell, Knut. (1896/1967). "A New Principle of Just Taxation." In R. A. Musgrave and A. T. Peacock, eds., *Classics in the Theory of Public Finance,* pp. 119–36. London: Macmillan Press.

Index

233